W9-CEG-818

MAIN LINE
WASP

ALSO BY DAN ROTTENBERG

FINDING OUR FATHERS:
A Guidebook to Jewish Genealogy

FIGHT ON, PENNSYLVANIA:
A Century of Red and Blue Football

WOLF, BLOCK, SCHORR AND SOLIS-COHEN:
An Informal History

Main Line WASP

The Education of

Thacher Longstreth

BY W. THACHER LONGSTRETH

WITH DAN ROTTENBERG

W·W·Norton & Company   New York   London

The text of this book is composed in 12/13.5 Garamond No. 3,
with display type set in Goudy Old Style and Garamond No. 3.
Composition and manufacturing by The Maple-Vail Book
Manufacturing Group.
Book design by Margaret M. Wagner.

First Edition

Library of Congress Cataloging-in-Publication Data

Longstreth, Thacher.
Main line wasp : the education of Thacher Longstreth / by Thacher
Longstreth with Dan Rottenberg.—1st ed.
     p.   cm.
     1. Longstreth, Thacher.   2. Politicians—Pennsylvania—
Philadelphia—Biography.   3. Philadelphia (Pa.)—Politics and
government—1865–   I. Rottenberg, Dan.   II. Title.
F158.54.L66A3 1990
974.8'1104'2—dc20

ISBN 0-393-02780-5

W. W. Norton & Company, Inc., 500 Fifth Avenue, New York, N. Y. 10110
W. W. Norton & Company Ltd., 37 Great Russell Street, London WC1B 3NU

1 2 3 4 5 6 7 8 9 0

TO ALL THE FRIENDS, COLLEAGUES, ACQUAINTANCES,
AND RIVALS WHO, SIMPLY BY CROSSING MY PATH,
MADE THIS BOOK POSSIBLE.

CONTENTS

MAIN LINE
WASP

The man who lives free from
folly is not so wise as he thinks.

— LA ROCHEFOUCAULD

PROLOGUE
1955

THE DAY AFTER Richardson Dilworth defeated me in the Philadelphia mayoral election, he phoned me and invited me to join him for breakfast.

Dilworth was then fifty-seven and already a living legend—the charismatic fighting district attorney and field general for Philadelphia's civic reform movement. Only a few years earlier he and Joseph Clark had joined forces to drive the Republican machine from City Hall for the first time in the twentieth century. I was thirty-four and a political neophyte, a mosquito challenging a steamroller whose time had come.

But Dilworth and I shared a few things in common. We both belonged to that class of Anglo-Saxon Protestants that had been running Philadelphia—and, for that matter, the Western world—for nearly three hundred years. As a result, both of us operated out of shared notions of manners and social obligations. It was typical of Dilworth that instead of gloating over his election triumph he would extend the hand of friendship to me in my darkest moment and thus enlist my support for the greater good of the city. That was one of Dilworth's strengths: He destroyed his enemies by making them his friends.

We met at the Racquet Club the next morning at seven-thirty and wound up staying there until ten-thirty, just shooting the breeze about the campaign. Dilworth graciously confessed that he had underestimated me as an opponent.

"It surprised us that you were such a quick study," he said. "We knew at the outset that you knew absolutely nothing about city government. It was quite obvious in our first few debates that I could eat you alive, because you were so ignorant and you didn't understand debating techniques. But by the fifth or sixth debate, you'd become so formidable that my people told me, 'Get out. This kid's showing you up.' So we canceled the last six."

This was nice to hear. So I tried to return the compliment.

"The thing that impressed me so much about *you*," I said, "was your unbelievable knowledge of city government. I have never heard of or imagined anybody who knew so much about every aspect of city government. I would study these things and come up with critiques of some of the things you and Joe Clark had done wrong, and you would always refute my arguments. You always had facts and figures to support everything you said. I was amazed at the breadth of background and the statistical data you had in your head. Where did you get all those facts and figures?"

"Oh," he said, "I made 'em up."

I assumed he was kidding. "Yeah, sure you did," I said.

"No, I'm serious," he insisted. "I'd hear you say something, and I wouldn't know the first thing about the point you were discussing. But I'd know *you* didn't either—you were just using something that had been put in front of you and that you'd memorized. So I'd refute it with figures that I'd make up and that seemed to have some relevance to what you'd already said. But there was no statistical data to back up any of that stuff."

I had a lot to learn about a lot of things. Still do, come to think of it.

CHAPTER 1
THE MAKING OF A WASP
(A.D. 900–1920)

MY GRANDMOTHER, Ella Hoover Thacher, moved through life with the serene confidence of those who are born to command. In any relationship, this frail little woman instinctively assumed the role of a queen directing her courtiers, and her manner was such that just about everyone who crossed her path instinctively deferred to her leadership. "Gah," as we called her—short for the baby-talk grandmotherly nickname "Gaga"—was an activist who believed that the individual can make a difference in society: Around the turn of the century she used to bust up saloons with her friend and fellow temperance crusader Carrie Nation, and she subsequently helped persuade Congress to write Prohibition into the U.S. Constitution.

In the summer of 1934, when I was thirteen, Gah took me on a three-month tour of Europe. She was eighty-five at the time but unwilling to concede anything to age. One hot day in Greece, she climbed with me to the top of Mars Hill, outside Athens. The notion that anything was impossible simply never occurred to Gah. Needless to add, I adored her.

On the boat coming home, perhaps two days out of New York, Gah found that she had used up all her money. The ship's purser wouldn't cash personal checks, and I thought our situation was desperate. Not Gah. At lunchtime she descended grandly to the dining room, carefully surveyed the diners, pointed one out to me, and whispered, "There he is."

"Who?" I asked.

"That's the man I'm going to borrow the money from to get us home."

She walked over to his table. I could see her speaking to the man, but I couldn't hear the conversation. As I watched, (a) Gah took out her checkbook and began writing in it, (b) the man reached into his pocket and took out some money, (c) she handed him a check, and (d) back she came to rejoin me. That total stranger had accepted her word that her check was good and had given her $100 or so—enough to get us from the pier in New York back home to Philadelphia.

In her day, Gah was a formidable woman: first cousin of Herbert Hoover, controlling stockholder of the prosperous Florence Thread Mill in New Jersey, and national president of the Women's Christian Temperance Union. But by the mid-1930s her day had clearly passed—and, come to think of it, so had the day of the WASPs throughout the Western world. Only Gah didn't know it, just as she didn't know she was in trouble when she ran out of money on the ship.

One day after she and I got back from Europe, over lunch at my parents' house in suburban Haverford, Gah got angry at some perceived slight and stormed imperiously out of the house. Unfortunately for her, she had left the keys to her car inside the house with us. Rather than swallow her pride and send her chauffeur back to retrieve them, Gah simply strode out of view as we watched her through the window. We assumed she'd return sooner or later, but she didn't.

Later that afternoon the phone rang. It was Gah, icily instructing my parents to return her chauffeur and her car. She was back home in her apartment in downtown Philadelphia.

"How did you get there?" asked my incredulous father.

"Well," Gah replied, "I went out and stood in front of a

car, and the driver stopped, and I told him I was Mrs. William
F. Thacher and to take me to Locust Street. And he did."

NOW JUMP AHEAD twenty years. It is 1955 and I am the
Republican candidate for mayor of Philadelphia. Unlike my
grandmother, I am a public figure whose name appears in the
papers every day.

In the course of campaigning one day in a black neighborhood, I stop in a bar (a mistake in itself because, as I subsequently discovered, people who hang out in bars don't vote).
Maybe thirty or forty men and women are clustered around a
circular bar, and I make my way along the crowded ring,
introducing myself and passing out cards bearing my name.
I've almost made it back it to the door when I come upon an
attractive but tough-looking woman in her mid-thirties, wearing a slit skirt and a low-cut blouse and sitting at the bar with
a shot glass and a beer chaser.

"Hello!" I greet her heartily. "I'm Thacher Longstreth. I'm
running for mayor."

She puts down the beer chaser and looks at me through
glazed eyes. "What you say?"

"My name is Thacher Longstreth, and I'm running for mayor,
and I hope you'll support me."

She looks at me again. "Man, I don't know what you're
talkin' about."

"I'm *Thacher Longstreth.* I'm running for mayor of Philadelphia, and I hope you'll vote for me."

I mistakenly perceive a glimmer of recognition in her eyes.
"How'd you like a little *poontang,* white boy?" she says.

SO THERE YOU HAVE IT: from grandmother to grandson, the
decline and fall of WASP authority in one easy lesson. Indeed,

to a large extent the story of my life is the story of someone continually forced to unlearn many of the cozy assumptions of his ancestors. That might strike some people as a frustrating process. But to me, the challenge of survival in the twentieth century is a source of continual amazement and fascination—even though, in my late sixties, I still haven't quite gotten the hang of it.

To be sure, my ancestors weren't merely WASPs; many of them were Quakers, too. Like other WASPs, the Quakers today have largely retired to the sidelines—even in Philadelphia, a city they founded. But they too bequeathed some of their instincts to me, and by and large those instincts have served me well throughout my life, however much they may sometimes seem to put me out of step with the rest of the world.

In 1965, the Teamsters Union went out on a wildcat strike against the Roadway trucking firm, which operated a big terminal in Philadelphia. It was a dangerous time for the city: The striking truckers were slashing the tires of Roadway's trucks, cutting the air hoses so the brakes wouldn't work, putting barricades in front of the trucks. One Roadway truck on Roosevelt Boulevard was carrying a trailer full of butter—this in July, when the temperature outside was 102 degrees. The strikers cut its hoses and wiring, destroying its electrical circuits so the refrigeration didn't work. And while the disabled truck sat there, that whole carload of butter melted and ran all over the boulevard.

The mayor, Jim Tate, was at Longport, his summer place at the New Jersey shore. It was his custom to go down there at the beginning of the summer, and you wouldn't hear from him again until Labor Day—as if somebody else were running the city. Governor Scranton refused to take any action, because he said the strike was a Philadelphia matter.

At the time, I was president of the Greater Philadelphia Chamber of Commerce. Thus one day at my office I received a phone call from the police commissioner, Howard Leary.

"Thacher, this thing is out of hand," Leary said. "The Teamsters are really getting out of line. But the mayor's down in Longport and he won't even answer the phone. The governor won't have anything to do with it. I don't know what to do. I realize that this isn't your baby. But at least you've run for mayor, you have some presence in the city, you care about the city."

"I tell you what I will do," I said. "I will go on television and I'll blast 'em—for the violence, how it's destroying Philadelphia's image, how Roadway's going to close up its business, and so on." So I did.

The immediate result of that appearance was that the Teamsters zeroed in on me. My home telephone number has always been listed, and the messages on my phone answering machine were terrible. Monday night somebody called up every five minutes and left a message on the phone. I had a limitless tape on the machine, so it accumulated fifty to sixty messages—all of them profane.

Tuesday night somebody shot a .30-30 through the front door of my house in Chestnut Hill—not with the intention of killing anybody, just to send me a message.

Wednesday night, all four front windows were broken by rocks thrown sometime during the night.

Thursday, during the late afternoon, when people were home, somebody called and got my daughter on the phone. He described her room to her in detail so she would know that he had either been there himself or had talked to someone who had been in it. Then he described how he was going to come in the middle of the night, rape her, cut open her belly and take out all of her insides, tie them to the newel post at the top of the stairs, and then throw her down the stairwell so that by the time she reached the bottom of the stairwell she wouldn't have any intestines in her. A nice thing to tell a thirteen-year-old kid. She was hysterical.

On Friday my car was stolen. We couldn't find it for about

twenty-four hours. Then it showed up in a quarry on the other side of Chestnut Hill, all smashed to pieces. A note had been left inside: "Next time you'll be in it."

Throughout this time, my family's only protection was a single Philadelphia policeman, whom the commissioner had assigned to stay at our house after the obscene phone calls began.

After eight or nine days of this kind of harassment, I received a call from Mike Hession, president of the local Teamsters. "I'd like you to come in and have breakfast with me," he said. And I did.

"Look, you're all right," Hession told me. "We really gave you a hard time, and you stood up to it. You've got guts, and we're going to lay off you." Then he added, "Incidentally, we're not the ones who did the automobile job. I know who did, but it wasn't us. The other stuff, we may have done it or we may not have done it, but the automobile we definitely didn't do. If we were going to do that, we'd make sure you *were* in it."

But that wasn't why he had called me. "We're having a hell of a time," he said. "We're having an election fight up here, and we're having a hell of a time with Jimmy Hoffa. There's this internal fight in the Teamsters Union. I wish you'd go down and talk to Hoffa for us in Washington and get him to meet with our faction. Also, I wish you'd go out and meet with the Roadway people, because they're talking about closing their depot here in Philadelphia. What the hell—we're going to go back to work again; we'll work this thing out. But it would be awful if they closed the depot, because we'd lose two hundred jobs."

So I met with Roadway's president and other Roadway executives and persuaded them, after a long session, to keep their unit open at least for another year. And when they did close it, they built a depot out near the Pennsylvania Turnpike. So the net effect was that they didn't really take jobs away from the Philadelphia area—they just relocated closer to the turn-pike. Thus the Roadway strike ultimately worked out satisfac-torily.

Then I made a date to go down to see Hoffa in Washington. But when I was ushered into his office, I couldn't find him. I looked around. "He's not here," I said to his secretary.

"Yes, he's here," she said. "Look on the other side of the desk."

So I looked, and sure enough, there was the international president of the Teamsters, down on the floor doing push-ups. Hoffa explained that he kept in shape by doing twenty push-ups in between every visitor. So I got down on the floor and started doing push-ups with him. I had played football at Princeton and was still in pretty good shape; in those days I'd do a hundred pushups every morning and another hundred at night.

When we got up to about fifty, Hoffa looked at me and said, "Jeez, you're pretty good. I think I've gone far enough."

We stood up. "Who are you?" Hoffa asked.

"I'm Thacher Longstreth from the Philadelphia Chamber of Commerce."

"Jesus H. Christ," Hoffa said. "What the hell does a Cham-ber of Commerce guy want to see *me* about?"

I explained that the local Teamsters in Philadelphia had asked me to come and speak to him about getting together.

"Why didn't they come themselves?" Hoffa asked.

"Well, they said they couldn't get to see you, but they thought I probably could, and they've been giving me a hard time for a while now, so we're kind of friendly enemies or hostile friends, but they felt I could present the story to you if only because of the curiosity of the matter—having a Chamber of Commerce guy representing a Teamsters local might have appealed to your sense of humor."

"It sure has, kid," Hoffa said. "Go ahead and tell me the story." And I did.

When I was through he said, "Okay. You tell Hession and the rest of those bums up there to come down and do their own dirty work next time. I really appreciate your coming; it's time we called off the feud. We'll be back to you in a few days."

Now, most people would consider me an incredible sap for helping the Teamsters after they damn near wrecked my house and family. But turning the other cheek is the Quaker way. It's an instinct I've inherited, whether I like it or not. And by the large I *do* like it. It worked well for me in the Teamsters situation. And it's served me well in most other situations throughout my life.

Take the time in 1980 when Ed Piszek came to me for help for his company, Mrs. Paul's Kitchens, the maker of frozen fish cakes. Piszek is no cheek-turner; he's a fighter who believes in head-on confrontation. His problem in this case was that one of his employees was accused of stealing water from the city, and it was being alleged that Piszek himself had known about this illegal diversion. Piszek called me at the Chamber of Commerce and asked me to use my influence with Philadelphia's Water Department to put an end to what he perceived as official harassment of his company.

I called the Water Department and pointed out that Piszek employed a thousand people, that he'd donated millions to the city, and that he deserved some special consideration. But my plea fell on deaf ears. "His employee's stealing water," I was told. "What do you expect us to to do?" The employee was subsequently convicted and went to prison, and Piszek's company suffered from all the accompanying bad publicity.

Subsequently, *Philadelphia Magazine* did a story on the case. Among other things, Piszek told the writer that no one in the city had done anything to help him, "not even Thacher Longstreth, him with his short pants. I'll give you a good description of Thacher Longstreth: He's the kind of guy who would be swimming fourteen miles an hour downstream when the stream was going at twenty!"

Naturally, the magazine writer called me and said, "I just thought you'd be interested to hear what Ed Piszek said about you." He read me Piszek's comments and asked if I'd like to respond.

"Sure," I replied. "Ed Piszek is a terrific guy, and he's obviously very upset, and he's got every right to abuse me. I was not able to help him. I tried, but I wasn't able to do it, so by his standards I failed. That's true."

"Aren't you upset about the language?" the writer asked.

"No," I replied, "Ed and I have been friends for a long time, and we'll be friends for a long time to come. There's nothing to be upset about."

Two weeks later *Philadelphia Magazine* appeared, with Piszek's comments about me and my turn-the-other-cheek reply: "Ed Piszek is probably the most honest, hardest-working, and generous man I have ever met."

The following day I got a phone call from Piszek.

"You Quakers are all alike," he laughed. "Goddammit, you have me so embarrassed. My wife is so angry at me. All my friends say, 'How in the world could you say such things about Thacher Longstreth, and then he comes back with such a gentle, kind answer?' All of a sudden, you're the good guy and I'm the villain. You've taught me a lesson, Thacher. I'm never going to say a mean word publicly about anyone again."

THE BENEVOLENT HAND of history has always rested gently but firmly on my shoulders. As a girl of ten in 1865, my paternal grandmother, Lucy Branson Longstreth, stood on the Railroad Avenue Bridge in Haverford, dropping pennies into the smokestack of the train bearing Abraham Lincoln's body from Washington to its final resting place in Springfield, Illinois, and she lived to tell me that tale. But then, as she pointed out to me, *her* grandfather had lived to tell her of seeing, as a boy in 1789, George Washington pass through Philadelphia en route to his inauguration in New York.

And I've always known that long before the Longstreths became Quakers—back as far as the Roman occupation of Britain—my ancestors were Saxons. They originally came from a little town in Yorkshire called Langstrothdale. I've been told that both the town and the family got the name in the ninth century during the days of King Alfred the Great, whose continual confrontations with the Danes kept him busy a good share of his reign. According to the family legend, during one of the periods when the Danes had driven Alfred from the throne, he was running through the woods from enemy soldiers when he came to the small farm that was manned by my ancestor, who went by some nondescript name such as Smith or Jones.

"Hide me," Alfred allegedly told my ancestor, "and I'll reward you when I regain my throne."

So my ancestor hid Alfred somewhere, and the soldiers were unable to find him when they came by. When Alfred subsequently proceeded on his way, he told my ancestor, in effect, "If I ever get back on my throne, don't forget I owe you one." Alfred apparently assumed that either (1) he would never regain his throne or (2) my ancestor would forget the incident. But Alfred was wrong on both counts: He did become king again, and my ancestor mounted his horse and rode nearly a hundred miles to Winchester. When he arrived he appeared before the king and asked, "Do you remember me?"

King Alfred looked at him blankly and said, "No."

"Well, I'm the guy who saved you when you were running away from the soldiers during the Danish occupation."

"So many people saved me, I can't keep them straight," Alfred replied. "Which one were you?"

Once my ancestor had demonstrated that he had indeed sheltered Alfred, the king asked how he could return the favor.

"I live in a long valley," my ancestor replied. "I would like to have that valley assigned to me."

That was how the long valley—or "Langstroth," in Old English— became the original Longstreth family landholding. And the family lived there as farmers until the mid-seventeenth century, when they embraced the teachings of George Fox and became Quakers. In the late 1600's Bartholomew Longstreth was a bachelor in his twenties, so it was easy for his Quaker friend William Penn to convince him to move to America, where Penn was developing a Quaker settlement around Bristol, just up the Delaware River from what is now Philadelphia. Penn's first shipload of settlers arrived aboard the *Welcome* in 1681; Bartholomew Longstreth arrived on the next trip.

But he was hardly what you would call a dedicated pioneer. The first winter was so grueling and bone-chilling that he went to William Penn—who had paid Bartholomew's way across the Atlantic—and begged to be sent back to England.

"No, no," Penn replied. "You didn't read your contract. I don't send people home. If you want to go home, you pay your own way."

So being a parsimonious Quaker and also being broke, Bartholomew stayed. And of course the family has been in the Philadelphia area ever since. I represent the eighth generation in the line of Philadelphia Quakers following Bartholomew's arrival.

Bartholomew moved out from Philadelphia to what is now suburban Bucks County in the late 1690s. The Longstreth Farm in which he lived is still there, complete with a plaque on the house that reads, "Bartholomew Longstreth, 1699."

There's also a Bartholomew Longstreth School in Horsham named for him. But the family sold the farm long ago.

Once he was established here, Bartholomew rather late in life—in his forties—married a woman named Ann Dawson, who was much younger. They had the usual large family, most of whom died either in childbirth or early life. Then the family began to split up. Some of the Longstreths followed Bartholomew when he moved out to Bucks County and stayed there. Others came back into Philadelphia, which was obviously a much more active place, particularly if you didn't want to be a farmer.

The subsequent Longstreth generations included a successful wool merchant and a fellow who started an iron mill which became Phoenix Steel. But the only truly rich and successful Longstreth in recent generations was my great-grandfather William C. Longstreth, a nineteenth-century Philadelphia Quaker who went to Haverford College—as most Longstreths did—and helped to found two major Quaker businesses that still flourish: Provident Bank and Provident Mutual Life Insurance Company. He later became a Philadelphia City Councilman. The William C. Longstreth School in West Philadelphia originally stood on land that once belonged to him.

Unfortunately for later generations of the family, Mrs. William C. Longstreth—my great-grandmother Abbe—outlived her husband to an improvident old age. The Longstreth holdings in the Provident Bank and Provident Mutual Life Insurance Company, which would have made the family wealthy, had to be sold off to pay her debts. But I can't really mourn the loss. If I hadn't had to make my way in the world, I would have lost out on a lot of fun.

There were two other slightly famous people in my family. Mary Anna Longstreth ran the Underground Railway during the abolitionist days before the Civil War; in fact, she was involved in a Philadelphia riot in the mid-1850s which very nearly took her life. A pro-slavery lynch mob apparently assembled a "hit list" of about a dozen abolitionists. Mary Anna was seized by this mob and dragged in a cart to Rittenhouse Square, where the crowd planned to hang her and several other abolitionists they had captured. But they only assembled about half of their victims, and so they decided to wait until the others were captured. Fortunately, the state militia came along, a pitched battle ensued, and the abolitionists escaped with their lives and their freedom.

Although slavery was illegal in the North at that time, riots of this sort were common in northern cities like Philadelphia, New York, and Baltimore. Many people who had come to America from other parts of the world didn't want to get involved in the slavery issue. They may not have supported slavery themselves, but they weren't anxious to go to war about it. Also, hard as it may be to believe today, the prevalent feeling in many areas in those days was that while slavery was a bad thing, nevertheless slaves were private property, and the rights of private property should not be abrogated.

Of course, the Quakers—including the Longstreths—were actively involved in the anti-slavery movement—so much so that most of my family memorabilia from the pre–Civil War period consist of anti-slavery propaganda.

My paternal grandmother, Lucy Branson Longstreth, had two relatively famous siblings. Her sister Mary Branson was one of America's earliest women doctors, graduating from Women's Medical College in 1870. And grandmother's brother, David Branson, was a brigadier general in the Union Army during the Civil War—an odd occupation for a devout Quaker. I have some of his letters in which he agonizes between his hatred of war (which derived from his Quaker beliefs) and his hatred of slavery (which led him to fight).

I also have the sword with which he commanded the Union troops at the battle of the Rio Grande in Texas in 1865, which turned out to be the last battle of the Civil War (it was fought a month after Lee surrendered to Grant at Appomattox). General Branson's problem was that he had been placed in command of black troops—at his specific request—and the Southerners refused to surrender to them. General Branson solved this standoff by agreeing to bring up some white troops too, so that his force would consist of both races. That apparently assuaged the Southerners' pride and enabled them to surrender.

Like the Longstreths, my Thacher ancestors also came from England—specifically, from Thacher Island, off the southwest coast. They were not Quakers—they wound up as Baptists—and no one seems to know what caused them to leave England. In the New World they originally settled on another Thacher Island in Massachusetts Bay before moving down to New Jersey in the early 1800s to become farmers.

My grandfather, William Franklin Thacher, was a farmer in Burlington County, New Jersey, who went off to the Civil War when he was sixteen. I still have the diary he kept during the war. He lost his arm at the Battle of Malvern Hill and consequently was invalided out of the service at age eighteen, shortly before the war ended.

Since he couldn't farm any more, William started a foundry in Florence, New Jersey—a fortuitous move, because the industrialization of America was just picking up steam, and also because William turned out to possess a good business head. This Florence Foundry, as he named it, led to the development of the Florence Thread Mill in nearby Riverside, New Jersey. This was a typical nineteenth-century textile works, except that instead of producing garments it turned out thread, much of which was subsequently sold to automobile makers for wiring insulation.

The thread mill was also a classic family business of its time: William ran it until he died; then my uncle Frank Thacher took it over and ran it until *he* died; then his nephew Wilkins

Thacher ran it; and then Fred Grauer, who was married to Frank Thacher's daughter, ran it. It didn't fold up until the late 1950s, when the textile industry moved south to escape the unions.

About 1870 my grandfather William Thacher married my grandmother, Ella Hoover—"Gah—who was twenty years old at the time; she lived to the age of ninety and died in 1940. Gah produced three children, but there were twenty-two years between her oldest and youngest kids. (They didn't have any birth control in her day, of course. When we used to ask her how she planned her children, she'd reply, "God sent them.")

Gah's youngest child, Nella, my mother, was an extraordinarily beautiful woman—the most beautiful woman in Philadelphia, I'm told by her contemporaries (a judgment which her pictures certainly support). With her beauty, her sparkling personality, and her intelligence, she never failed to light up a room simply by entering it. She brought a formidable combination of traits to the world—accompanied, unfortunately, by one fatal flaw.

My mother went to Miss Wright's School, a girls' finishing school in Bryn Mawr. Early in the game she because enamored of a man named Colin Cameron, who at that time was a senior at the University of Pennsylvania and a very glamorous figure. He was the grandson of Simon Cameron, the longtime Pennsylvania Republican boss who had been Secretary of War under Lincoln, not to mention a thief of major magnitude. In an effort to shake the unsavory reputation which he developed during the Civil War, Simon Cameron moved after the war to Arizona and apparently bought some Spanish land grants, which gave him a very substantial share—about half—of what subsequently became the state of Arizona. Simon had a son, Donald Cameron, who lived on the Camerons' big ranch near Tucson. And Donald Cameron had a son named Colin Cameron, who was my mother's first husband.

She met him at Penn. He was a good-looking fellow, a

marvelous rider, a marvelous dancer—a snake in the grass, but a very attractive one. My mother fell for him and married him when she was nineteen. She had been sent to Smith College on her graduation from Miss Wright's, but when she got to Smith she decided she just wanted to get married. Against her mother's wishes, she returned to Philadelphia and married Colin Cameron, and off they went to Arizona.

In the meantime my father, William Collins Longstreth, had entered his thirties both wifeless and fatherless—his father, an attorney named Thomas K. Longstreth, had died at the age of thirty-two, a few months after William was born—and was under increasing pressure from his mother to get married. One day, when he was thirty-two himself, William came into the house to inform his mother that he had finally met the girl he intended to marry.

"That's wonderful!" my grandmother rejoiced. "Who is she?"

"Nella Thacher," my father replied.

"Goodness!" his mother said. "Nella Thacher! If it's the person I think it is, where did you meet her?"

"I met her at a party yesterday," my father said.

"What was the party for?" his mother asked, with increasing trepidation.

"Well, she was announcing her engagement to Colin Cameron."

"That's not a very good bet, is it, to fall in love at first sight with somebody on the day she announces her engagement to someone else?"

"I can't help it," my father said. "I didn't do it because I wanted to, but that's the way it is. I don't know—something will happen. I'm going to wait awhile and see."

So my mother married Colin Cameron and moved with him to Tucson. Arizona just after the turn of the century was a far cry from Philadelphia. The Apache chief Geronimo had been defeated by U.S. troops, and his people had been moved off their land and onto reservations. But every now and then they would escape from the reservations and take their revenge on nearby settlers. One night a group of Apaches showed up at the next ranch down the road and murdered all the inhabitants, including my mother's best friend.

The frontier living conditions were exacerbated by three other problems. First, it turned out that Colin Cameron, who had represented himself as a teetotaler, was in fact a drunk. Second, it turned out that he also suffered from tuberculosis, which my mother discovered on their wedding night when he hemorrhaged. (Indeed, he died of it not too long afterward.) And third, she discovered that Colin had a lady friend in every corner of Arizona.

So here she was—this young, proud, willful, beautiful woman from Philadelphia, moving out to Arizona and ending up lonely, frightened, sick (she caught her husband's tuberculosis), and unhappy. She lost her first child, had a second child—Nella, my half-sister, who's still living—and after about five years decided that this life was not for her. So she headed for Reno and got a divorce.

In 1910, of course, a divorce was a disgrace. To make matters worse, my mother went to Hollywood—which in those days was considered even less respectable than it is now—and appeared in two movies as an extra.

By this time my grandfather Thacher had died and my grandmother Gah had moved to Washington, the better to attend to her work with the Women's Christian Temperance Union. Gah had been horrified by my mother's divorce, so my mother never even told Gah about her movie career; she just wrote and said she was going to live out on the West Coast for a while.

But eventually word seeped back to Gah: Nella's in the movies. Gah got on the next train out to Hollywood and brought her back to Washington to live with her for a while.

Thus the stage was set for my father, William Longstreth, to reenter my mother's life. He had never seen her or contacted her during the time she was married. But, he told me many years later, "There was never a month when I didn't know where she was." When she returned to Washington, from Hollywood, he began writing to her periodically—just cheery, chatty letters from a friend back home in Philadelphia. After a bit he went down to Washington. Within a month of that first visit, my mother and father went to my grandmother and said, "We want to get married."

"Absolutely not," Gah replied. "That would be indecent. You can't do anything until she's been divorced at least a year." So they waited. They were married in 1916, and this marriage lasted for forty-two years—until my mother died in 1958 at the age of seventy.

For the first few years of their marriage my parents lived downtown in Philadelphia, where their first son, Sammy, died at birth. The "big house" in Haverford—the Longstreth family estate on the Main Line, built in the 1880s—was being rented at the time. But when the tenants moved out, my parents moved in, and that is where they were living when I was born on November 4, 1920. In the course of a thousand years or so, the events of my ancestors' lives had strangely conspired to bring me into the world in such a manner that hardly anyone would perceive me as a product of anti-abolitionist riots, Civil War battles, prohibitionist crusades, and detours to the Wild West and Hollywood. Instead, they would see only what my name and place of birth suggested: a proper and respectable Main Line Philadelphia gentleman.

CHAPTER 2
BOOM AND BUST
(1920–35)

I WISH YOU COULD SEE the enormous house in Haverford where I grew up in the 1920s. It's no longer there, of course—it was torn down in 1980 to make way for a luxury apartment complex. But for a century it stood on Montgomery Avenue, next to the Haverford mansions and four doors down from the Merion Cricket Club—a huge, rambling thirty-room house built for carriages and horses and servants.

My grandmother Longstreth moved out from Philadelphia and built that house near the new Haverford train station after the Civil War. The Pennsylvania Railroad—in which my great-grandfather had been involved—had just constructed its Main Line to the suburbs and in the process had introduced Philadelphians to the then-novel concept of commuting. From then on, five generations of Longstreths lived in that house at one time or another; my father lived there and my brother Frank and I were born there; and by its sheer size and persistence the house proclaimed to us and to the rest of the world the solidity and permanence of its owners and of the values we represented.

But of course appearances can deceive. Throughout the life of the house there were long periods when no Longstreth lived there because no Longstreth wanted to live there. And there was another long period of thirteen years—after we were wiped out in the stock market crash of 1929—when the Longstreths yearned to live there but couldn't afford to, even though we owned the house. The upkeep was simply beyond our suddenly depleted means, and so we were forced to close the mansion and move into the carriage house in the rear.

The family into which I was born was decidedly upper-middle-class—comfortable, but certainly not rich. But by the time I was old enough to be aware of things, the stock market had taken off and, like many another American family in the 1920s, we were living the life of the wealthy. We had the huge house in Haverford, seven servants, a place at the shore, motorboats and automobiles. My mother and father went abroad every year.

Of course, in those days it was easier to be wealthy. Father never made more than $50,000 or $60,000 a year, but the dollar was worth perhaps ten times its present value, and there were no income taxes to speak of. So a $50,000 income approached the purchasing power of a $1 million income today. Household servants cost only $15 a week, and even that was generous: You could get them for $12 if you bargained. So seven servants cost barely $100 a week, and that was only 10 percent of my father's income.

It was my father's good fortune—or bad fortune, depending on your perspective—to have gone into the investment business in 1914. Work-wise, his first love was neither stocks nor bonds but the automobile, a novel contraption that had barely been introduced when Father graduated from Haverford College in 1902. Father's driver's license—License Number 12—must have been one of the first in Philadelphia. After earning his master's degree at Haverford, he went into the automobile business, and he was very happy there for about ten years—until the used car became significant. Father contended that it was wonderful fun to go out and introduce people to the horseless carriage. But when the basis of making or losing a sale became "How much are you going to give me for my trade-in?" the business lost its appeal for him and he took a partnership with Brooke, Stokes & Co., a Philadelphia investment firm.

My mother and father were always happily married—there was very little friction between them, primarily because he adored her. He let her take the lead, and she took it. She was a very happy and successful woman by 1920s standards, which were almost entirely self-oriented. Her garden, her servants, her house, her travels abroad, her automobile—she had everything a woman of her day could want, and she was very happy with it.

The thought of putting money aside for a rainy day didn't occur to my parents in those heady years. For one thing, my maternal grandmother, Gah Thacher, was genuinely rich. When her husband died she had inherited the controlling interest in the Florence Thread Mill—an interest worth more than $1 million, most of which, my father assumed (wrongly, as it turned out), would pass to us when Gah died.

For another thing, nobody else saved, either. The interest rate offered by savings instruments in those days was very low—2 percent. And there had been so many financial panics and crashes since the mid-nineteenth century that the general feeling was, "What the hell, it may be gone tomorrow, so let's have a good time." My father subscribed to that philosophy just as everyone else did. Years later, when all the money *was* gone, he told me, "You know, I'm so happy I spent all the money I spent in the 1920s, because if I'd saved every nickel of it, it would have gone the same day everything else went."

One Thursday in October 1929 I was home in bed with scarlet fever—a blessing of sorts for a nine-year-old boy, because my absence from school enabled me to hear all five World Series games on the radio. That was the great World Series between the Athletics and the Cubs, in which washed-up

Howard Ehmke struck out thirteen Cubs in the opener and the Athletics won the third game with a ten-run seventh inning after trailing eight to nothing.

Father came home that night very upset because there'd been an enormous break in the stock market that day. But he had no concept at all that it was anything more than a temporary setback—a bad day at the market. It never occurred to him that the market wouldn't recover for a generation, or that the life our family had known would be irreparably shattered as a result.

The magnitude of our financial disaster crept up on us only gradually and indirectly, because father himself was not very heavily invested in the market. But he *did* own a small partnership investment in Brooke, Stokes & Co., the brokerage house where he worked. Like other investment houses then and now, the firm used the partners' capital for two purposes: to pay the office operating costs and to play the stock market.

So the firm was investing heavily in the market, and my father was spending money, secure in the belief that when my grandmother Gah (his mother-in-law) died, a lot of money would be passed on to him.

Two developments subsequently shattered his serene confidence. First, Gah's business—the Florence Thread Mill—went to hell along with everything else, so that instead of generating an income of $100,000 or $120,000 a year for her, the mill earned her virtually nothing. As a result, she began selling off her securities for cash to meet her living expenses—but of course the value of the securities was rapidly shrinking, too. Thus by the time Gah died in 1940, about 90 percent of her fortune had been dissipated. All that was left was two hundred thousand dollars, which is what my mother and father essentially lived on for the rest of their lives.

Meanwhile, my father's brokerage house—like every other brokerage house—had done all of its stock investing on margin. Under the pre-1933 rules, investors could buy stock by putting up a "margin" of only 10 percent of the purchase price; the rest could be paid in the future, presumably after the investor sold his stock at a profit. Thus if you bought a $100 stock on margin, you had to put down only $10—the investment house lent you the rest of the price—and if the stock went up to $110 you could sell it and receive $20, less the investment house fees—doubling your money. But if the stock went down to $95, your share of its worth would be reduced to $5, and the investment house would ask you for an additional $4.50 to keep your share of at least 10 percent of the worth. If you weren't willing to put up the additional money, the investment house would sell the stock and give you only $5, less its fees. If the stock kept falling, you would have to keep meeting these calls for additional margin or let the investment house sell the stock.

On a much larger scale, this is how the Crash of '29 gradually destroyed my father and his firm and just about everyone else on Wall Street. Each week as the market went down, the major partner Francis Brooke would come to the partners, calculate their percentage of the firm, and assess the amount each man would have to kick in to cover the new margin requirement.

"OK, Bill," he might tell my father one week, "you've got six percent of the business, so your share today is ten thousand dollars." So father would put it up. Then a week later father would be told, "You owe another six." So father would put it up. Then another week Brooke would say, "You owe twenty-two." So he would put it up. But by now it's pretty tough; he'd borrowed money from my mother, and he'd put a mortgage on the house, and he'd taken a personal loan. Ultimately even that money was all gone—everything father could beg or borrow. The only thing we had left was our house, which had a huge mortgage on it—and the only reason the bank never took it was that the bank couldn't have done anything with it. The bankers figured that if they took the house, they couldn't get anybody to live in it and it would fall apart. But as long as *we* lived in it, at least we were housekeepers and house-sitters, and someday we might be able to pay it off. And we did, but not until the late 1940s.

If you haven't been through it yourself, it's hard to understand what it's like to be wiped out clean-clean. Our family went from an income of $50,000 or $60,000 a year to exactly $997 in 1935. When you've lived in the lap of luxury, and particularly if you're like my mother—accustomed to having your own way, to having everybody notice you and fawn over you because of your looks and social position—and suddenly you find yourself penniless, without new clothes, without servants, unable to send your kids to the schools you want them to attend, you respond in one of two ways: Either you buckle down, or you fall apart. My mother, as it turned out, did both.

At first, when the impact of the crash hit us, my mother was the pillar of strength who picked up the family responsibilities, went out, got a job, earned the money, and kept the family together. It wasn't that my father fell apart; it was just that there was nothing he could do. Nobody wanted him. There were no jobs, no money, nothing to do. During this period, Father would go to his brokerage office every day and work like hell, but no customers bought anything. His customers had lost everything as the result of investments he had sold them, so they had no confidence in him. And he had no confidence in himself.

"Father," I'd say typically, years later, "what would you recommend that I buy?"

"War bonds," he'd reply. "That's the only thing you can be reasonably sure of. These other things might go down."

"But Father," I'd protest, "look at this—"

"No, don't do that," he'd say in a shell-shocked voice. "Everything crashed. You've got to be very careful." The stock market crash did more than wipe him out financially; it destroyed him as a salesman as well.

But my mother sold dresses. She tutored children. She also got involved in the sale of Prosperity Pens, which was nothing more than a pyramid scheme: I sell you a pen, and then you sell two pens to someone else, and they sell two pens to somebody else, and I get a small commission on each one and you get a small commission. Everybody was going to buy a pen, and that was going to extricate us from the Depression!

That I survived this period with reasonably good humor was largely due to the companionship of my younger brother Frank, my best friend and constant companion until I went off to college. We loved all the same things—to ride bicycles, play baseball, play soldiers, and just enjoy each other's company. I've often thought that between the two of us we would have made a fine athlete—mixing my size and strength and his speed and stamina. When the Depression hit, Frank and I created our own little form of welfare. We didn't perceive it as welfare at the time, but that's what it was. There was a field out in back of our house that grew beautiful violets in the spring. We'd spend two or three hours every day picking violets. Then we'd assemble them in little bunches, wrap a string around the stems, and put them in a basket. We'd walk around the neighborhood ringing doorbells: "Would you like to buy our violets for twenty-five cents?" They were probably worth a penny, but we found out that people would pay a quarter, so that's what we asked.

Years later I found out that our neighbors were saying, "Isn't this cute? The Longstreth kids haven't got a penny, and they're out there trying to keep things together." So the 25 cents—which we thought was part of a legitimate business transaction—was really given to us merely as a form of charity. Frank and I used to make $3 or $4 a week this way, and that was all the money we had. This money didn't go for Tootsie rolls or toys; it went into the family exchequer to buy food.

We actually went through periods when the only thing we had to eat for perhaps a week at a time was turnips. The year Roosevelt closed the banks—1933—we had no cash in the house at all, and I remember my mother going out of the house to visit friends and coming back with some canned goods. Again, that was all we had to eat.

BY 1931, father was no longer able to pay his share of the margin calls at Brooke, Stokes & Co., and suddenly he was out of a job. Shortly after that he was approached by a man named Fuller Parsley, who had an investment firm in town.

"Bill," Parsley said, "I know you're one of the fine salesmen and you've got great contacts, and I want you to join my firm. I'm not going to make you a partner—I own the whole firm, and I don't want any partners—but I'll bring you in here and pay you a salary and then you'll have a commission." My father was in no position to bargain; he accepted a three-year contract with a guaranteed draw of $10,000 a year. His commissions were to be charged against the $10,000, and then he'd get a share of anything in excess of $10,000.

But in the first year my father sold nothing—nothing at all—and at the end of the first year Parsley said to him, "Bill, I know how hard you tried. You've been a wonderful addition to our firm, and I hope you'll stay with me for a long, long time. But I only made four thousand dollars last year out of the business, and I can't keep on paying you ten thousand. You have a contract, but if you insist on holding me to it, I'll have to close the firm."

"Forget the contract," Father said. "I'll go on straight commissions." Thus he had one year at $10,000, but in the imme-

diate following years our income was more like one-tenth of
that. Nevertheless, Father worked for Parsley the rest of his
life, and the two of them remained great friends. Father stopped
working when he was about eighty-eight and died in 1974 at
the age of ninty-three. He'd make a few dollars here and there,
but his customers gradually died off. Never again for the rest
of his life did he earn $10,000 in a single year.

THE STRAIN of the Depression finally began to tell on my
mother. In 1933 she went to the doctor and told him she
thought she was going to have a nervous breakdown.

"I think you are too," he agreed, "and I think what you'd
better do is find ways to relax." One of his suggestions was
that she take a little whiskey every day.

So she started drinking—something she had never done
before, and something that had been strictly forbidden by her
prohibitionist mother, Gah. Too late my mother discovered
that she was one of those people who couldn't handle it at all.

Within weeks she was an alcoholic. All of a sudden we saw
a terrible change come over my mother. You could tell in a
moment if she'd had one drink. She who had once been the
sweetest, most loving person in the world suddenly became
argumentative, unfriendly, unreasonable, irrational. I've never
seen anyone else undergo such a character turn. She'd stagger
around, slur her words, become quarrelsome. She'd talk end-
lessly on the telephone, in a loud voice, about bridge hands,
business, fancied slights, repeating the same conversations over
and over with several different friends, so that it was impossible for Frank and me to concentrate on our studies. The carriage house was not the big house; it was more like living in a
tenement, where everybody hears and sees everyone else's business. Ultimately Frank began staying at school to study, and
I'd study at a friend's house.

Compounding the problem was the fact that as time passed, her looks went; she just didn't take care of herself at all. She didn't eat anything, but her figure went; her legs got skinny the way drunks' legs do. But my father went right on adoring her and would never do anything about it, would never acknowledge that she was an alcoholic.

When I was about thirteen or fourteen and beginning to understand what was happening to Mother, I went to her and pleaded with her to do something. She was furious at me. I had been her absolute pet; in her eyes I could do no wrong, and she was never the same to me after that. She never forgave me for telling her the truth. She didn't want to hear it; she wasn't going to believe it.

This estrangement was almost unbearable to me. When Frank and I were small boys, we had worshipped my mother as a goddess; she was our fairy godmother, and we were the two most adoring little boys you'd ever want to see. And now, to see her destroying herself! From that time—about 1933 or 1934—she was never really my mother again.

She continued to enjoy moments of rationality. In fact, the funny part of it was that she followed a strict rule: She never drank before lunch. Thus you could do things with her in the morning. The trouble was that she usually got so drunk at night that she'd sleep halfway through the morning. She'd get pretty well in the bag at lunchtime, then she'd lay off in the afternoon—but the evenings were just horrible.

My grandmother, Gah Thacher, had always been adamantly anti-booze. My father never took a drink and was a happy, easygoing person. My mother drank and was miserable and unhappy and died a wretched person. Between my admiration for Gah and the experience of watching alcohol ruin my mother, I decided never to touch the stuff myself. I always feared that, like my mother, I might be an incipient alcoholic, so I figured the wise thing to do was simply not expose myself to it at all—and I've avoided it ever since, with one spectacular exception which I will get to in due course.

AS IT HAPPENED, my mother's best friend belonged to the wealthiest family in Philadelphia—the Pews of Sun Oil. Mabel Myrin, a daughter of Sun Oil founder Joseph Newton Pew, had been my mother's roommate at Miss Wright's School. In those days—shortly after the turn of the century—the Pews hadn't yet moved to Philadelphia and they weren't yet super-rich; Mabel Pew was just a shy, introverted little girl from Pittsburgh. My mother, on the other hand, was president of the class, the top student in her grade, captain of the basketball team—the biggest girls' sport then—the most beautiful girl in the class, and the most popular girl in the school. Mother and Mabel were total opposites, but they took a great liking to each other which never died.

Aunt Mabel, as I called her, married a handsome, charming Swede named Alarik Myrin (pronounced Mew-REEN) in the early 1920s, and he and my father became good friends. The Myrins moved down to Argentina, bought an enormous section of the country, built ranch houses, and raised cattle and drilled for oil. But it didn't work out for them, and after ten years or so—about 1931—they sold it, came back to the United States, and bought an estate in Kimberton, outside of Phoenixville, a Philadelphia exurb. So here they were, back again, and Mother and Mabel picked up where they had left off—except that in the interim my father had been wiped out financially and my mother had become an alcoholic.

With the combination of what was happening to mother and the fact that we had no money at all through 1933, 1934, and 1935, one year mother and father decided we were going to have a Christmas without Christmas—that is, no one in the family would buy presents. We had a tree that we cut down from the backyard, and we used the ornaments that we'd saved from previous years. But presents were forbidden. I remember my father got Mother something, causing Mother to burst into tears in fury because he had abrogated the agreement. She hadn't bought him anything, and she felt put down by that.

My half-sister Nella was married and gone by that time. But my brother and I were still home and feeling pretty badly about life: Here it was Christmas and we had no gifts to show for it.

"Now," my mother told me, "we have two presents for you—one for you and one for Frank."

"I thought there weren't going to be any presents," I said. "That's not fair, because we didn't get you anything."

"This isn't from us," Mother said. "It's from Aunt Mabel."

We had always thought of Aunt Mabel Myrin as a fairy godmother. In past Christmases she had given us toy soldiers and a toy suit of armor. Her presents were always glamorous and expensive, and they came from the F.A.O. Schwarz catalogue—classy stuff. So we were very excited at this news. Until that moment, we hadn't been sure whether or not she'd been included in the "Christmas without presents" agreement.

Frank and I were each given a slender box, which we opened in great anticipation. But instead of a glamorous toy or game, all we found inside was a leather belt. I didn't want to seem ungrateful, but I felt like throwing myself on the floor and crying, because this was the ultimate disappointment—to get a goddam belt for Christmas. ("What did you get for Christmas?" "Oh, I got a bat and a ball and a toy." "Well, I got a belt.")

My brother felt the same way, and neither of us could hide his disappointment. I remember sitting there and wanting to cry out to Aunt Mabel. Why this one year, when we weren't going to get anything from our parents, would she give us belts? I lacked the maturity to realize that this was Mabel's way of saying, "You're thirteen and you're mature now, and therefore I'm going to give you things I would give an adult; I'm not going to give you children's toys anymore." This was one year I really *wanted* a child's toy.

We were sitting there in the living room bemoaning our fate when all of a sudden my brother said, "Hey, Thacher, look at this." As he held out the belt, I saw a zipper in the back.

"Oh," I said. "I wonder what *this* is." Frank pulled the zipper, the belt opened up slightly, and there, inside the pocket, was a $100 bill.

My God, I can't tell you what $100 was in those days. It was like getting $1,000 today. A $100 bill for each of us— that was $200, when the entire family income for that year had been less than $1,000. Suddenly we were beside ourselves with our newfound good fortune.

Finally Frank and I went upstairs to the room we shared together. We used to talk a lot in bed when the lights were out, and after a while I heard him say, "Thacher."

"What?"

"Come over on the bed a second." So I went over and sat on his bed.

"I don't feel good," he said.

"What do you mean? What's the matter?"

"Well," he said, "it isn't right for us to have two hundred dollars while Mother and Father have nothing."

"Yeah," I said, "you're right."

And almost simultaneously, we got up out of bed, took one of the $100 bills, went downstairs, and gave it to our mother. "This is for you," we said.

Of course, my mother just broke apart, and so did my father. It was a very emotional scene. But obviously it was the right thing to do. Frank and I took the other $100 and got some things for ourselves—a suit and even a few things that weren't quite as prosaic. But my mother told Aunt Mabel what we'd done.

The following year, when Christmastime came, Frank and I found a letter from Aunt Mabel to each of us. "Your mother told me what you did with my present last year," the letter said. "I think that's the most perfect example of Christmas that I've ever heard of. I want you to know that I'm going to give you a hundred shares of Sun Oil each Christmas as long as I live." Thus we received a hundred Sun Oil shares from Aunt Mabel every year until she died in 1972—nearly forty years later. All told, I would guess she gave each of us about $100,000 worth of Sun Oil stock. It was a case of kids doing what they ought to do, and of an adult responding in kindness. And it offered us the hope that one day we would awaken from our financial nightmare.

We could never resume our old, idyllic fairy-tale life of the twenties. The Great Depression had permanently endowed me with an innate fear of poverty—a fear far more acute than, say, the fear of being killed or robbed. Yet at the same time, it permanently snuffed out any attraction I might have had to the business of making money—for what was the point of accumulating wealth in a world where fortunes could be wiped out overnight? Thus the Quaker maxim "Do well before you do good" underwent a modification in my case: It became "Do good, have fun, and don't hurt anyone along the way."

From now on my brother and I would find our pleasures in something other than material comfort. In effect we had traded wealth for wisdom, and our lives would be more satisfying as a result.

CHAPTER 3
LOVE AND MARRIAGE, MAIN LINE STYLE
(1931–41)

THE STOCK MARKET CRASH may have decimated my family and others like ours, but it barely touched many of our Main Line friends and relatives. Some of them, like the Pews, fell back on the cushion of inherited wealth. Others enjoyed professions that the national economy couldn't damage. A doctor in the mid-1930s, for example, might have gone right on making $15,000 or $18,000 a year, a fortune in those days—and he worked with the assurance of regular income and without fear of losing his job, assuming his patients were able to pay fully and promptly.

Thus despite our family's sudden crushing poverty, as a teenager in the mid to late 1930s I found myself plunged into an awesome—and, in retrospect, ludicrous—round of debutante parties, dances, balls, and theater outings among my friends whose lives had been blissfully unaffected by the Depression. During the year that a girl "came out" she and her friends might be invited to a hundred parties. That's no exaggeration: A single wealthy debutante like Frances Pew, the daughter of Sun Oil's chairman, J. Howard Pew, might be the guest of honor at four or five different parties—some thrown by her parents, some by her aunts and uncles, and so on.

All this lavish partying in the midst of staggering national poverty was of course grossly insensitive. Even for the participants themselves it was often pointless and monotonous: You went to so many parties, and at every party you met the same people, drank the same champagne, ate the same filet mignon, danced to the same Meyer Davis Orchestra playing the same music. But if you were too poor to afford other entertainment, as I was, they were wonderful parties. I especially loved theater parties. Since my family couldn't afford theater tickets, a theater party was the only way I got to see *DuBarry Was a Lady, Red Hot and Blue,* and other hit shows of the thirties.

And yet there was an underlying serious purpose to all this surface frivolity. The whole party-going exercise was really something of a mating ritual. In the process of all these parties, dances, and theater outings, it was expected that you would find your mate and, subsequently, marry and settle down in a manner that would cause the least possible disruption to the larger society. No doubt every primitive society provides similar mating rituals. But ours on the Main Line seemed to drag on for a very long time, especially given the terrible poverty around us.

Actually, I first encountered *my* eventual mate in another much earlier Main Line mating ritual. If you lived on the Main Line in the 1930s, at the age of ten or so you were sent to the Wednesday Afternoon Dancing Class at the Merion Cricket Club, and you continued to attend this class until you were about thirteen. (If you lived in Chestnut Hill, of course, you attended the *Tuesday* Afternoon Dancing Class, which was conducted at the *Philadelphia* Cricket Club.) At fifteen, you went on to the Friday and Saturday Evening dances in Philadelphia (at the Warwick Hotel).

Both of these classes were conducted by Mrs. S. Naudain Duer, a tiny, peppy, immaculately groomed matron then in her late sixties, whose primary claim to fame was her membership in the prominent Poe family of Baltimore: She was the former Josephine Poe; her brothers had been All-America football players at Princeton in the 1890s and heroes in the First World War, and they were all related to Edgar Allan Poe. Mrs. Duer lived in the Warwick Hotel downtown, but through the strength of her social connections she had built a network of dancing classes in several East Coast cities; she also operated Camp Beaver for girls in Rockland, Maine, from 1911 to 1948. Nobody seemed to know who *Mr.* Duer was, although much later I learned that he had been an invalid who had died in 1922.

Mrs. Duer's dancing classes were steeped in all the tradition and mystique of a two-hundred-year-old event like Philadelphia's Assembly Ball, but in fact they dated back only to the end of World War I. Nevertheless, Mrs. Duer had developed them into such a vehicle of social prestige that mothers would kill to get their daughters into one of her classes, in much the same way that parents today assume that admission to the "right" nursery school or kindergarten will make or break a child for life.

In those days girls in my circle rarely attended college, so an invitation to Mrs. Duer's dancing classes was a critical factor in the only thing that mattered to their families: meeting a suitable prospective husband. It was never difficult for boys to get into Mrs. Duer's classes—we were always in short supply, partly because so many boys in our circle were away at boarding school. But among girls, the number of places was limited and the competition was fierce—a situation which enhanced Mrs. Duer's status and the prestige of her classes. But of course the dance classes were nothing more than an invention which Mrs. Duer's fertile mind had concocted in order to provide herself with a regular income when her husband had become disabled.

Admission to the classes was controlled by Mrs. Duer and a handful of *grandes dames* who decided among themselves whom to invite and whom to exclude—a process then not unlike admission to the *Social Register,* the Union League, or the Philadelphia Club. At each stage of the game you applied for admission and then were "evaluated," largely on the basis of your family background. The selection committee members didn't much care if you were handsome or ugly or charming or mean; their concern was "Who knows her?" and the acceptable answer would be something like "Oh, yes, that's Jack Walton's family; they're all right—I went to school with his daughter."

To be sure, Mrs. Duer was ideally suited for her chosen profession. She was a bundle of upbeat energy, constantly moving as she gathered us timid ten-year-old students in a circle, leading us into a collective dance step while singing, "Have you seen my new shoes?" Having broken the ice among us, she'd then pick out couples to do the step in pairs. She was a wonderfully friendly woman who seemed immensely interested in everything each of us was doing—no small feat for an adult dealing with prepubescent kids. And no matter how much she bounded about the dance floor, her hair, dress, and makeup always remained perfectly in place. You might say she was the ideal Main Line role model.

Each of Mrs. Duer's dancing classes was divided into several age groups so that budding adolescents like myself were always kept with our own contemporaries. In theory, if you attended these Tuesday or Wednesday classes faithfully for three or four years, you then graduated at age fifteen or sixteen to the Friday Evening Dancing Classes at the Warwick—which drew boys and girls from a much broader geographical area—and then to the Saturday Evening Dancing Classes in your mid-teens and ultimately to the debutante parties. Indeed, that was the whole point of attending these classes for so many years: All the guest lists for the debutante parties were culled from the survivors of these dancing classes as they progressed from Tuesday or

Wednesday afternoon to Friday and Saturday evening and from the Merion and Philadelphia Cricket Clubs to the Warwick.

Since I lived in Haverford and Nancy Claghorn lived in Chestnut Hill, our paths never crossed at the afternoon dancing classes. We didn't meet until I was fifteen and we had both been "promoted" to the Friday Evening Dancing Class in town. I remember the first time I set eyes on her. She was a year younger than I and absolutely stunning—the most gorgeous girl you'd ever want to see in your life, five feet, seven inches tall, 125 pounds, built like a showgirl with long perfect legs. Along with all that went sparkling blue eyes, white teeth, flawless skin, and dark brown hair. She was a real "show stopper," with an enthusiastic personality and friendly manner that ingratiated her to everyone.

"Who is that?" I asked a friend on that first night.

"Her name's Nancy Claghorn," I was told. "Why don't you dance with her?"

I recoiled. "I don't want to dance with her. I mean, she wouldn't want to dance with *me*." I was tall and skinny and pimple-faced and plagued with all the customary self-conscious obsessions of a gawky teenager, and I assumed she was much too good for me. So for a year thereafter I never even said hello to her, much less asked her to dance.

Relating to girls did not come easily to me. By the time I was fifteen I stood six foot four but weighed only 155 pounds. As a younger boy I had been a good athlete—and would later become one again—but at this interlude I was simply awkward. I was terribly embarrassed by my pimples. As I became more interested in girls, it seemed my constant fate to be attracted to pretty girls who wouldn't give me the time of day because they were so much in demand.

One of my obsessions in those days was a lovely girl named Natalie Wood (not the late film actress), a wonderful dancer whom I knew from the Friday Evening Dancing Class and who lived just about a mile from me on Valley Road in Ardmore. I'd dance with her at the classes and go out with her occasionally, but in my bumbling way I couldn't seem to advance our relationship beyond the "friendly" stage.

At the time my best friend at Haverford School was a fellow named Peter Page, who was everything I was not—a good athlete, dashing, self-assured (he was subsequently killed in the Battle of Guadalcanal in early 1943). One day I broached my problem to him: "I really would like to make a run on Natalie Wood," I said. "You're so successful with girls—you must have some idea of what I should do to romance her. All I want to do is kiss her."

I had, in fact, tried to kiss Natalie Wood one night at the Friday Evening Dancing Class: While we were dancing, I sort of reached for her in the corner and slipped and fell to the floor. She was so busy laughing at me that she didn't even realize that I had been working myself up to kiss her.

"Is there anything you can do well that a girl might like?" Peter asked.

"Yeah," I said. "I can sing like Fred Astaire."

"Well, sing to her."

A fine idea—but where? I couldn't sing to her at the movies. I couldn't sing to her at the dancing class—someone was always cutting in. And I was too young to drive.

Peter insisted we could find a way. Together we scouted Natalie's house in Ardmore. Her room was on the third floor, but I had never been above the first floor. We noticed a large tree outside her window.

"I tell you what we're going to do," Peter said. "Next week we'll come down here after supper. I'll boost you up into that tree, and you climb outside her window. The windows will be open"—this was May, and the evenings were warm, and air conditioning wasn't available yet—"and you can just lean in and sing 'Isn't This a Lovely Day to be Caught in the Rain?'

We'll wait until we get a night when it's raining a bit, so it'll be very romantic."

I thought Peter's idea was terrific. So about a week later—one of those misty, moisty spring evenings when the bugs are just starting to come out—he phoned me and said, "This is the night." I sneaked out the back door of my house—my parents thought I was upstairs studying—and got into Peter's car and headed for Natalie's house.

We parked the car, walked down the street to her house, and studied the situation. Natalie's third-floor light was on. Her window was open. What's more, the tree contained a vast series of branches and seemed easy to climb; at the third-floor level I saw a good-sized branch which actually brushed against the house near Natalie's room, so I'd be able to get within three or four feet of her window. Everything seemed perfect.

Peter boosted me into the tree, and up I went. But as I ascended I noticed a light shining on the second floor, so I swung behind the tree trunk to prevent myself from being seen. But as I pulled myself over a branch, my face swung around in such a way that I could see directly into the room and whoever was in there could see me clearly in the light. And there *was* somebody in the room—which, I now realized, was the bathroom. The somebody was Natalie's mother, and she was sitting on the toilet.

I can imagine how she must have felt, sitting on the second floor and suddenly seeing a face come into her line of vision. I watched the horror begin to appear on her face, and in no time she was screaming, *"Peeping Tom! Peeping Tom! Peeping Tom!"*

So there I was. All I had wanted to do was climb to the third floor and sing Fred Astaire songs to Mrs. Wood's daughter. But now, I knew, my evening was ruined, if not my whole life. I wanted to let go of the branch, crash to the ground, and expire as Natalie held my head in her lap—but I figured I'd probably screw *that* up somehow, too. So I painstakingly made my way down the tree as quickly as I could—which was not very quickly, given the size of the tree.

To compound my problems, my friend Peter had jumped into the car and taken off as soon as the screaming started. When I let go of the last branch, I fell the final six feet to the grass and found myself down on all fours, looking up into a melange of lights and legs hovering over me. Natalie's father was there, and her brothers Vincent and Tom, both of whom I knew as upperclassmen at Haverford School, as well as a few neighbors—all older, stronger, and angrier than I.

For a moment nobody said anything. Then Mr. Wood looked at me. "Thacher," he said, "I must say I'm very surprised to see you here. Could you please explain to me what you were doing up that tree looking through the window at my wife?"

I earnestly started to describe the whole stunt Peter Page and I had concocted, but it was too ludicrous to explain, and I knew that anything I said would be all over Haverford School the next day, thanks to Tommy and Vincent Wood. "Aw, Mr. Wood," I said in a woebegone voice, throwing up my hands, "if I told you, you wouldn't believe me anyway. Let's just say I'm a peeping Tom."

Well, it was fairly obvious to them that I *wasn't* a peeping Tom, just as it was obvious that I wasn't about to burglarize the house. Mr. Wood started smiling, and I began to hope that I might get out of this situation alive.

"Well, Thacher," Natalie's father said, "let's just chalk this up to your youth. Everybody's entitled to one mistake. Obviously, don't do it again. But I do have one thing I want you to do. When you go home, I want you to be sure to tell your mother what happened."

A fate *worse* than death! Kids were more afraid of their parents in those days than they are now—even though, in retrospect, there wasn't much my parents could do to me or take away from me by way of punishment. I didn't receive any allowance because we had no money. And I wasn't old enough to drive, so they couldn't take away my car privileges. The only thing they could deprive me of was their approval. But their approval—especially my mother's—was terribly important to me. When Mr. Wood told me to tell my mother what had happened, he picked the severest punishment I could have imagined.

"Aw, Mr. Wood," I pleaded. "Do I have to?"

"You tell your mother," he insisted. "That's your punishment."

I walked the mile back to my home and into our house. Mother and Father were sitting in the front room. "What are you doing?" my mother asked. "I thought you were upstairs studying."

"I went out for a minute," I said.

"Oh. Where did you go?"

"Well," I said, "I went out and I got into the car with Peter Page, and we went over to see Natalie Wood. I climbed up the tree, and I was going to sing like Fred Astaire in her window, but then I went by the window where Mrs. Wood was on the toilet, and she saw me in the tree and started to scream 'Peeping Tom,' so I came down the tree, and Mr. Wood was there, and he told me I had to come home and tell you what happened."

"Now, wait a minute," my mother said. Then she turned to my father: "Bill, did you hear this story? This boy's been reading too many books." She turned back to me. "That's the craziest thing I ever heard in my life," she said. "Now, get upstairs and get back to work."

In retrospect, my mother knew I'd been outside doing *something* I shouldn't have been doing—getting a pack of chewing gum, maybe. I wasn't supposed to leave the house at night. But she also knew that I didn't drink and I didn't smoke, and we didn't have drugs in those days—so whatever I had done, it couldn't have been outrageous. She just figured that my Natalie Wood story was my way of saying I didn't want to tell her what had happened and that it wasn't worth making an issue over. In effect she trusted her intuition about me, and her intuition was right.

THAT WAS THE END of my courtship of Natalie Wood. But in the best adolescent fashion, I rapidly shifted my affections—soon to become adoration—to Nancy Claghorn, even though I hadn't yet said a word to her. If this was puppy love, I was soon to become an adult dog.

When we graduated from Friday evenings to Saturday evenings, for some reason Nancy wasn't "invited" back by Mrs. Duer. No reason was ever given, of course, and on the face of it her rejection seemed outrageous: Nancy had been the most beautiful, most popular, most sought-after girl at the Friday classes. On the other hand, perhaps that *was* the reason: The pettiness and jealousy of other girls' mothers shouldn't be underestimated.

My mother was friendly with Mrs. Duer at the time, and I remember telling her, "Mother, I'm not gonna go to the goddam thing if Nancy doesn't go. I don't dare dance with her, but I want to *look* at her."

My mother phoned Mrs. Duer to tell her my feelings about inviting Nancy Claghorn to the Saturday Evening Dancing Class.

"Of course she's going!" Mrs. Duer insisted.

"Thacher says she's not."

Mrs. Duer phoned her back a bit later. "There's been some mistake," she said. "It's all been taken care of."

Even then, though, I didn't speak to Nancy directly. But one afternoon in the spring of eleventh grade at Haverford School, a classmate named Pete Childs pulled me aside during recess.

"You know Nancy Claghorn?" he asked.

"Sure," I said. Which was true, but only in a limited sense: I still hadn't actually spoken to her. "Everybody knows her."

"Oh, good," Pete said. "I'm bringing her to the Haverford dance." The Haverford School dance was a "card dance"—that is, girls were expected to have a committed partner for each dance beforehand, lest they suffer the embarrassment of sitting one out alone—and so Pete asked, "Would you dance with her?"

Thus it came to pass that my name was entered on Nancy Claghorn's card and I got to dance with her for the first time. And to my great surprise, I found she was as friendly as she was beautiful. Most good-looking girls tended to be stuck-up, but Nancy was easy to get along with and a lot of fun, to boot. As the saying went at that time, I fell for her like a ton of bricks.

The following fall at Haverford we had the big football dance. By this time I had made the football team and had been chosen for the All-Scholastic team and the All-Inter-Academic League team, and it dawned on me that I was going to be somebody in the world—and, therefore, I didn't have to be scared of girls anymore. How best to proclaim my new stature to the world? The best way, I concluded, was to bring Nancy Claghorn to Haverford School's football dance.

I dialed her home. "I'd like you to come to the Haverford School dance with me," I said.

"Well, I'll have to ask my mother," she replied. She came back on the phone a few minutes later. "I can go to the dance with you," she said. "But my father has to bring me, and he has to take me home."

That upset me a bit; by this time I was old enough to drive. But I figured: Beggars can't be choosers. "Fine," I told her. "It's wonderful."

So the night of the dance, Nancy's father brought her over to my house and took her home—a show of parental concern that impressed my family no end. And I never looked at another girl from that night until we announced our engagement in the middle of my junior year of college.

Nancy and I have been married ever since. We were parents in our early twenties and grandparents by our mid-forties, and we'll be great-grandparents before we're out of our sixties. In retrospect I can see Mrs. Duer's dancing classes for the contrivances they were. Yet what strikes me as I look back from the perspective of more than half a century is how well that system actually worked, for me and others in my circle. I literally met my wife through the dancing class. My brother, too, met his wife at dancing class. And to a large extent most of the marriages of my generation stuck.

To be sure, much of this marital longevity was related to our lack of mobility during our adolescence. All of my adolescent friends grew up together, married mutual friends, stayed at home, and remained friends as we grew older, and we still see a great deal of each other today. We were—and are—nowhere near as cosmopolitan as the generations that followed us. But we *were* more stable.

World War II changed all that. It threw together people from all over the country, so that friends of mine who married after, say, 1942 as likely as not married spouses who were not Philadelphians. Thus when everyone returned after the war, the role of the dancing classes in matching suitable boys and girls had diminished in some imperceptible but critical manner.

True, both of my daughters went through the same dancing-class system in the fifties, and both were given big coming-out parties of their own. And one of them met and married a boy through this system. But he was a boy who had moved to Philadelphia from Virginia because his father had come to Philadelphia for business reasons—the sort of family that wouldn't have been invited to the dancing classes in the old insular days.

More important, by the time my daughters passed through the system it had ceased to be the be-all and end-all of a Philadelphia girl's life. Like other girls in their generation, they knew they were going on to college; the dancing classes would not constitute their only chance at the brass ring. My daughters were perfectly willing to attend the dancing classes and become debutantes. But if we had denied these experiences to either of them, I doubt they would have objected very strenuously.

Mrs. Duer lived on to 1951, when she was eighty-three. By then, I think, even she would have agreed that her time had passed. But in retrospect even I would have to agree that, in her own day, she fulfilled a service and performed it well.

CHAPTER 4
BIG MAN ON CAMPUS
(1937–41)

I WAS NOT YET SEVENTEEN when I entered Princeton University in the fall of 1937. Between my age and my Haverford School background, I started off at some disadvantage in campus politics, which were really just an extension of prep-school politics. Campus activities, which were such a vital part of the college experience, were essentially run by students who had come to Princeton from the big boarding schools like Exeter, Lawrenceville, the Hill, Deerfield, Hotchkiss, Choate, and St. Paul's. Although I was one of fourteen entering freshmen from Haverford School, our numbers paled next to those of a Princeton feeder school like Lawrenceville, which might send seventy or eighty.

What's more, the boarding-school boys tended to look down on us day-school boys (and we, in turn, looked down on the public-school boys). Thus the president of the Princeton freshman class invariably came from Lawrenceville, for the simple reason that a Lawrenceville alumnus entered the election with an automatic seventy or eighty votes from his loyal prep-school classmates.

Thus it was something of a surprise to me when I was elected class secretary and treasurer. It wasn't the sort of office you campaigned for; indeed, campaigning was forbidden. At Haverford School I'd always been so young, so immature, so badly behaved that I never became head of anything. Being chosen one of three class officers was a heady experience—my first taste of popularity and politics—so heady that, in retrospect, it hooked me for life.

As a sophomore and junior I was elected vice president of my class; in my senior year, finally, I became president. Yet class office was not something I had expected or worked toward; it seemed simply a natural consequence of playing football, of saying hello to everybody, of remembering people's names and being nice to them. And of course it didn't hurt to be tall and stand out in a crowd. The fact that my roommate—my cousin Stanley Pearson—was the best athlete in the university helped, too.

At night I sold sandwiches and milk door-to-door in the dorms. I did it to pay my way through school and simultaneously feed myself for nothing, but this job generated another fringe benefit as well: I got to know just about everyone on campus, and vice versa.

But my critical experience at Princeton was football. Remember, when I entered Princeton in the fall of '37 only one school year had passed since a remarkable run of three seasons—1933 through 1935—during which Princeton had lost only one game and had been ranked week after week among the top three or four teams in the country. It was a heady time to be a Princeton football player.

By the time I arrived, to be sure, our material had thinned out somewhat. Coach Fritz Crisler, who had built Princeton into a national football powerhouse, left for Michigan after my freshman year, offering a curiously economic explanation for his departure:

"The Depression," he said, "is exerting an important influence on colleges, which they are just beginning to feel. The high tuition of privately endowed Eastern schools is turning

many kids toward land-grant state institutions. . . . The days
of large endowments and big returns on invested capital are
gone. Inheritance taxes will rise steadily. And high income
taxes, cutting into money which could have sent boys to the
rich social schools, will turn them to state colleges with cheap
tuition. Reduced registration and endowments add up to curtailed sports activity. I think it's best to leave Princeton while
my reputation is still worth something."

Crisler was wrong on the details—the Ivy League colleges
have flourished as America's middle class has grown more
affluent. But he was right on his central point. Schools like
Princeton no longer dominate the national college football scene,
for a reason Crisler neglected to mention: the rise—just as I
arrived and Crisler left—of the Ivy League philosophy, by which
sports emphasis was carefully limited so that the athletic tail
didn't wag the academic dog, as it did at so many schools.
Some Princeton football players, like myself, were there on
scholarships—but these were *academic* scholarships: No one was
required to play football in order to keep his scholarship. In
an age when many schools were virtually hiring football players who rarely saw the inside of a classroom, most of our
Princeton players were reasonably good students, and one—a
guard named Jim Worth—was a Phi Beta Kappa. The few
players who *were* poor students would be sent over to the nearby
Hun School in their spare time to be tutored by that school's
founder, John E. Hun. And most of the Princeton football
players did graduate—not as high a ratio as today, perhaps,
but an impressive proportion for those days.

Thus I was playing for Princeton at the time of its last gasp
as a national football power. Still, we *were* a power: In my
junior year—1939—we were ranked among the top ten football schools in the country, and so were two other Ivy League
schools, Penn and Cornell. To have been a part of that, to have
played football at a time when football was important, remains

one of the most rewarding experiences of my life—even if my association with Princeton football ended on a bitter note.

I WAS A GOOD DEFENSIVE END at Princeton because I was strong and quick and not afraid of physical contact. On the other hand, I was a lousy offensive player. I was too tall to be an effective blocker: I could never get my legs under and drive the other guy—an important ability in Princeton's single-wing formation. It wasn't enough to contain the defensive tackle where he stood; you had to move him out of the way. And you had to move him by yourself; we didn't play with a wingback.

I suffered from one other slight problem as an offensive player: I have 20/200 vision—that is, I can see at one foot what the normal person sees at a distance of twenty feet. So as a pass receiver I was almost useless. I could catch a ball within ten yards of the line of scrimmage, and I was so tall that sometimes our passer could float the ball up there and I could catch it among the surrounding group of pygmy defenders. But when it came to a big, important pass play, where I was required to run long and deep, I simply couldn't find the ball.

Compounding that problem was the fact that my hands weren't all that good to begin with, so the forward passes that did find their way to me often slipped through my fingers. Thus while I was a very good defensive player, I was such a mediocre offensive player that my few attempts to throw or catch passes resulted in tremendous embarrassment—not only for me, but for my university.

Sophomore year they didn't pass to me very much, although in my junior year I caught several short passes. But by then the word had gotten around among our Ivy League opponents that I couldn't see, thanks in part to feature stories in the newspapers about "Princeton's blind end"—that sort of thing. On pass plays I'd run deep patterns in the hope of taking the defensive halfback or safety out of the play. But the defensive backs knew no one was going to throw to me, so they paid no attention to me. Often I ran these deep patterns without knowing where I was or where the defensive backs were but blissfully confident that the ball wouldn't be thrown to me.

Thus there was a certain perfunctory manner in which I went through the motions of running out these pass patterns. Needless to add, the day came that I regretted this attitude. We were playing Harvard and I was running my usual charade of a pass pattern, chugging along deep in the Harvard secondary where no Harvard back was within twenty yards of me. In the meantime, our tailback, Dave Allerdice, was back in the pocket being rushed and desperately looking for a receiver. He saw a black jersey out in the distance, all alone; he forgot that the fellow in the jersey was me; and he let go a pass—a pass so perfect that it hit me squarely on the helmet.

I looked like an idiot, but the story gets worse. Allerdice's pass not only hit me in the helmet, the ball bounced straight up in the air, so that all I had to do was look up and catch it as it came down—which of course I didn't do. The ball came down and hit me on the shoulder pad. The Princeton fans who seconds before had been screaming in anticipation of a sure touchdown were now booing and shaking their fists, and Coach Wieman added insult to injury by taking me out of the game at this precise moment—perhaps the most horrible moment of my life up to that point.

As a result of such humiliations, I played most of the time when we were ahead. But whenever we fell behind I played much less often, because in those situations the team needed a better offensive end. The coaches thought about making me a tackle, but I lacked the thick, heavy legs that you need to play that position. I was a track man; I could run and I was quick; but I was no football tackle. So in an age of one-platoon football—when everyone on the field was expected to play both offense and defense—at Princeton we switched around a lot to the extent that the substitution rules permitted so that, in effect, I was two-platooned. Whereas most football teams had two regular ends, at Princeton we had four: Two of us were better on offense, two of us were stronger on defense. I started most of the games and played more than most of the other ends, but I played nowhere near sixty minutes of every game.

Then too, I was injury-prone. In the course of four years I suffered a separated shoulder, a knee job, a broken ankle, broken ribs, a broken toe, and a sprained thumb—the result of someone's throwing the ball at me too hard.

Sometimes my injuries and my eyesight teamed up to compound my problems. In my sophomore year I injured my knee before our sixth game, and rather than jeopardize me for the rest of the season, Coach Tad Wieman decided to use me only sparingly in our sixth game, against Rutgers. "If I don't have to use you," he said, "I won't. But if we get in trouble, I want you to get in there and play defense."

Well, we did pretty well in the first half against Rutgers, so I didn't get into the game at all. But in the second half Rutgers began to move the ball. Midway through the third quarter they mounted a drive that brought them about to the Princeton twenty-yard line, or just about opposite the point where I was sitting on the bench. At this moment Wieman looked over and shouted, "Longstreth—get in there at end!"

Now, ordinarily I was a member of the starting team, so I was unfamiliar with the procedures for reporting into a game as a substitute. But I had tried to prepare myself for this moment as best I could. In those days when you went into a game you had to report to the referee. And the first play you went in, you were required to stand apart from your teammates until the ball was put in play, lest you communicate any message to them from the sidelines. (Strange as it may seem today, in those innocent days it was believed that the game belonged to the kids and that players should do their own thinking on the field without interference from their coaches.) You were not allowed to speak to your teammates or huddle with them until one play had transpired.

My particular problem in this regard, of course, was my vision. Without my glasses, anything on a football field more than three feet away from me looked like a blur of shapeless forms moving around. Thus I had arranged in advance with the team's manager that I would watch the game with my glasses on. If I was sent into the game, I'd pick out the white shirt—the referee—hand my glasses to the manager, and run onto the field in the direction of the white shirt in order to report my entry into the game.

When Coach Wieman called my name, I leaped to my feet, gave the manager my glasses, pulled on my helmet, and dashed into the game as quickly as I could, so as to avoid the five-yard penalty assessed against substitutes who fail to report promptly. Like all nearsighted people, without my glasses I was groping my way around—but in this case I was groping at high speed.

Unfortunately for my well-laid plans, Rutgers had just made a first down at the very moment I—*sans* glasses—was dashing toward the field. I sensed the presence of two men and so took care to run in between them so I wouldn't bump into them. What I failed to notice in my haste was that these two men were the linesmen, that each of them was holding a pole, and that the pole was connected by ten yards of chain stretched between them. Racing onto the field at top speed, I tripped on the chain and went down as if someone had hit me with a two-by-four. In the process I reinjured my knee, so that when I stood up, I collapsed on the ground again and began rolling around on the ground in agony. I had to be carried off the field on a stretcher before I'd even been *on* the field. I often wonder what it must have been like to watch this spectacle from the stands—to see this tall figure suddenly jump up from the bench, pull on his helmet, rush onto the field, crash to the ground, jump up, crash to the ground again and then be carried off.

We lost that game by two points, incidentally—the first time Princeton had ever lost to Rutgers since the two schools played the very first college football game in 1869. But Coach Wieman's compensation was the laughter he derived thereafter whenever he retold the story—as he did on many occasions. "You know," he used to say, "it was the best game Longstreth ever played."

THROUGHOUT MY FOUR YEARS at Princeton my coaches refused to admit that my eyesight was a lost cause. As a freshman I played extremely well defensively without glasses, and the coaches deluded themselves into believing that modern optical science could make me a good offensive player as well. So sophomore year they fixed me up with a special pair of glasses coated with rubber around the edges. Then they fashioned a mask for my helmet in order to protect the glasses. It was a little frightening to me, because the eyeglass lenses were thick and heavy, and I was afraid the glasses would dig into my face, as they sometimes did even when I *wasn't* playing football. The lenses were supposedly shatterproof. But I couldn't help wondering what would happen if, in a game, my helmet was knocked awry; even with the rubber protection, I envisioned cuts on my cheeks or forehead. That never happened, but the special glasses did get bent constantly when I played. And then there were two rainy games when I couldn't see because my glasses were covered with mud.

So by my junior year I had decided not to play with the glasses at all. Perhaps coincidentally, I had a pretty spectacular year: At the end of the season I was an honorable mention All-America selection. But my success without glasses simply revived the coaches' belief that I'd be an even more successful player with glasses.

Thus at the end of my junior year, courtesy of Princeton University, I became the first football player in America to play with contact lenses. They were huge lenses—very difficult to insert—and I discovered that whenever I got a good belt around the head, the lens would pop and a bubble of air would form between the lens and my eye, after which I couldn't see anything at all. So the contact-lens experiment was less than a success.

Ultimately I developed a more or less manageable routine: I'd wear the lenses at the start of a game. But once I got belted or a bubble of air formed behind a lens, I'd remove them. Sounds easy? The only problem was that in the middle of a game I had no time to take the lens out. And free substitution wasn't permitted in those days—which meant that if I left the game to remove my lens, I couldn't return until the next quarter.

LENSES OR NOT, I lacked hands capable of holding on to a football. But I did possess a great talent for throwing a football which my nearsightedness rendered useless. I could easily throw a football sixty or seventy yards. One afternoon in my senior year we were fooling around before practice. I was retrieving kicks for the punters, and the kicking coach was impressed by the strength of my passes.

"Thacher," he said, "how far can you throw a ball?"

"I don't know," I said. "As far as those guys can kick it, I know that."

The coach put me on the forty-yard line, and I threw the ball into the opposite end zone—a toss of sixty yards. Then he moved me back to the thirty-yard line; I threw the ball into the end zone again. When I tossed a ball into the end zone from the twenty-yard line—a distance of eighty yards—the kicking coach ran off to get Coach Wieman. Eyes or no eyes, they were going to make a passer out of me.

They developed an end-around play in which I would come around from left end, take a handoff, fade back, and then uncork the pass. We had a halfback named Jackson who could run the hundred-yard dash in 9.7 seconds (at a time when the world record was 9.4); in theory, he would outrun the defensive backs—who, again in theory, wouldn't chase him sixty or seventy yards down the field because they'd assume no pass could travel that far. He would run this pattern three or four times in a game so the defense would let its guard down and stop paying attention to him. And on the appointed play, I (who couldn't see) would count a specific number of seconds and then let the ball fly to a specific point seventy yards or so downfield—where Jackson, unmolested by defenders, would gather it in and head for an easy touchdown.

We tried it in practice against the junior varsity, and it worked. So we decided to use it against Navy. On a first down from our own twenty-yard line, I came around, took the ball, faded back . . .

At this point theory and practice parted company. For one thing, Navy's line was all over me, so I had no time to get set or even squint around to look for receivers. All I could do was run back as fast as I could and throw the ball like hell. Which is what I did. From close to my own goal line I let fly a beautiful straight-arrow pass of some eighty yards.

Unfortunately, unbeknownst to me, Jackson had fallen at the line of scrimmage. So there was no one within fifty yards of my beautiful pass. The play did earn me some notoriety: It was the subject of a vignette in *The New Yorker*, titled "Princeton's Mystery Play." Some mystery. We never tried it again.

IN MY SOPHOMORE YEAR I was approached by the head of the classics department, Dr. Duane Stewart, who asked if I'd be interested in majoring in the classics. I shook my head: "Too tough," I said.

Dr. Stewart had anticipated that response. "We have only ten classics majors," he said. "But we have a faculty to serve thirty. We need to show the students that you don't have to be a genius to major in the classics. You're a prominent student, and you're no genius. Your presence here could attract others."

Thus he proposed a deal: "If you sign up, we'll make sure you get through. And when other students see that you got through without working too hard, they'll sign up for the classics, too."

That's how I came to major in Latin and Greek at Princeton. In my zeal to take advantage of what seemed like a free lunch, it didn't occur to me that Dr. Stewart was selling his department's soul for a larger enrollment. So I had only myself to blame when, after one year, the only thing that could go wrong with this ingenious arrangement did go wrong: Dr. Stewart died, and his promise to me died with him, leaving me stuck in a major I was somewhat unqualified to handle.

Indeed, three weeks into my senior year, the new head of the classics department—who'd been hired from Williams College—called me into his office. "I can't figure out why you're here," he said. "Unless you buckle down, I'll kick you out."

I survived my senior year only with the aid of an unsuccessful Princeton Ph.D. candidate who decided to coach me as a means of revenge upon the classics department which had rejected him. Since I was beyond comprehending most of the works we studied, he salvaged me through a "visualization technique": Bits and pieces of everything we studied were marked on a single huge cardboard chart, and I simply stared at that chart until I had committed the whole damned thing to memory. And what I remembered was sufficient for me not only to graduate, but to graduate with honors.

Perhaps as a result, within three years Princeton's classics department grew from ten majors to forty. And one of those majors—my younger brother Frank—became a prep-school Latin teacher, which he still is today, more than forty years later. Wherever Dr. Stewart is today, I'm sure he's smiling at the success of his strategy—even if it succeeded for the wrong reasons.

THE MOST WONDERFUL MAN I knew at Princeton was the football trainer, Eddie Zanfrini—a beloved uncle figure who listened to the troubles of Princeton players for some thirty years. Eddie knew just the way to handle the dumb situations college kids sometimes get themselves into, as I discovered firsthand.

Aside from food at the training table—better food than other Princeton students got, and more of it—Princeton football players received no special privileges, with one exception. It was accepted that during football season, each day you could exchange your white socks, your white T-shirt, and your jockey shorts for a fresh set. In other words, you got clean laundry every day—but only during the season. Most of us were poor kids, and a clean change of undies every day meant a great deal to us. By the time you approached the end of your senior football season, you were thinking seriously about finding a way to continue the supply into the off-season.

One day at lunch my cousin, roommate, and teammate Stanley Pearson pulled me away from the training table. "I got big news," he whispered conspiratorially. "They just got a new shipment of brand-new beautiful T-shirts. I think today's the day."

Stanley and I lived at the Ivy Club, just across Prospect Street from University Field, where the team practiced. We devised a plan and executed it that afternoon. Before practice, when no one was in the team's shower room, we balled up newspaper pages, put them in the shower, and set them afire. The smoke and flames diverted everyone to the shower room, and in the ensuing confusion Stanley and I ran around to the momentarily abandoned equipment room, where each of us grabbed a box of half a dozen T-shirts. We hid the boxes in our lockers and ran out to the field to practice.

Later that night, on the pretext of getting a rubdown, we retrieved the boxes from our lockers, concealed them under our coats, and spirited them back to our room, where we hid the boxes in the bottoms of our dresser drawers. We didn't need the T-shirts until the football season was over, of course, so for a month or so we didn't examine the boxes. But I often sat in class, thinking about those six beautiful T-shirts.

About a week after the season ended, I decided to try out one of the shirts. I opened my dresser drawer, took out the box, and lifted the cover. Inside, where I'd expected to find six new T-shirts, I saw apple cores, orange rinds, two old jock straps, a dirty towel, and some used adhesive tape—and a note which read, "Crime does not pay. The Shadow."

What had happened? Well, Eddie Zanfrini, the team's trainer, had figured out what had happened. Somehow, the moment he heard the shirts were missing, he knew exactly where they were. He never said a word to us—just went to our rooms while we were in class, retrieved the stolen goods, and substituted his own boxes filled with worthless junk. It was the sort of thing Eddie would do—teach you a lesson without forcing a public scene. But he didn't own up to it until years later.

"Eddie," we'd say to him, "it was you, wasn't it?"

"Me what?" he'd reply.

"It was you who took those T-shirts."

"What are ya talkin' about? What were you doing with T-shirts?"

"Oh," we'd say, "we had some shirts."

"And where'd you get them?" Eddie would exclaim in mock amazement. "You mean to tell me you stole shirts? Well, I'm glad I never heard about that."

IN RETROSPECT it's curious that the stealing of the shirts earned me no public disgrace and was dismissed by Eddie as a bit of good-natured fun. But the incident that did earn me my first public disgrace caused no discernible harm to anyone and came about not because I was dishonest, but because I was honest to a fault.

In my senior year I became class president, and at the end of the year I was voted best all-around man in the class. It was immensely enjoyable to know everyone on campus and be liked by most everyone. All the more reason, then, to be frustrated by my poor play during my senior football season. When I should have been going out in a blaze of glory, I was mostly relegated to the bench by one injury after another.

The fifth week of the 1940 season I thought I was back in good shape and ready for the Harvard game. I had a very good week in practice, and the coaches moved me back up to the starting team for the first time in weeks. But prior to the game, at Cambridge, it had rained, and as a result Coach Wieman changed his mind.

"We're going to receive the opening kickoff," he told me, "and I want to pass while the ball is still dry." So the starting end would be someone who, unlike me, could catch passes; I would play later on.

But as things turned out, (1) it didn't rain very much after that, so we continued to throw passes, (2) neither team scored in the entire game, and (3) I didn't get to play until the fourth quarter, and then only for a few minutes, because our pressing need was not defense but offense. So against Harvard—which should have been one of the biggest games of my biggest year—

I played barely five minutes. When the game ended I was furious.

In a destructive mood, I dressed, left Harvard Stadium, and looked up a couple of my Harvard friends. They were at a postgame party in the dorms, and I took them aside to an empty room.

"I'm pissed off at the coach," I told them, with all the bravado of a college boy whose greatest frustration is a football game, "pissed off at this afternoon, pissed off at life. I want to get drunk."

Their reaction was amusement; they knew I'd never had a drink in my life. "We can sell tickets to this one!" they chortled.

"No," I said. "I'm serious. Get me something that's so strong that I'll be drunk. It's so repugnant to me that I won't be able to keep it down. So get me something that will get me drunk quick. I've got to do this to the old man"—that is, Coach Wieman.

We went through the dorms from party to party, looking for something I could drink. Whiskey smelled horrible to me; I had no interest in beer; drinking gin seemed to me like drinking rubbing alcohol. Ultimately I found something called "fishhouse punch," which was palatable but also pretty powerful: There's no whiskey in it, but plenty of rum. I chugalugged two iced-tea glasses full of the stuff.

The effect of consuming this alcohol so quickly was strange. Instead of making me tipsy, it made my lachrymose: I went on a crying jag, weeping to three or four friends about the son-of-a-bitch coach who'd said he would start me and then barely put me in, and goddamm it, I'm a senior . . .

But even the crying jag and the accompanying dizziness didn't last very long; the drinks never really made me drunk (an experience which suggests that I've been right to avoid drink all my life: alcoholics seem to have a genetic disposition to tolerate large quantities of booze). In short order I went back to the party and was my happy old self.

The team caught an eight o'clock train back to Princeton. Most of the players boarded at South Station, but I got on about five minutes later, at Boston's Back Bay Station. Princeton's athletic director, Ken Fairman, was waiting on the platform with me, and we chatted about the game. He didn't seem to notice anything unusual about me.

But when I boarded the train and climbed into my bunk to go to sleep, I started thinking. I was chairman of Princeton's honor committee. I knew there was nothing in the honor code about breaking training or breaking rules; the code applied only to academic life. Still, I *was* the head of the honor committee, and by taking two drinks I had broken the football team's training rules. I started to brood. I felt ashamed and embarrassed. I'd acted like a little boy, I'd done a stupid thing, and only a punishment could absolve me of my guilt. In my younger days, my mother would have spanked me or withheld my allowance, and that would have done the trick. Now someone else would have to fill that role, and I'd get more of a punishment than I bargained for.

So the next day I went to see Coach Wieman, which was no easy thing. Tad Wieman was a very stiff, straightforward guy— a good football tactician, but not much on personal chemistry.

"Coach," I said, "I have to tell you something. I went out and broke training last night."

Wieman looked astonished. "You broke training?" he said incredulously. "But you don't drink or smoke!"

"I know," I said. "But last night I took a drink. First drink I ever had in my life. Probably the last one." Which it was, incidentally.

"I can't believe that!" Tad said.

"Well, I'm sorry, Tad, but it's true."

"Why did you do this?"

I launched into my whole catalogue of grievances: He had said he would start me, it was my senior year, and I'd barely played at all.

"But you play on a *team*," he said. "You should put the team's interests first. You know we were tied; you know we weren't looking for someone to play defense. You know that Wilson's a better offensive player than you are. You're a better all-around player, but for that day and that game, he was the proper person to have in there."

"Well, Tad," I said, "everything you say is right, and I'm very embarrassed and ashamed, and I just wanted to come and tell you and get it off my chest."

He paused. "You know," he said, "I'm going to have to ask you to turn in your suit."

My jaw dropped. "You can't be serious!"

"Yes," he said, "I'm deadly serious. You know we have rules. And the rules say you can't break training."

I sat there and thought to myself: I wonder if he knows that after the Vanderbilt game, his star tailback, Allerdice, got so drunk that Stanley Pearson and I had to carry him home and put him to bed. I wonder if he knows about the others.

But I said nothing. I'd acted enough like a jerk already, and now I'd gotten what I deserved—more than I deserved, really. This was no time to exacerbate matters. Let's recover with honor, I said to myself.

It wasn't easy to tell my parents what had happened, and that I wouldn't be playing in the Dartmouth game the following week. Nor was it easy to face anyone else. After the story got out that Monday, athletic director Ken Fairman—who had stood with me on the train platform in Boston the previous Saturday night—phoned me, flabbergasted.

"What the hell is this all about?" he said. "You and I were together. When was this? After you got on the train?"

"No, it was beforehand," I said.

"When beforehand? The game ended at five and we got on the train around eight, and you were fine."

Then I got a call from a New York sportswriter, who seemed equally mystified.

"I understand you got kicked off the team," he said. "I can't believe that somebody who'd never had a drink before takes two drinks and the coach is kicking you off. The guy must be crazy."

"As far as I'm concerned," I said, "I got what was coming to me, and that's all I have to say."

I never said another word. And it turned out that was the right way to handle it. Instead of being perceived as a villain or a bum, I became an object of sympathy and even some admiration on campus—so much so that despite this episode of stupidity, later that year I was voted the best all-around man in the class and the most popular man in the class.

But if I never complained about my punishment, my mother did. Unknown to me, until the day she died—this was 1940, and she died in 1958—each year on the anniversary of my suspension from the team she telephoned Tad Wieman. He went on to become athletic director at the University of Denver and president of the National Association of Football Coaches. But wherever he went, once a year my mother found him. "This is Nella Longstreth," she would say. "I just want you to know that I have neither forgiven nor forgotten."

I didn't learn of her phone calls until 1970, when I ran into Wieman by chance in the lobby of the Bellevue-Stratford Hotel in Philadelphia. From behind I saw a man whom I immediately recognized, even after thirty years, by his distinctly shiny bald head—the baldest I'd ever seen (with the exception of Harold Stassen's, before he got his toupee).

My God, I thought to myself, that's the Teddy Bear—our nickname for Wieman. I walked across the lobby, spun the guy around, and gave him a big bear hug.

"Tad, how are you doing?" I said. "It's Thacher Long-streth."

He looked up at me once; then he looked up at me again, and his eyes filled with tears. "Thacher, I'm so glad to see you," he said. He said he'd read about me in the papers over the years and was glad to see me looking and feeling so well. "But above all," he said, "I'm so happy to see that you have no rancor for me. Your handclasp and your hug have told me—more than anything you could have said—that anything that happened between us thirty years ago is long forgotten."

"Tad," I said, "it sure is. I'll just say to you what I said in the newspapers then: I got just what was coming to me."

We sat down for a long conversation of who was who and what was what. Just as I was leaving, he stopped me. "Let me ask you one question," he said. "Did you ever know about your mother's phone calls?" I said I didn't. And then he told me.

"Well, Tad," I said, "I'm embarrassed. But what the hell. I mean, she felt bad about it."

"Thacher, she didn't feel as bad as I did," Tad said. "If I'd been a little older and a little wiser then, I would have handled it totally differently. That wasn't the way to handle you—the circumstances weren't appropriate. But I'm just happy it had no ill effects on either of us." Just a few years later he was dead of a heart attack.

IN THE FALL OF 1940, of course, even a sports nut like me had bigger things to worry about than suspension from the football team. World War II had started the previous fall, and the Germans had overrun Poland, Norway, Holland, Belgium, and France. The United States wasn't in the war yet, but the whole world was becoming preoccupied with the need to defeat Hitler, which made it hard to maintain any interest in academics or sports. I waited on tables at college and carried a sandwich basket and worked summers at Camp La Jeunesse for boys in upstate New York. But I never gave a thought to a job or a career after college, because there was no question that we were going to war. I was majoring in the classics; I'd sit in the library and read about Rome and Greece, and I loved it. But I wondered: Will there ever be a world where this knowledge will be any use at all? Shouldn't I study engineering or learn how to work with my hands? If we're all going back to living in caves, wouldn't that leave me better prepared to survive than I am now?

WHILE I PLAYED and studied at Princeton, Nancy remained in Philadelphia, attending Springside School in Chestnut Hill and then working as a retail sales clerk at Wanamaker's with her best friend and fellow debutante, the department-store heiress Fernanda Wanamaker—notwithstanding the fact that Nancy's maternal relatives owned Wanamaker's primary rival, Strawbridge & Clothier.

In the course of those four years I somehow managed to write her a letter nearly every day—really sappy stuff when I reread the letters today. But for a guy who was in love, those letters were serious business. Once a girl was out of school in those days, she wanted to get married right away; she wasn't likely to wait while her intended went off to college for four years. My first cousin had lost his fiancée in just this manner.

So by my junior year at Princeton I had worked out my schedule so I was spending almost as much time with Nancy as I did at school. I'd spend Friday night, Saturday, and Sunday at her house in Chestnut Hill. Then Monday morning I'd hitchhike back to Princeton for classes Monday and Tuesday. I had no classes Wednesday, so Tuesday night I'd hitchhike back to Chestnut Hill. Thursday morning I'd hitchhike back to Princeton again for classes Thursday and Friday.

We were married in 1941, four days after my graduation from Princeton, at St. Martin's-in-the-Field, an Episcopal church in Chestnut Hill. My mother, anticipating that I'd be participating in a lot of weddings (she was right: I've been an usher at twenty-one), and perceiving that it's difficult to rent a morning suit for someone who's six foot six, had put together her savings of several years and bought me a morning suit to ensure that I'd be married in style. In spite of my family's straitened circumstances, it was an enormous wedding, because, of course, the bride's family pays for the wedding, and in a moment of weakness my wife's maternal grandparents—the Strawbridges of the department-store family—had agreed to foot the cost of the wedding. Thus relieved of direct responsibility for the bill, Nancy's family and mine—figuring that this was the only chance we'd ever have to entertain—invited virtually everyone we'd ever known. So in hundred-degree weather—this in an age when men wore wool morning suits and air conditioning was still in its infancy—more than a thousand guests crowded into the Claghorns' substantial house just a block from the church.

Actually, the Strawbridges *had* placed some limits on their generosity. They had agreed to pay for the food, the music, the tent, and virtually everything else—but not for any liquor; the Strawbridges were teetotalers. Thus the liquor bill at the party was the Claghorn family's responsibility, and so the Claghorns were watching the consumption of champagne and hard liquor very closely and trying to hold it to a minimum.

I had contributed to their nervousness because, at my urging, they had invited my entire Princeton graduating class—some five hundred men—on my insistence that virtually all of them were friends of mine. I had assured my father-in-law that the act of inviting my classmates was merely a token gesture. "Who," I asked rhetorically, "is going to hang around for four days after graduation just to attend my wedding?"

As it turned out, of course, more than a hundred of my

classmates *did* show up at the wedding. And most of them perceived the event as our last big party before we would all be shipped off to war: Although the United States hadn't yet been drawn into World War II, it was obviously going to be, and more than half the members of our class were going directly from graduation into the Army or Navy or ROTC units. Thus they hung around campus for four days of celebration and then came down to Philadelphia for my wedding.

And did they drink! Remember, young men in those days didn't fool around with narcotics, and perhaps for that reason they drank more hard liquor than they do today—especially when it was free. There was simply no limit to the booze capacity of this horde of Princeton seniors who descended on our wedding.

Not long after the reception had begun, as I was standing in the reception line, my father-in-law, John Claghorn, came over to me and whispered in my ear. "*All* those Princeton students who weren't coming and who are here," he said, "have consumed *all* the alcohol that I bought, which I was told would be enough for two thousand people, and I now have to go over to the club and buy additional whiskey and gin to take care of those Princeton students who are still here and still drinking." He never let me forget it. To the day he died at age ninety, he'd bring up that subject whenever a wedding was mentioned.

IN THE EARLY 1980S, while I was still president of the Greater Philadelphia Chamber of Commerce, I was one of several local boosters who went down to Washington to testify before a U.S. Senate committee regarding projects for the Philadelphia Navy Yard. William Proxmire, the well-known curmudgeon from Wisconsin, was the committee's chairman. At the start of the session, he studied the agenda and frowned.

"Let's see here," he announced. "Our first witness is Thacher

Longstreth. There can only be one person in the world with that name. Mr. Longstreth, will you stand up, please?"

I rose. "Yessir."

"You are Thacher Longstreth?"

"Yes."

"You went to Princeton?"

"Yes, that's right."

"You played football there, I believe?"

"Yeah, I did."

"Would you tell us how tall you are?"

"Six feet, six inches."

"And how much do you weigh?"

"Well, I weigh about two hundred and thirty-five pounds."

"How much did you weigh in 1938?" he asked.

"I weighed about two hundred and twenty-five then," I said.

"Umm-hmm. Are you fast?"

"Not anymore, Senator."

"Were you fast at the time?"

"Well, I held my college high-hurdles record."

"Umm-hmm. Weren't you a wrestler, too?"

"Yes, I was."

"Now, I'm going to stand up," Proxmire said, and he rose to face me. "I'm five feet ten," he said. "I weight one hundred and eighty pounds now. I weighed one hundred and seventy-five in 1938. I'm not only not a wrestler, I'm not strong enough to break an egg." He paused. "I was the slowest man on the Yale football squad." Then, turning to the audience: "I want you to look at the obvious mismatch that stands before you." Then, turning back to me: "Now, I want to recount an incident to you, Mr. Longstreth, which you may not remember. I was the fourth-string fullback at Yale. I played on the junior varsity until my senior year. And then, because I was a senior, they let me sit on the bench. I never got into the games unless we were way, way ahead or way, way behind. And this particular year that I am speaking of, we were usually way, way behind. For that reason I got into a fair number of games.

"In this particular game, we played Princeton very hard the first half, and the score was tied. Just before the half ended, our first-string fullback went to block his man and was rendered unconscious. He was carried off the field and did not return to the game that day. Halfway through the third quarter, our second-string fullback, in carrying a ball on a smash over the line, was tackled by this man—and he too failed to rise from the contact. It then became my turn, because our third-string fullback had a bad leg.

"So the coach said to me, 'Proxmire, on the first play I want you to hit that number 41 and get him out. He's been playing in our backfield all day. Just hit him as hard as you can. Get him out of the game!'

"On the first play I didn't pay any attention to the play or anything else—I just ran into that guy and hit him as hard as I could."

Proxmire paused for dramatic effect. "I woke up three days later in the Princeton infirmary. I'd been unconscious for seventy-two hours." He turned to me. "I've been waiting for forty years to get even with you, Mr. Longstreth. I don't know what your testimony is going to be, but it sure as hell had better be good."

Old football players never forget. Which is why I haven't.

Overleaf above. The "big house" in Haverford—a huge, rambling, thirty-room mansion built by my grandmother shortly after the Civil War—is central to my memory, even though the stock market crash forced us to move out when I was barely 13.

Opposite below. The carriage house in Haverford, where my parents moved us in 1933 when we couldn't afford to staff or heat the "big house."
Above right. My maternal grandfather, William Franklin Thacher, lost his arm in the Civil War and subsequently opened the Florence Foundry in New Jersey.
Right. My maternal grandmother, the indomitable Ella Hoover ("Gah") Thacher, was one of the nation's leading temperance crusaders. I adored her.

Opposite left. My father, William C. Longstreth, chose his intended bride on the day she announced her engagement to another man.

Opposite right. The author, 1921, with my mother, Nella Thacher Longstreth.

Opposite below. Brother Frank, myself, and our father about 1931—after the stock market crash but before we moved out of the "big house" (pictured behind us).

Above. Camp La Jeunesse, Saranac Lake, New York, 1933. That's me in the front row at far left, age 12. Next to me is my lifelong friend, Charles ("Chizzy") Anderson.

Right. December 1936: The author as a Haverford School senior, just after I was named to the *Evening Bulletin*'s All-Inter-Academic football team.

Left. Fall 1938: As a sophomore on Princeton's varsity football team, I started my first game.

Above. Spring 1941: My Princeton graduation portrait. I was 4-F and a Quaker to boot, but all my friends were going to war, and I could do no less.

Below. Fall 1939: That's me applying a flying tackle to Brown ball carrier Richard High.

Opposite. Nancy at 17, vacationing at Miami Beach shortly after our engagement was announced. What a build!

Left. Nancy and I at the Princeton junior prom. By my junior year I had worked out my schedule so that I spent almost as much time with her in Chestnut Hill as I did at school. I made better marks with her.

Below. The in-laws: my parents, Bill and Nella Longstreth, with Nancy's parents, Anne and Jack Claghorn, whom I loved as much as I did my own parents.

Above. June 1941: With Nancy on our honeymoon in Brandon, Vermont.
Below. June 1966: On our twenty-fifth anniversary we returned to the same spot in Vermont.

Opposite above left. The author
(left, in Navy gear) with my
brother Frank (a Marine) at
North Philadelphia station
during World War II.
Opposite above right. June 1944:
The author, aboard the USS
Wasp in the Pacific.
Opposite below. January 1945:
U.S. Task Force 58 at Ulithi,
prior to the battles of Iwo
Jima and Okinawa.

Above. In the Pacific, February
1945: That's me at left,
receiving the Bronze Star from
Vice Admiral John Sidney
McCain.

Near the end of World War II our growing family consisted of Peter (left), age four months, and Anne, three years. A third child was on the way, much to the mystification of our neighbors—since I was still in the Pacific.

CHAPTER 5
WAR
(1941–45)

I WAS PROBABLY the number-one potential employee in Princeton's 1941 senior class. I had already been declared 4-F because of my vision, so I seemed unlikely to go into the armed forces. I was president of my senior class, an honors graduate, and an athlete, so I was highly visible.

I flirted briefly with an offer to play professional football for the Cleveland Rams for $100 a game—but I wouldn't get to play: I'd simply sit on the bench in case one of the starters got hurt. I asked the coach—a tough old gladiator named Dutch Clark—if he thought I was good enough to make a professional football player.

"If I had a Princeton education and was married to a beautiful girl like you are," he replied, "I'd get the hell out of here. Everybody on this team is either out of the mines or off the farms." (The NFL didn't have black players in those days.) "If you're going to play football, you're going to be playing with guys who are inherently much tougher than you are. They're not physically any stronger or quicker, but they're tougher. And they have a much different attitude toward life, because they're never going to improve themselves, except through the vehicle of football. You've got all kinds of ways to make it. I think the least of them is going to be football. Unless you're

97

trying to prove something, or unless you love the game, I'd take a walk." So I did.

Joyously released from the need ever again to endure the physical pain of being banged around on a football field, I considered three other concrete job offers. One was a trainee position at Macy's which paid $35 a week—a fortune in those days. But that meant moving to New York City. Then I had a $30 offer from IBM, but that meant going to Endicott, in southeastern New York state. Nancy and I were just getting married, and she preferred to stay in Philadelphia. So did I, for that matter: All the things that were important to me at age twenty—my parents, my friends, Haverford School, Princeton—were right in the Philadelphia area. Also, though I didn't know it, we were only six months from Pearl Harbor.

But even if there hadn't been a war on the horizon, and even if I hadn't felt constrained by loyalty to my wife and family and friends, I suspect I would have stayed in Philadelphia anyway, simply out of fear. In high school and college I'd been the big frog in a little pond; now I was about to take my place in the big pond, and it seemed to me that I could manage the transition more smoothly if I stayed in Philadelphia. After the war, when *Life* magazine sent me to Detroit, I was no longer afraid of the outside world. But in 1941 that apprehension deeply influenced me, even though I perceive that today only in retrospect.

Thus I went to the Insurance Company of North America in Philadelphia for $25 a week. But within six months the United States was at war, and I went to enlist in the Army— my atrocious vision and my Quaker heritage notwithstanding. At Princeton I had read Arthur Koestler's *Darkness at Noon,* and for the first time I began to realize that what Hitler was doing to the Jews in Germany could happen to people like me. In 1939 the Nazis and Russians had systematically exterminated Poland's leadership class; I assumed they'd do the same if they ever came here, and I instinctively perceived of myself as a member of that class. Instead of thinking like a Quaker— that it's wrong to go to war—I came to see the war as a classic struggle between the forces of good and evil.

Beyond that logic I yielded to the macho implications: When there's a war, men fight. All my friends were going to war, and I could do no less than my friends. I had always been an earnest student of American history and particularly America's wars; now, I realized, we were going to have the greatest war in our history. I had to be part of it, or I would never again feel that I was a man.

"YOU'RE 4-F," I was told at the Army recruiting office after submitting to a physical which included an eye examination.

"Yes," I said, "but that was before Pearl Harbor."

"You can't see, period," said the sergeant. "You'll never get into the Army. If we ever get to the point where we have to take people like you in the Army, the war's lost. Go away and do something else—get a job in a war factory—but don't bother us."

I realized there was no way I could change my medical record. But I judged—correctly—that the Navy didn't know what the Army was doing, and vice versa. So I went over to the Navy to enlist, and this time I anticipated that sooner or later they'd discover how bad my eyes were if I didn't find some way to deceive them.

I still had my Rohm and Haas Plexiglas contact lenses— miserable, oval things, about the size of elongated quarters— which Princeton's football team had purchased for me in 1939 and which I'd used in 1940. To avoid irritation when you wore them, you had to put synthetic tears in them with a dropper. Then you'd work the thick lenses into your eyes, blinking and squinting and agonizing throughout the process. I got to the point where I could wear them for four hours. Then when you took them out, you'd usually need a little suction cup. It was a very unpleasant procedure at both ends. But I did have the lenses, and when I wore them I could see as well as I could with glasses on.

So when I went to enlist in the Navy, I took the contact lenses along. I was also wise enough to get a pair of my regular glasses fitted up with plain glass. Thus according to my plan, I'd walk in wearing my contact lenses. Had I worn them under my regular glasses, the effect would have been like looking out of the bottom of a Coca-Cola bottle. But with plain glass lenses in my eyeglasses over the contact lenses in my eyes, I could read the charts perfectly. Then when I was told to take the glasses off, I would pretend that I could only read part of the way down the eye chart—with 20/15 vision you could still get in.

In this fashion I got through the preliminary eye examination with no trouble. I sailed through the physical exam and all the other procedures until April of 1942, when I received my commission as an ensign, with orders to leave for Washington in four days for preliminary duty and further reassignment. Nancy was about to give birth to our first child—two days later, as it turned out—so I was noticeably nervous when I went down to the Philadelphia Navy office for one final physical exam, again wearing my contact lenses under my eyeglasses.

At first my physical went just as it had before—I stripped down, took off all my clothes, went in, and got examined. When they got around to the eye exam, I read the chart just as I had before. In each of my previous three physicals, I had read the eye chart with my glasses on, then read it without my glasses, and then proceeded to the next test. But this time, when I was finished, the eye examiner—a Navy yeoman—said, "Now, sit down in the chair here."

"What for?" I said.

"When you go on active duty we refract your eyes," he said.

"What's that?" I asked.

"Well, we put an anesthesia in your eyes, and then we examine them to make sure you don't have glaucoma or cataracts or anything like that."

Well, I knew that the moment they put drops in my eyes and the drops bounced off my contact lenses, they'd catch me. Desperately, I looked around for some place where I could take the lenses out. Just as I started to sit down in the chair, I clutched my belly and threw myself on the floor and made retching noises.

"What's the matter?" asked the flabbergasted yeoman. "Are you all right?"

"Oh, my god," I said, retching and gasping. "I've got this terrible stomachache. I think I'm going to be sick."

"Christ," he said, "don't get sick on that floor—I just cleaned it up fifteen minutes ago."

"Where's the bathroom, where's the bathroom?" I wailed. He pointed to the next room.

So I crawled, stark naked, on my hands and knees—still making retching noises—across the floor and into one of the stalls in the men's room, where I closed the door, continuing my retching sounds while the bewildered yeoman stood just outside the stall door, calling, "Are you all right? Are you all right?"

"Yeah, I'll be out in a minute," I said. "I'll be all right." Meanwhile, I had to take those goddam lenses out. As I said, ordinarily it required a suction cup to pull them out—but my suction cup was back in my clothes at the other end of the building. So I'd have to pry them out with my fingernails.

Try to picture my situation. There I was on my knees—so as to appear to be throwing up in the toilet—trying to pry out a lens with one hand and cupping the other hand so that when the lens did pop out it wouldn't fall into the toilet (in which case I'd really be licked). My hands were trembling from the stress.

"Hurry up," the yeoman was saying. "Come on, we've got twelve guys waiting in line out here." I could feel the sweat pouring off my forehead. Here my whole life hinged on whether this guy caught me with those goddam lenses or not. If he didn't catch me, I'd get into the Navy for four years and become a hero and emerge from the war with medals and decorations. But if he caught me, I'd spend the rest of the war making artillery shells in some factory, humiliated at the thought of walking down the street while everyone who passed me wondered: Why isn't he in the war?

After scratching my eyeballs several times, I finally got my fingernail in under each lens and pulled it out.

But where to hide them? I had no clothes, no pockets. So I put the lenses in my left hand, figuring that my hands were large enough that if I kept my hand sort of closed, the lenses wouldn't be noticed. Soon I was back in the examination chair and the yeoman fetched the doctor to put the drops in my eyes.

"My God," the doctor said when he looked at me, "your eyes are really red, aren't they?"

"Yeah," I said, "too much celebrating last night." He proceeded with the refraction and concluded that my eyes were healthy.

But I was not yet home free. From here the yeoman took me into the next room for a blood-pressure test. I sat down at a table, where the yeoman wrapped my left arm and pumped up the pressure device. "Now open your hand," he instructed.

If I did that, of course, he'd see the lenses I was clutching. Once again, I had to think fast.

"I can't do that," I said. "I got a cramp in my hand. I can't get it open."

"Jesus!" the yeoman muttered. "What the hell's the matter

with you, for Christ's sake? One moment you're retching on the floor and now you've got a cramp in your hand. You really don't want to go to war, do you?"

"I can't open it," I insisted. "My goddam hand is cramped."

"My god," he said. "I'll go get you a relaxant." So he went to get a pill for me, and while he was gone I shifted the lenses over to my right hand.

The yeoman returned and give me the relaxant, after which I allowed him to pry my fingers open. But when he pumped up my arm and took my pressure, I had a new problem.

"Unbelievable!" he shouted. "You got a blood pressure of two-twenty over one-ninety. You're almost dead. What the hell's the matter with you?"

"Well, my wife's having a baby," I suggested.

The yeoman hurried off to get the doctor, who asked how old I was. "I'm twenty-one," I said.

"I never saw anyone with such high blood pressure for twenty-one. Are you worried about anything?"

Of course I was worried—I was terrified that they'd find the contact lenses in my right hand and throw me out of the Navy, and for the previous twenty-five minutes I'd been worried about prying out my contact lenses without blinding myself or giving myself away. But all I said was, "Yeah, I'm worried. My wife's having a baby. It's due tonight, and I don't want to have to go away before it's born."

"Oh, hell," the doctor said. "That's simple. Tell you what we'll do. We'll finish the physical, because you've never had any problems with your blood pressure before. You go back and get that baby and then come back here and we'll complete your physical and away you'll go."

"Doctor," I asked, "do I have to take this whole physical all over again?" I knew I couldn't get away with my retching act a second time.

"Oh, no," he said. "We'll just do your blood pressure." So

I left the Navy center—not to go home to my wife, but to return to the Insurance Company of North America, where I'd been in the middle of taking an exam. The exam was another matter weighing heavily on my mind that day. It had cost $15 to take it—more than half a week's pay—so I couldn't leave it unfinished. And it was very important that I score 90 or better—because in that case I'd get my money back. I *did* get my 90 and my refund, and from there I raced out to Lankenau Hospital, where our first child was about to be born.

By the time I arrived at the hospital, Nancy was in labor—and also very angry at me because I hadn't come sooner. In those days hospitals were more casual than they are now. They didn't have air conditioning; the windows were open. And as I walked up the hospital steps I could hear Nancy shouting, "Thacher, you son of a bitch, where are you?"

I got in there just in time to be present when our daughter Anne was born. The following day I returned to the Navy center and took my blood pressure, which was back to normal. And I was off to war.

ONE DAY I was saying goodbye to my friends at the Insurance Company of North America; the next day I was walking into the labyrinthine halls of the Office of Naval Intelligence on Constitution Avenue in Washington. I'd had no indoctrination. It was now the first week in April of 1942 and the United States of America was getting its clock cleaned in every battlefront across the world. The Navy Department wasn't exactly a center of laughter and good cheer—at least until I arrived.

I reported to my commanding officer wearing a uniform I'd purchased at the only source I knew of—Wanamaker's in Philadelphia. (Officers, unlike enlisted men, were responsible for buying their own equipment.) But the largest uniform I could find there was intended for someone about four inches shorter and fifty pounds lighter than I was. Also, what with getting through my physical and becoming a father and taking my insurance examination and saying goodbye, I'd let my hair grow longer than Navy regulations permitted. One other thing—my electric razor had been separated from me in transit, so I hadn't shaved in three days.

At the end of my first day in Washington—about four o'clock—my boss came over and asked me where I was going to spend the night. I told him I had a place with some friends. "Tomorrow morning," he said, "when you come in, get here half an hour early." He explained that Admiral Jack Towers, an old sundowner who was chief of the Bureau of Aeronautics, would be there to inspect all the new officers.

So I came in there the next morning at eight o'clock and found myself in a reception office with about ten other naval officers, most of them lieutenants; I might have been the only ensign in the room. We were all standing around, talking or reading the papers. I picked up a copy of the *Washington Post* and was studying the sports pages intensely—the baseball season had just begun—when suddenly I heard, "Uh *huh!*" It didn't sound like anything that you could understand, and I kept on reading the baseball scores; I thought perhaps someone was coughing. Then again came the sound: "Uh *huh!*" Still I kept on looking at the paper. Finally a voice barked, "Ensign Longstreth, come to attention!" Uh-*huh,* it turned out, was the aide's way of bringing us to attention. It was supposed to mean "Ten-*shun.*" But how was I to know that?

I dropped the paper and Admiral Towers entered the room. He shook hands with each of us and invited us into his office, where the ten or twelve of us sat in various chairs. He gave us a pep talk about the Bureau of Aeronautics: Our mission was to provide for the troops in the field, he said; the young men flying for the American Navy were the finest young men in the world; we were going to help them whip the Japs—that sort of thing. After a few minutes he dismissed us—everyone that is, except me.

"Ensign," he addressed me when the others had gone, "I assume you're a college man. Where did you go to college?"

"I went to Princeton, sir."

"Thought so. Where do you live?"

"I live in Philadelphia."

"Do you live on the Main Line?"

"Yessir."

"I thought so. What did you do when you were in college?"

"I played football, sir."

"I thought so."

Gradually I deduced the admiral's purpose in thus cross-examining me: He had singled me out because I was obviously bigger, stronger, and brighter than the rest of the new officers. No doubt he was about to issue me a secret assignment. I was to be dropped in a parachute over Nagoya or smuggled onto a tropical island aboard an American submarine to subdue a battalion of Japs with my bare hands. I was ready to go—thrilled, actually.

Admiral Towers' voice grew quiet. "Ensign Longstreth," he said, "my first order to you is: *Go get a haircut!* My second order to you is: *Go get a uniform that fits!* My third order to you is: *Go shave!* You're the most slovenly-looking, disgraceful-looking officer that I've ever seen in my thirty-five years in the Navy. When you go do those things and at least appear to be a naval officer, then you come back here and we'll try to make an officer out of you. Dismissed."

Towers didn't cross my path again for another three and a half years, in late September of 1945. I had become assistant operations officer on the staff of Admiral John Sidney McCain, commander of the Second Fast Carrier Task Force in the South Pacific. With the end of the war that month, McCain had been sent back to the United States. Two days after his arrival he attended a large reception in his honor; that night he died in his sleep. His replacement in command of the Second Fast Carrier Task Force turned out to be none other than Admiral John Towers.

On his first day on board, Towers assembled his staff at attention and walked down the line, greeting each of us with a handshake and a "Well done." I received the same perfunctory handshake and greeting, but just as he was about to pass on to the next man, the admiral turned and looked at me a second time.

"What was your name again?" he asked.

"Longstreth, sir."

"Lieutenant Longstreth, haven't I seen you somewhere before?"

"No, sir," I lied. "Not to my knowledge."

"Funny," he said. "I have a feeling I've seen you somewhere before. Oh well, I'll think of it." But he never did.

WHEN I WAS ASSIGNED to the Bureau of Aeronautics in Washington, I was put in charge of all the top-secret messages sent to the bureau, even though I'd been in the Navy just a few months. Every night I'd gather all these secret messages, lock them in a huge safe, and then set a time lock so no one could open it until it unlocked automatically at eight the following morning, at which time I'd be there to supervise the opening personally.

Security was very tight at this point. The Japanese seemed to know too much about our fleet movements, so concern about spies was rampant. I used to work at the office late into the night, trying to learn my job and keep abreast of all the correspondence in my care.

About six or seven o'clock every night, Mamie, the black cleaning woman, would come in. Among those who came out of my socioeconomic set—white Anglo-Saxon Main Line Protestant, Haverford School, Princeton, naval officer—our only exposure to blacks was to family servants. In those days the gulf between white and black—between upstairs and downstairs—was wide in many respects but remarkably narrow in others. To me as I grew up there were two types of black people. There were those mysterious people who lived in ghettos somewhere—whom we heard about but never saw because they weren't allowed to come downtown. And then there were those wonderful people who lived in your house, bandaged your hand when you cut it, or even let you crawl into bed with them at night when thunder struck and your parents were out.

Since Mamie fitted into the second category, and since I was the only one there when she worked, we got to be pretty friendly. Once when Mamie complained about her rheumatism, I gave her an old sweater I had at home. On her children's birthdays I'd bring candy for them. It was a nice relationship.

After I'd been there maybe two months, I was at home one night in my little apartment in Arlington, Virginia. I'd finished my customary office routine—work late, gather my secret messages, put them in the safe, set the time lock, close the safe and go home. I was eating my dinner when the phone rang.

"Ensign Longstreth?" said the voice.

"Yes."

"This is Mamie."

"Hi, Mamie!" I said. "Got something wrong with you?"

"No," I heard her say, "I ain't got nuttin' wrong with me. But you got a lot wrong with *you*."

"My God, Mamie, what's the trouble?"

"I'm down here cleaning up," she said. "This safe's open."

"*What?*"

"Yeah, it is. The safe's open!"

I panicked. "Oh my God. How'd it get open?"

"I don't know. When I came in here, it was open."

"Mamie," I insisted, "it *can't* be open. Once you put that time lock on, that safe can't be opened until tomorrow morning."

"Well then," she said, "you musta forgotten to close it, 'cause it ain't closed!"

"Don't make a move," I instructed her. "Just please stay right there, and I'll be right on down."

I got in my car, drove down as fast as I could, signed in with the duty officer—"I've got to go up and get some papers," I explained—and raced to my little office. Mamie was sitting at the desk. The safe door *was* open—just barely open, but open nevertheless. Immediately I realized that in closing it I had pushed the door but had forgotten to pull the clamp down.

"Mamie," I asked her, "what are you supposed to do in a case like this?"

"I's supposed to call the duty officer the moment I find anything like this happening," she said. "But I remember a young man they had down here and what happened to him. They raised hell over it, court-martialed him and everything. I don't want to let anything like that happen to you. So I just figured I'd call you up, and then you'd come down here and close it up and that'd be the end of it."

"Mamie," I breathed a sigh of relief, "you and I have the same attitude toward life." She and I shook hands. I closed the safe, set the time lock, returned home, and never heard a word about it.

Which was very lucky for me. Because if Mamie had done what ninety-nine out of one hundred people would have done in her place—called the duty officer—the best that would have happened is that we would have taken an inventory of every communication in the place to see if anything was missing. The worst? I could have been court-martialed for carelessness and thrown out of the Navy. Mamie had saved my career.

Was I the same Thacher Longstreth who two years earlier

had turned himself in to coach Wieman for consuming two drinks after a football game? Yes—but in the interim I'd developed a more sophisticated concept of the enormity of my offense. When I broke the Princeton football team's training rule against drinking, I really had caused no harm—but I felt I had done something in the presence of other people, that therefore I couldn't conceal it and the best response would be to turn myself in. Had Mamie *not* discovered the open safe, I probably *would* have mentioned it to my superiors the next day, because of the risk that some important documents might have been stolen. But the next day I conducted my own inventory and found that nothing was missing. And since no harm had been done, I concluded that the best course of action was to let sleeping dogs lie. I had come a long way in two years.

IN THIS FASHION I spent my first year in the Navy, behind a desk in Washington, in keeping with an understanding Nancy and I had reached: "I won't squeal on you if you don't go to war," she said. That is, if I stayed out of harm's way, she'd keep my secret about the contact lenses that got me into the Navy. That was fine with me: By the end of 1942 we had a child and a second on the way.

But all that changed on the 13th of February, 1943, when my friend Peter Page was shot down at the battle of Guadalcanal—my best friend, and also the first of my friends to be killed in the war. When my mother phoned me with the news, I spent the night walking the deserted streets of Washington, crying. Beautiful Peter—my classmate at Haverford and Princeton, who'd driven me to sing outside Natalie Wood's window—was gone forever. Suddenly the war took on new meaning to me. And the thought of remaining at my cushy desk job was something I couldn't stand.

The next morning I walked into the office of my bureau

chief, Admiral Ralph Davison. "My best friend just got killed," I said, and I burst into tears again. "I want to go to war."

"You want to come with me?" he asked. "I'm putting together a carrier task force." I told him to count me in. But later, when Davison's task force was delayed, I told him I couldn't wait. That's when he assigned me to an air group on the new aircraft carrier *Wasp,* scheduled for the Pacific.

Nancy was beside herself. "You can't do that," she cried. "You can't leave." But I wasn't listening to her, or to reason. As has so often been the case with me, I was operating from my gut. Looking back now, I'm appalled at how little thought I've devoted to the direction of my life and how much I've relied instead on my instincts. But as I've frequently found, that's not so terrible: As long as your instincts are somehow tied to your brain, your gut reaction is likely to be the right reaction.

TO TOUGHEN ME UP for mortal combat against Hirohito and Tojo, my Navy superiors found a unique expedient: I was sent into combat on a baseball field against Dom DiMaggio—the great Boston Red Sox center fielder and brother of the even greater Joe DiMaggio. The place was the Quonset Point Naval Air Station in Rhode Island; the time was the summer of 1943, when DiMaggio was at the peak of his baseball career. I was, too, come to think of it—but the resemblance between us ended there.

As a young man I had been blessed with the ability to throw a baseball very hard and very far. I didn't play baseball at Princeton, but I once impressed the team by standing at home plate in Princeton Stadium and throwing the ball into the right-field stands—something no one had ever done before (and no one ever will do again, since the stadium has been torn down). I didn't play varsity baseball for the same reason that had dogged my football career: I could barely see. As a pitcher, I was unhittable when I threw the ball anywhere near the plate. But I rarely did.

Nevertheless, in the summer of 1943 I found myself at the Quonset Naval Air Station having a catch one night when Pete Appleton—a former major-league pitcher who was Quonset's baseball coach—walked by. He was so impressed by the power and speed of my throwing arm that he resolved to make me into a pitcher, despite my warnings about my poor vision and lack of control. My utter lack of baseball experience—which struck me as a solid liability—merely enhanced his interest in me.

"You're just what I've been looking for all my life," he told me. "Raw, primitive talent that's completely unspoiled by experience and knowledge. I'm going to make you a big-leaguer by the time this war's over."

He convinced me that it would be fun to go out for baseball because the baseball players were excused from the rigorous daily calisthenics regimen imposed on everyone else at the base. Instead I sat around, shagged flies, and worked on my pitching each day with Pete Appleton. Finally one day Appleton decided I was ready to be tested in a real game against the Boston Coast Guard—the best of all the service teams in New England. Whereas our Quonset team consisted of semi-pro and college players, the Boston Coast Guard included three major-leaguers: Jim Hegan, the Philadelphia Athletics catcher; a Boston Red Sox catcher-outfielder named Peacock; and, of course, Dom DiMaggio. Needless to add, the Boston Coast Guard beat everybody easily.

After five innings of our game, we were trailing, ten to one, and there was no question who was going to win. At this point Appleton came over to me and said, "Warm up! You're going in the next inning."

The first batter I faced in my official baseball career was

none other than Dom DiMaggio. I was scared to death. Appleton, who had convinced me thus far that I had what it took to pitch in the big time, came out to the mound to reassure me yet again.

"Now, I don't want you to worry about it," he said. "Just stick your foot up in the air and throw that ball as hard as you can. That's the first thing you do. Just loosen him up a little bit. If he sees you at your top speed, he'll know he's got something to reckon with."

So I took my first windup and stuck my foot up in the air and let the ball go. It sailed over DiMaggio's head and into the screen behind home plate with a sizzling *dinnnnnnnggggggg*, sticking in the screen and quivering back and forth from the burning heat of my powerful pitch.

DiMaggio never said a word. He put down his bat, walked back into the dugout, put on his jacket, waved to his teammates, walked over to a jeep, and drove away. They sent out a pinch hitter for him.

There was no need for words; his message was clear: Why should such a gifted athlete risk his major-league career against a bush-league wild man like me?

I pitched the remaining three innings of the game and gave up about seven runs. I never pitched again in formal competition. Now I had more serious business to attend to.

I SPENT FOUR YEARS in the Navy and outlasted four aircraft carriers. But I never stood a watch, never touched a line, and never gave an order. I was always on staff duty or with an air group, never in a position of authority. I was as careful as I could be to stay out of harm's way—although, now and then, I got there in spite of myself. The four aircraft carriers to which I was assigned—the *Wasp,* the *Shangri-La,* the *Hancock,* and the *Ticonderoga*—brought me into every major engagement in the Pacific Ocean from the invasion of the Marshall Islands in February 1944 to the end of World War II in September 1945.

As an air group intelligence officer, I flew on bomber and torpedo missions as an observer, supervised the taking of photos of enemy aircraft carriers, analyzed the photos, plotted tactics, and briefed and debriefed pilots before and after their bombing missions—all this for a group that consisted of eighteen aircraft and thirty pilots. After a year, Admiral John Sidney McCain, commander of the Pacific Fast Carrier Task Force, came on board—and his third in command, Commander John Thach, asked me to stay on as his assistant. Thus at the age of twenty-four, I found myself running one phase of the Pacific war—pulling together everything that had happened each day and deciding on the next day's targets for eleven hundred carrier planes. It remains by far the most interesting job I ever held.

Also, needless to add, the most dangerous. It was at the battle of Leyte Gulf in 1944 that, for the first time, the Japanese used kamikaze fighters—pilots who deliberately sacrificed their lives, crashing their planes into our ships. These kamikaze attacks were to continue until the end of the war, and they made an enormous difference. Until that time, it was relatively dangerous to be in the air because the Japanese had formidable fighter pilots, but relatively safe to be in our ships because the Japanese rarely hit them. By 1944, Japan's first team of pilots had been exterminated, and their replacements weren't very good at hitting our ships. But with the arrival of the kamikazes, the percentage of American ships hit and American seamen killed rose sharply.

To defend our ships against the kamikazes, we developed a strategy of sending out air patrols and stationing destroyers beyond the ordinary range of the fleet in order to sight the kamikazes or pick them up on radar well before they reached our main force. But after a while we concluded that there was

a better way: Figure out where the kamikaze strikes were coming from and keep our combat air patrols over the enemy airfields, where we could hit the kamikazes when they were on
the ground or as they were taking off.

Thus this newly-created "target combat air patrol" would
accompany our initial fighters and bombers each morning to
the Japanese airfields scattered throughout the Philippines—
but when the bombers returned, the fighter planes would remain
over the Japanese airfields until relieved to drop bombs and
otherwise harass the enemy. At night these fighter planes would
be relieved by night fighters which would continue the harassment, keeping the Japanese pilots awake in addition to damaging their planes. In this fashion we destroyed hundreds of
Japanese planes and reduced the frequency of kamikaze attacks.

The trouble was that we couldn't be *sure* how many we'd
destroyed and thus how effective the program was. It was easy
enough to know when a pilot hit an enemy plane in the air:
The plane went down, for all to see. But these target combat
air patrols would zoom over an enemy field, fire away and drop
bombs, and then zoom off, never knowing with certainty how
much damage they'd done.

Consequently, we decided to send out a photographic strike
force to take pictures of forty Japanese air fields early in the
morning and again late the same afternoon. By comparing the
morning and evening photos, we reasoned, we could calculate
the number of enemy planes our pilots had destroyed in one
day. I was put in charge of working out the logistics—how
many photo planes we would need, which fields they would
cover, at what altitudes and what hours they would fly.

The two days we chose for this experiment—November 6
and 7, 1944—were days on which we knew the Japanese were
bringing a huge number of planes down from Formosa. We
knew this because we had broken their radio code and inter-
cepted their messages over the air. At the end of two days'

bombardment of Japanese airfields, we examined our photos—
we managed to get thirty-two of the forty Japanese airfields—
and couldn't believe what we found: In just two days we had
destroyed more than four hundred Japanese planes on the
ground.

This was a tremendous figure—as many Japanese planes as
had been destroyed in the Battle of the Philippine Sea. It was
so tremendous that when we sent it to Admiral Halsey for
forwarding to Admiral Nimitz and, from him, to be released
to the American public, Nimitz didn't believe it; he thought
we were padding our figures. Nimitz had no use for our Admiral McCain anyway—the two admirals belonged to different
factions in the Byzantine world of Navy politics. So Nimitz
refused to announce the figures and instead sent a dispatch
chastising McCain for making outrageously optimistic claims.

The dispatch came in to our ship about one in the morning.
McCain read it, went through the roof and called for Jimmy
Thach, who was his operations officer and my superior. Thach
told him that I had supplied the figures and that he would
vouch for my reliability.

At two in the morning I was shaken awake and taken to
Admiral McCain's cabin. He was a bundle of nerves: shaking,
smoking cigarettes, his false teeth out on the table. His word
was being questioned by his superiors, which to him meant
that his whole career was at stake.

"Son," he said to me, "they're trying to get me. Where'd
you get these figures?"

"Admiral, I got them off the photographs," I replied. He
sent me to bring him the photos, and after I'd reviewed about
ten of them for him, he asked, "About how many of these
planes have you got?"

"I've got three hundred and twenty of them for forty fields,"
I said. "We've estimated an additional eighty planes for the
fields that were not photographed."

"Can you put that in a presentation form?" he asked. "Admiral Halsey wants to see me on the flagship at eight o'clock tomorrow to question me on what Admiral Nimitz considers inflated claims. And Halsey's very upset. You'll only have Billy Halsey's attention for about three minutes. So you'll have to make a convincing case within that time."

I spent the rest of the night assembling my documentation. The next morning McCain, Thach, and I were pulled aboard Halsey's flagship, the battleship *New Jersey*, by a big, powerful guy who introduced himself as Harold Stassen—the same Harold Stassen who in peacetime had been governor of Minnesota but was now serving as Admiral Halsey's flag secretary. He took the three of us into a cabin, where McCain went in to talk to Halsey for fifteen minutes while Thach and I waited. Finally McCain came to the door and beckoned to us. "Jimmy, Stretch, come on in," he said.

Once inside we had no time for pleasantries. "Now, show Admiral Halsey what you showed me last night," McCain said to me.

I took out my pictures. Halsey picked up one of them. "How many planes are destroyed here?" he asked.

"Seven," I said.

"Well, where are they?"

"They're the red circles," I replied.

"Oh, yeah," he said. "Yeah—they're burned. Now, where were those planes at the beginning of the day?"

"Over here," I said, indicating another photo of the same field. "They're the green circles."

He studied the two photos, visibly impressed. "These are the planes at eight o'clock in the morning," he asked, "and this is what's left at night?"

"Yes sir, that's right."

"No question about it," he said. "Seven planes there. Okay, let me look at the next group."

I showed him photos of the second field and then the third. Then he asked, "You've got all forty fields?"

"No, sir," I acknowledged. "We got pictorial coverage of thirty-two fields, and we took the pilots' claims on the other eight and adjusted them downward by about twenty-eight percent to reflect the percentages on the fields where we *did* have pictorial coverage."

"That's fair enough," he said. "Gee, this is great stuff. Have we ever had stuff like this before?"

"No, sir," I said. "This is the first time we've ever done this. This is the most accurate appraisal of damage done on the ground that we've ever had."

Halsey stood up, bringing to a conclusion my only encounter with the commander of America's Pacific fleet. "Son," he said, "that's all I wanted to hear. Thank you very much." And from that day on, as far as Admiral McCain was concerned, I could do no wrong.

AT EIGHT IN THE MORNING on January 18, 1945, the USS *Hancock* was passing through the Formosa Strait between Formosa and the Philippines—bringing in the first flight morning attack. Three of us were up on the "island" on the flight deck—a photo interpreter named Hudson; my immediate boss, Lieutenant Commander George Worthington; and myself. The *Hancock* was slowly fighting its way forward—the Japs were giving us a hard time—and as our planes came in to land I turned away to begin assembling data for my report on the first strike. Worthington started down to the war room to get a cup of coffee; Hudson stayed with me to watch the last three or four planes land.

At that moment a kamikaze plane glided out of the clouds— we never fired a shot its way—and smashed into the flight deck right at the base of our island, taking Hudson's head off and putting a piece of steel into Worthington's eye as the plane's bomb exploded. He had just started down the steps when this piece of shrapnel bomb casing passed through the side of the ship and into his eye, blinding it to this day. Yet somehow his body was untouched and his senses were unimpaired, so that he was able to walk down to sick bay on his own steam.

I was knocked flat by the impact but was untouched. I got to my feet and saw a huge hole in the deck, smoke coming out of it, and bodies scattered everywhere. General quarters was sounding, so I staggered up into my battle station in the flag plot—the lower-level structure where the admiral was head-quartered, just below the captain's bridge. Here everything was pandemonium—and I, as a member of the admiral's staff, was not a member of the ship's company and thus had no battle station nor any command responsibility. So I figured the best thing to do was to stay out of the way until somebody needed me. As ludicrous as it may sound today, I settled down in a corner of the flag plot, picked up a book—*A Tree Grows in Brooklyn*, I believe it was—and started to read.

At this point the ship's fire marshal, a lieutenant named Smith, came into the flag plot, surveyed the chaotic scene of people running in all directions in the wake of the explosion, and noticed me.

"Stretch," he shouted to me, "I need some help right away!"

"Sure, Smitty," I said. "What can I do?"

"I'm trying to get a message up to the captain's bridge"—which was on top of the flag plot above our "island" structure.

"Fine," I said. "What message can I get up?"

"I want to get a seven-degree list for the ship."

"Why can't we just tell the bridge on the speakerphone?" I asked.

"All the lines up there are out. I'm trying to get word down to damage control in the bowels of the ship that we have no communication. We do understand they have communications from the captain's bridge. So if you can get that message up to the captain's bridge, he in turn can get it down to damage control and we'll get the seven-degree list I need."

"Smitty, I'll just run right up the ladder and take it to him," I said.

"No. The ladder's been blown away by the explosion. You can't get up there."

"How *can* you get up there?"

"Up the rope," he said.

The rope of which he spoke was a very long rope which we always dropped out of the captain's bridge when we went to battle stations. Thus if we had to abandon ship, instead of jumping sixty or seventy feet to the water, we could shinny down the rope and improve our chances of survival. At this moment, because of the wreckage from the bomb explosion, the rope represented the only means of climbing up the ten feet or so to the captain's bridge.

"Fine," I said, and I swung out onto the rope and climbed upward—a very frightening experience, because the ship was taking evasive actions at a speed of about thirty knots, swinging me back and forth as I clung to the rope. It wasn't a long climb—maybe ten feet—but a very harrowing one. And, of course, if I fell, no one would notice me amid all the noise and confusion.

I swung myself onto the captain's bridge and found more pandemonium: Fires were breaking out, more Japanese planes were attacking, and we were also trying not to collide with the ship next to us.

I rushed to the captain and tapped him on the shoulder. "Captain!" I said. "Captain!"

Of course he paid no attention to me. So I shook him, and shouted, *"Captain! Captain!"*

"Waddaya want?" he snapped at me. "Waddaya want?"

"Fire Marshal Smith wants a seven-degree list right away."

The captain picked up the speaking tube and shouted to damage control: "Seven-degree list!"

Then, from the bowels of the ship, a voice replied: "Port or starboard?"

The captain turned to me. "Port or starboard?"

Well, I didn't know. And I don't think anybody had told me. But something had to be done right away. I couldn't go back and find Fire Marshal Smith—God knew where he was by this time. But I could see I had to say something.

So I made the decision myself. Since it's faster to say "port" than "starboard," I answered, "Port!"

"Port!" repeated the captain into the tube.

"Aye aye, sir," came the answer from below.

I shinnied back down the rope to my flag-plot battle station when I heard on the ship's loudspeaker, "Lieutenant Longstreth, report to sick bay on the double!"

Sick bay was the ship's hospital, of course. And at this moment it was inundated with hundreds of people, killed and wounded in the bomb explosion. (All told there were perhaps thirty-three hundred men aboard the *Hancock*—three thousand seamen and three hundred officers.)

So in circuitous fashion I made my way down through the flames and wreckage to sick bay. Not knowing where to go amid the chaos down there, I walked over to the chaplain.

"Father, somebody called me," I said. "I'm Thacher Longstreth."

"Oh yes, Thacher, sure. The guy over here wants to see you."

I walked over to a patient slumped in the corner with a big hunk of metal sticking out where his eye used to be. I didn't know who it was. "Hi, I'm Thacher Longstreth," I said. "Can I help you?"

"Thacher, God almighty," the man said. "Don't you recognize me? It's George Worthington."

I did not recognize him. His face was puffed up beyond recognition. His own mother wouldn't have recognized him.

"My God, George!" I said. "What happened?"

"I got hit by this piece that came through the side."

"Are you all right?"

"No," he said, "I'm dying."

"Oh, George, come on," I said. "You must be all right. I understand you walked in here."

"I don't care," he said. "I'm dying. I wanted to give you a message for Betty"—his wife. "I want you to give it to her."

"George, you're not dying!" I cried.

"Thacher, believe me, I'm dying. Will you take my message, please?" And he started to cry.

So I took the message—not really paying much attention to it because I was so alarmed by George's conviction that he had been mortally wounded. I ran over to one of the doctors, whom I knew as a poker companion.

"Doc, Doc!" I shouted. "This guy over here—George Worthington—is in bad shape."

"Thacher, he *walked* in," the doctor said. "I've got guys here that are dying. I'll get to him in a while, but he's all right for now."

So I went to another doctor. He was so overwhelmed with dead and dying that he couldn't even come over to look at George. Then I saw the ship's dentist, whom I knew because his room was right next to mine.

I grabbed him. "Doc, you've got to come look at Worthington."

He started to give me the same response as the physicians had. "Doc," I insisted, "either you come over or I'm *taking* you over there!"

"All right, all right!" he said. "I'll come."

The dentist found that George had been right: He was losing blood so fast that he was almost gone. The medics got some blood, gave him a transfusion, and within half an hour it was obvious that he would survive. He subsequently underwent operations on his eye. But there is no question that at that moment he was fairly close to death—and that he would have died had I gone back up topside to make myself useful. On that thread of circumstance hung the life of my friend.

More than forty years have passed, but every January 18 I get a phone call from San Diego. "This is George," he says. "Thanks."

Somehow that day came to an end. We put out the fires and got everything under control. We fought our way through the Formosa Strait and got out into the open sea. I went down to the wardroom, which is one of the nice things about the Navy: When you got through fighting, you usually had a chance to live reasonably comfortably. They were serving us a big meal, and we officers were feeling pleased with ourselves: The Japs had done their worst to us, and we'd held them off and survived.

As we sat there, Fire Marshal Smith walked in. His shirt was ripped, his face was crimson, and he had burn marks all over his body. (In fact, he received a Navy Cross for his heroism that day.) He sat down and the steward brought him some food.

"Stretch, I want to thank you," he said. "You really helped me out a lot on that message."

"Smitty, what was that all about—seven degrees?" I asked.

"Well," he explained, "we had a hell of a fire on the hangar deck, where the bomb had set some airplanes on fire. We were afraid the whole deck would catch. And we were trying to keep those planes wetted down. But we had a lot of burning gasoline and oil—combustibles—that were sloshing around the deck as the ship rolled. We opened the curtains on the side of the ship and then we used these huge hoses to flush the burning stuff over the side."

"Oh, I see."

"The list meant we could just wash the stuff right off."

"Well," I asked, "would it have mattered whether it was port or starboard?"

He looked at me strangely. "My God," he said, "just the difference between our being here and our *not* being here!"

"Why? Why did it matter?"

"Well, the hatchway on the starboard side was wedged open. It was open when the bomb exploded. And after the explosion, you couldn't close the hatch. And that hatch goes down into the magazine area. So if the list had been starboard, it would have washed all that burning stuff down into the open hatch with the distinct probability of it going into the magazines and blowing up the whole forward section of the ship. The port side was okay, so that's why I told you port when I asked for the seven-degree list."

I thought to myself: The hell you told me. . . .

I never did tell him what really happened. But I did subsequently tell Admiral McCain. He laughed and laughed. "You know," he said, "some day somebody's going to write the story of the great American Navy and how a handful of Annapolis men were able to sufficiently contain and control a million reservists, so that we won the war in spite of you guys."

THE 24TH OF DECEMBER, 1944, found us at anchorage at Samar Island in the central Philippines, preparing for the attack on Lingayen Gulf and the reinvasion of Luzon. But this was the day before Christmas and everyone was getting into the spirit. Later that day we'd have a turkey dinner, and we were to see a special movie—that is, a film that was only five years old instead of twenty-five years old. We were all feeling good already when we heard the ultimate good news.

"Now hear this," the speaker announced. "On the starboard

fantail, landing barge bringing mail—Christmas mail and presents from the States."

A landing barge is a relatively small landing ship which fills up with infantry at one end of a troop transport ship and then runs onto the beach, where its front flops down and the men on board pour onto the beach and into battle. The Navy was very good about flying our mail from the States to the airfield at Samar and, from there, bringing it to the various aircraft carriers via these landing craft.

At the news of the craft's approach, a huge cheer went up and everybody came pouring onto the hangar deck—a thousand guys leaning over the side, cheering, waving, and singing to the approaching vessel.

The pilot in the landing craft—a kid of maybe nineteen—was so tickled by all this attention that he responded in kind, waving and laughing and shouting "Merry Christmas!" Amid all this showboating, unfortunately, he neglected to watch where he was going: The vessel smashed head-on into the side of our carrier and sank right there—in just sixty feet of water—taking all our mail and presents to the bottom with it.

In an instant, the mood on board shifted from total euphoria to total gloom. As the pilot floundered around in the water, one of the guys leaned over the rail. "Don't swim too close to this ship, you bastard," he shouted, "or I'll jump in and drown you."

VICE ADMIRAL MCCAIN was a nice old man but not a dynamic leader. He knew little about aerial warfare, and by 1944, when I served under him, he was sixty-three and pretty well worn out. But McCain and his alternate commander of the Fast Carrier Task Force, Vice Admiral Mark Mitcher, were both smart enough to get themselves the brightest chief operations officers—Commanders Jimmy Thach and Jim Flatley, respectively.

Thach had shot down five Japanese planes at Midway in 1942. Early in the war he'd developed the "Thach Weave," a flight pattern which enabled the bigger, slower American planes to evade the faster Japanese fighters. When I was with him later in the air, he developed the Target Combat Air Patrol, a system for battling kamikazes. His concept: If we kept harassing their airfields—about thirty fields on Luzon in the northern Philippines—the kamikaze pilots wouldn't be able to get off the ground to fly their suicide missions. Under Thach's direction, we maintained TCAP patrols from dawn to dusk and developed a night fighter force so the Japanese couldn't land their planes at night. This strategy cut our losses from kamikazes by 75 percent during the last month of the Philippine campaign.

Thach was also a wonderful boss. If I did something good, he always saw to it that I got the credit—but if I made a mistake, he always took the blame on his own shoulders. When the Korean conflict erupted in 1950, I sent Thach a telex: "If you want me, I'm ready." That's how I felt about him. We all did.

Thach and Flatley were close friends, and so much alike that one man might have been the other's clone. While Thach was piloting fighter planes at the Battle of Midway, Flatley was doing the same at the Battle of the Coral Sea. They were good friends who'd attended Annapolis together, Thach in the class of '27 and Flatley in the class of '29. The two of them literally never made a serious mistake in their magnificent naval careers.

I became friendly with Flatley after the war when we spent two weeks at Norfolk briefing our replacements and I stayed with the Flatleys and their nine-year-old son. Years later, in the early 1980s, I got a visit and a call from that son—by now Captain James Flatley, commander of the USS *Saratoga*—when his carrier came into the Philadelphia Navy Yard for an extensive overhaul.

Thach subsequently rose to a four-star admiral and died in his seventies; Flatley died much earlier, of cancer, in his fifties. In 1985, when both men were inducted into the Carrier Hall of Fame aboard the USS *Yorktown* in Charleston harbor, I was invited to represent Thach, and Flatley's widow appeared on his behalf. At the close of the ceremony, each of the representatives of the inductees was instructed to throw a wreath into the water. The deck of the carrier was some sixty feet above the water, but somehow the wreath I threw in for Jimmy Thach and the wreath Mrs. Flatley threw for her husband landed one on top of the other, and the two wreaths floated off together. At this, Mrs. Flatley turned to me and started to cry. "That's the way they always were," she said, "inseparable friends."

G. MENNEN WILLIAMS was a bright but rather stolid fellow, nicknamed "Soapy" because of the Mennen family's soap fortune. He served as air intelligence officer under Admiral Montgomery, just as I was air intelligence officer under Admiral McCain. Soapy was nearly ten years older than I and held the rank of lieutenant commander, whereas I was a mere lieutenant. But since his boss, Montgomery, was one of four admirals who answered to my boss—McCain, the commander of Task Force 38—I was actually higher in the bureaucratic hierarchy than Williams was. Beginning with our old school tie—he was Princeton '33—we worked together for a number of months and got to be good friends.

One day after we made a series of air strikes against the Philippines, we returned to Ulithi, an atoll in the Caroline Islands from which we operated regularly—one of the great anchorages for the Pacific Fleet.

It was a typical coral atoll—a sort of necklace of islands

which had been formed by sand washing up on the coral and palm trees. All the natives lived on two or three islands, which we were never allowed to go near. Another island housed a small landing strip, which only a few of us were able to use on local flights.

Then there was an island called Mogmog, which was the R&R island—rest and recreation—and whose sole claim to fame was the largest bar in the world—a circular bar whose perimeter measured a quarter mile, served by 100 to 150 bartenders at any given moment. And with good reason: There might be 30,000 officers and enlisted men on Mogmog at any time, and there was nothing to do there but swim, look for shells on the beach . . . and drink. But it could be quite an impressive sight to watch five thousand officers urinating simultaneously on the sand, in the water, or on each other. I often wondered what that island smelled like after the war ended.

At any rate, one day while I and maybe ten thousand other men were looking for seashells on the beach at Mogmog, Soapy Williams came up to me.

"Thacher," he said, "I want to talk to you for a minute."

"Sure," I said.

"I've been recommended for the Legion of Merit."

I said that sounded wonderful.

"It's not so wonderful," he replied. "You know, our staff recommends decorations to Admiral McCain, but Admiral McCain determines whether or not the recommendations are approved and the awards are made. In my case, the award was turned down. I don't know why Admiral McCain turned it down, but he did."

"Gee, that's too bad, Soapy," I said. "What are you going to do about it?"

"I hoped that maybe you could help me."

"Jeez, I don't know how. I'm just a lousy lieutenant, way down the totem pole."

"Well, you know," he said, "usually that stuff is handled through the flag secretary. Who's your flag secretary?"

"It's a guy named Charlie Sisson."

"Do you know him well?"

"Yeah," I said. "He has the room right next to mine. I know him very well. He's a wonderful guy from Mississippi. Why don't I talk to Charlie Sisson and find out what happened?"

The question of what Soapy had done to deserve a medal never came up in our conversation—but then, for our practical purposes it was really irrelevant. What concerned us fighting Navy men then was the fact that the Air Force was handing out medals to anyone who flew a bombing mission, whereas the Navy was insisting on a fussier standard of heroism; when we proposed medals for our sailor colleagues, our own Navy brass in Washington often rejected them. Thus our concern was not so much whether a specific individual deserved a medal as bringing our aggregate medal total more into parity with that of our interservice rival, the Air Force.

So the next day I went in to see Charlie Sisson. "Charlie, how do we handle the awards around here?" I asked.

"Well," he said, "they're usually started at the ship level or at the air group level or what-have-you, and then they're approved by the commanding officer, and then they get bucked up to the next-highest commanding officer, and then they get to the task group commander—a rear admiral—and then they come over to us. We approve them or disapprove them. If it's a Congressional Medal, why, it has to go to the president of the United States. But for a Navy Cross on down, it can be approved by us. We go through the routine of getting Admiral Halsey to approve them, but he always approves whoever we send over."

"Oh," I said. "Did you ever hear of a guy named Mennen Williams?"

Charlie said he hadn't.

"Well," I continued, "he got an awards recommendation

from Admiral Montgomery about a week or so ago and got turned down."

Charlie went to the file cabinet, pulled out a folder, and began to leaf through it. "Oh, yeah," he cried in recognition as he found the appropriate paper.

"Who turned it down?" I asked.

"I did," he said. "I make all the decisions on these things. I take them in to the chief of staff, and he signs the admiral's name on them, and that's the end of that. But they don't know anything about these guys. It's pretty much up to me."

"Why'd you turn this guy down?"

"Christ, Thach, he didn't *do* anything. What the hell. He's just a guy out here like you, riding around in a boat. *You* never got the Legion of Merit. This guy's some rich guy, thinks he can buy his way—"

"No," I said, "he's a hell of a good guy. Works his ass off. Charlie, you've got the wrong idea."

"Ah, Thacher, come on!"

We argued back and forth for a while. "Look," Charlie said finally, "does this guy mean something to you?"

"Well, he's a friend of mine . . . and I think he—"

"That's all you have to say," Charlie said. "If he's a friend of yours and you think he ought to get it, and it's important in his life and yours—go ahead. Tell him to send it in again and I'll approve it."

So Soapy resubmitted the application in slightly different language. "Is this the one you meant?" Sisson asked me when it arrived.

"Yeah," I said.

So Charlie scribbled his initials and passed the recommendation on to the chief of staff, and a few weeks later Soapy Williams was standing on the deck of the USS *Smyrna* being decorated with the Legion of Merit.

About a week after that, Soapy showed up at my office aboard the *Wasp* with a case—twelve bottles—of Scotch to show his gratitude. In those days, at sea or in combat, you could get $50 to $100 for a bottle for Scotch. In effect Soapy was giving me goods worth perhaps $1,000 in 1944 dollars—the equivalent of something like $10,000 today.

"Soapy, I don't drink!" I said. "I don't even want this stuff around."

"It's just something I wanted to do," he said. "I don't drink either, but this case was put away for me, and I wanted to show my appreciation."

I took one bottle to pass on to a friend who *did* drink and returned the rest of the case. "The only question I have," I said, "is what the hell do you care about this Legion of Merit? You're not gonna stay in the Navy, are you?"

"I'm gonna go back to Detroit and go into politics," he said. "I want to run for governor. Getting the Legion of Merit in this war will be a very helpful thing in my campaign."

"Well, that's wonderful, Soapy," I said. "Anytime I can help a good Princetonian and a good Republican, I'll always break my neck to do so."

Soapy smiled slightly. "Thacher, I'm a Democrat," he said.

"You son of a bitch," I laughed. "Give me that award back!"

As things turned out, Soapy Williams was elected governor of Michigan in 1948, just a year after *Life* magazine had moved me to Detroit. One day early in his term I was calling on my accounts in Lansing, the state capital, and I said to myself: What the hell, I'll look him up. Wonder if he'll remember me?

I wandered into the governor's office in the capitol building, told the receptionist I was an old friend of the governor, and handed her my card. Two minutes later Soapy came bounding out of his office.

"Stretch! How are ya? Gee whiz!" And he invited Nancy and me to dinner in the Executive Mansion—a pleasant reward for my small part in the making of a governor. The greater reward I got from this episode was my insight into how things happen in the real world.

IN MY FOUR YEARS in the Navy I won over $10,000 playing poker—plus perhaps another $2,000 which I never collected from guys who were killed. One of my victims was a pilot in our air group, a Southerner named Bill Davidson, who was into me for about $1,000. When his plane was shot down over Formosa—now Taiwan—I assumed that was the last I'd see of Bill or of my $1,000. But three months later I received a letter from his wife, Ruth, saying Bill had left a letter written before his death instructing her to pay his debt to me out of his GI insurance.

"If you will let me know how much he owes you," Ruth Davidson wrote, "I'll send you a check."

Now, how are you going to collect a gambling debt from a friend and squadron mate who's no longer alive? I wrote back and told her that the debt had been settled and to forget it.

But one evening nearly ten years later—say about 1955—Nancy and I were just finishing dinner in our house in Chestnut Hill, Philadelphia, when we heard a knock. I opened the front door and there was Bill Davidson. It turned out he'd been shot down over Formosa but not killed; the Japanese had captured him and taken him to Japan, where he'd spent a year and a half in a prison camp, emerging at the war's end as a bare skeleton of his former self. But I had known nothing of his survival. Seeing him before me now, alive and healthy, I burst into tears and couldn't stop crying.

"I know you're dead," I said. "I don't understand what's going on, but this can't be taking place." He hadn't been an especially close friend of mine, but I was so unprepared for the emotional impact of seeing him that I just stood there blubbering.

"Stretch," he said finally in his Southern drawl, "you just gonna stand there and cry, or are you gonna ask me in for a drink?"

It turned out he'd stayed in the Navy; he happened to be passing through Philadelphia to attend to the affairs of an aunt who'd just died. We talked for a while and then he reached in his pocket and pulled out his checkbook.

"Stretch," he said, "I know I owe you some money."

"Jesus Christ, Bill," I said. "The day you got shot down, the clock stopped running."

He insisted on paying me, and I refused to take anything from him, and soon we were arguing back and forth until Nancy stormed into the room and settled the thing.

"Will you shut up?" she told Bill. "He's not going to take your money. Don't you understand that? All this garbage about Southern obligations and an honor debt—if you give him the check, I guarantee you we'll tear it up. Now, I never want to hear about it again!"

Bill looked at me and rolled his eyes. "Well, Thacher," he said, "I tried."

"You sure did, Bill," I said.

CHAPTER 6

THE PRIVATE SECTOR: SELLING FOR *LIFE* (1945–50)

I CAME OUT OF THE NAVY as a lieutenant commander with a reasonably good record, a few decorations, some exhilarating and frightening memories, and $10,000 which I had won in two years of poker games aboard various aircraft carriers. I sent it all home, except for $800 I won aboard the *Shangri-La,* the carrier that brought us from Hawaii back to Long Beach, California, in November 1945. From there we came home via the *Super Chief,* then one of the two great transcontinental trains. The trip took two days; you left Long Beach in the late afternoon and got to Chicago the following morning, and then you caught a train from Chicago to Philadelphia. On the way to Chicago I got into a coast-to-coast gin rummy game with another Princeton man named Ash Lee. We played a penny a point, 25 cents a frame, $1 a game—and by the time we reached Chicago he had all my money.

The following morning I stepped off the sleeper at 30th Street Station in Philadelphia and waited for the commuter train out to our home in Chestnut Hill. I would be getting out of the service in a few weeks, and obviously I was beginning to think about what to do with the rest of my life—thoughts which had been intensified by my overnight loss of the $800.

In college before the war I had never given the slightest thought to making a living, because all of us knew we were going to war. Even as a boy, my only ambition was to be a big-league baseball player. And the only vocational advice I had received from my father about the world of work was "For God's sake, don't go into the stock market."

I suppose it's difficult for anybody today to realize that when I attended high school and college, there were no opportunities. During the Depression, people were grateful for any job they could get. My brother-in-law, for example, graduated from Haverford College with an outstanding record—and for three years trimmed hedges as a gardener for $15 a week. When the war started in Europe in the fall of '39—my junior year in college—almost everybody foresaw that we were going to be getting into it. So you stopped even *thinking* about jobs.

As I stood there on the 30th Street Station platform that morning in November 1945, wondering what I was going to do with the rest of my life, a fellow named Charles Muldaur walked up and said hello. I had known him casually because, like me, he was a former Princeton football player, about ten years older than I. You might say he and I were friendly without being friends. He was a feisty little fellow who had been classified 4-F, much to his dismay, and he spent the rest of his life apologizing for not having fought in the war. At any rate, Muldaur said hello and we chatted a bit about where I'd been.

"What are you going to do now?" he asked.

"I'm gonna look for a job, " I said.

"Ever think about working for *Life?*" he asked.

"No," I answered instinctively, thinking of my brief pre-Navy stint at the Insurance Company of North America. "I know I don't want to be in the insurance business."

"No, no," he said. "I don't mean life insurance. I mean *Life* magazine."

"*Life* magazine—that's pictures and things," I said. "I don't know anything about taking pictures."

"No, no," he said again. "This would be in the advertising end, the merchandising end."

"I don't know what you're talking about. What do you mean, the advertising end?"

"You know the ads that are in the magazine?" he asked, as if instructing a child. "Well, you know, somebody sells them."

That thought had never occurred to me. I knew the ads were there, but I had never considered how they got there.

"Look," Muldaur said, "*Life* magazine is going to hire a hundred young fellows right out of the service. We're gonna pay you forty bucks a week, and then you'll have an opportunity to be trained and get into the flow of the business. Some of you will be promoted within the *Life* structure and others will go into other Time Inc. publications. Or with this background and training, you can go into advertising agencies or other areas of business."

"That sounds pretty interesting," I said. "I'd like to come in and talk to you about it some day."

"If you're interested," he said, "you'll have to talk to me before four o'clock today, because by four o'clock I will have completed my hiring."

"Gee whiz," I said. "I've been away for a long time. I want to go home and see my wife."

"Please do. But if you want to work for me, you'll have to come back into town a little later today and be interviewed."

So I caught the commuter train home to Chestnut Hill, had a short celebration with my wife, and then told her, "I've got to go back into town"—thus establishing what was to become a pattern of domestic absenteeism for the next forty years.

"What for?" Nancy asked.

"I think I'm gonna get a job."

"You just got home," Nancy said. "What are you worried about a job for?"

"Because we'll soon have three little children under three years old, and I've got to figure out some way of paying for them, and this is an opportunity and it might be an interesting one."

Nancy was furious: I had been gone twenty-seven months out of the four years of the war, so she had spent better than two years alone with little kids. And our third child, Ellen, would be born in just a few days. Worse still, all that summer Nancy had suffered the raised eyebrows that accompanied her unexplained (and unexplainable) pregnancy. You see, when my aircraft carrier was wrecked in March 1945, I was brought back to Washington with my superiors for a few weeks—enough time for Nancy and me to conceive our third child. But military secrecy demanded that no one be *told* I was back in the U.S.

So Nancy had every right to be angry when I told her I was running off once again. But I got on the train and went back downtown for a two-o'clock interview with Charles Muldaur.

"You look pretty good to me," he said when the interview was over. "But I'd like you to come to New York and meet the big boss with me, because he has to okay it."

So then and there we got on the train to New York, and I was hired by *Life* that afternoon, at $40 a week.

How could I make such a major career decision on the spur of the moment? In retrospect, that decision—like so many of my seemingly spontaneous decisions about my life—*did* result from a great deal of inner thought; it's just that in my case this thinking process seems to take place more rapidly than it does with most people. When I'm faced with an emergency— like a job change, a family crisis, or being asked to give a speech when I have no idea of what I'm going to say—my mind or my instincts seem to crystallize so that it becomes relatively easy to make what I think is the right decision. Conversely, the more time I have to think about a decision, the more muddled I get with weighing the pros and cons.

I've often felt, too, that my instincts were honed by the enormous amount of reading I did as a student. As a boy I read hundreds of books a year; each Friday afternoon on my way home from school I'd stop at the Ardmore public library and take out seven books—the maximum limit—which I'd return, all read, on my way to school the following Monday. All this reading took me vicariously into all sorts of situations and into detailed discussions of how the characters reacted, all of which somehow seeped into my subconscious.

The third element to my spontaneity was the fact that Nancy and I had often talked by the hour about what we wanted to do with our lives, so that each of us knew where the other stood. Thus what often may have appeared to have been foolish or casual or lighthearted decisions on my part were not really foolish at all. If I didn't check with Nancy before accepting the offer from *Life,* that was because, in essence, we had been talking about just such decisions all along.

After accepting the job that day in New York, I went out with the *Life* people for a little celebration—I ordered Coke while they drank whiskey sours—and finally got back on the train to Philadelphia. I didn't get home until ten o'clock that night. Nancy was absolutely livid. Here it was, my first day back after more than a year overseas, and I was up in New York sitting in a bar talking business with a bunch of *Life* guys I'd just met. But I suspect what upset her most was that she perceived it—accurately—as an indication that I would be away a lot in the years to come.

At *Life,* as in the Navy, I was traveling all the time, so I *was* away a lot at night. And when I subsequently went into the advertising agency business, I was often away nights visiting out-of-town clients. Even later, when I became president of the Greater Philadelphia Chamber of Commerce in the sixties, I'd often be up in Scranton and Wilkes-Barre or out in Pittsburgh or down in Baltimore and Washington and Richmond. And of course my subsequent political activities kept me busy almost every night, even though I wasn't away from Philadelphia: Over a period of maybe twenty years, I averaged three hundred speeches a year.

To be sure, on such occasions Nancy was with me much of the time, but there was also a lot of the time that she wasn't, particularly when the children were small. Once the children grew up, she came along with me on many occasions. But while the children were smaller she had a lot of time at home while I was somewhere else. And that was something she never accepted with equanimity or anything other than passionate opposition.

I was out of the Navy by the end of December and started working for *Life* in January of 1946.

At first I worked out of Philadelphia as what they called a retail representative. I wasn't actually selling ads; instead, I went around and called on retailers and persuaded them to promote products that were advertised in *Life,* and particularly encouraged them to put up "Advertised in *Life*" posters around the store and to feature products in their store windows at the same time the ads for those products were appearing in the magazine.

I would call on maybe 100 to 150 stores a week, popping in and out of stores in the Philadelphia area all day. The idea was to remind the retailer that this national magazine—which seemed like such a distant operation to a merchant—actually reached thousands of local readers who were his potential customers.

One of our ploys was to show the retailer the local telephone book. "Do you know," we would say, "*Life* has more readers in this area than there are names in this phone book?" That was pretty heavy stuff for merchants, some of whom might be selling a hundred products that were advertised in *Life.* Some of them got so excited when we pointed out the possibilities of their connection to *Life* that they would go through copies of the *Life* magazines that they were selling and actually put little stickers on all the ads for products that were stocked in their stores.

My big coup came with the Boston Store in Wilkes-Barre, where I arranged a two-week storewide "Advertised in *Life*" promotion. When it was done, I compiled "before" and "after" sales figures to show how much better products had sold when the "Advertised in *Life*" signs were used. Well, the retailers just fell all over themselves—they had never seen anything so sophisticated before. (Remember, this was 1946 and '47.) And in the meantime, of course, *Life*'s advertising salesmen, in making their presentations to ad agencies and manufacturers, would point to retail reps like me as an example of "that extra dimension that you get for your advertising dollar when you're in *Life*." The combination worked like a charm, and it added a dimension to magazine advertising which had never really existed before—a glamorous impact that nothing matched until television came on the scene.

After about a year of this, I became what they called a zone manager. That meant I supervised seven guys who were doing what I had done. I'd accompany them on calls and make sure they were doing it right. Then I became the regional manager, which meant I was in charge of all the retail representatives in the Eastern region. But I held that job only a few weeks before I was promoted to everybody's goal: to be a space salesman for *Life*.

I WENT FROM COLLEGE, which was a relatively lighthearted place, to the Navy, which was also, in its own rough way, a humorous place: In the face of death you *needed* humor to preserve your sanity. So it wasn't until I got into the business world and went to work for *Life* that I began to understand the determination, the tenacity, the grim commitment to success that's required of business people. And I began to recognize that personal traits which had served me well in other chapters of my life were not necessarily going to work as well in business. I particularly discovered that my willingness to play the fool in any given situation—a prime source of my popularity in high school and college—was not going to be perceived as an asset in the business world.

When I first went to work, almost everybody wore a hat. Thus when I came back from the war in the fall of 1945 my brother-in-law, James Downward—a successful salesman and an executive with *Time* magazine—told me, "Now that you're working for Time Inc., you've got to wear a hat. It's just something you've got to do. If you don't wear one, it'll hurt your business career."

I was astounded that anybody could think that wearing or not wearing a hat could have any effect at all on how you did in the business world. First I tried to laugh it off, but then I realized Jim was serious. I had a birthday on November 4, and, sure enough, he gave me a beautiful Stetson fedora. It cost $10—a lot of money for a hat in those days. "You really have to wear it," he said. "You've got to promise me you'll wear it."

So I wore it all that day. And I grew angrier and angrier as the day progressed. I didn't like the hat. It happened to be a very windy day, and the hat blew off a few times. I felt like a fool—as if everyone were looking at me and saying, "You've sold out to the establishment."

I thought it would be rude to throw the hat away, since Jim had given it to me as a gesture of friendship and affection. On the other hand, if something accidentally happened to that hat. . .

So I walked across the Market Street Bridge to Time Inc.'s office that first day and let the wind do what good manners had precluded me from doing myself. The result was the same: The hat wound up in the Schuylkill River.

That was the last time I wore a hat. But it was the first time I realized what a grim attitude a lot of people took toward business. So the question arose: Do I owe it to myself and my wife and family to eschew the actions and deeds of a young fool and become a pompous young man instead? Or is there a happy medium where perhaps I can do both—be pompous as the occasion demands and frivolous when I feel like it? And that's essentially what I've done most of my business life.

LIFE *SENT ME TO DETROIT* in the spring of 1947, and we lived there for more than three years. When we arrived, Nancy and I owned a 1941 Chevrolet which she had driven throughout the war years and which had about eighty thousand miles on it. It was hardly the sort of car that you would take to Detroit, where a car was an important status symbol and where I was hoping to make a good impression on prospects throughout the state of Michigan. So we sold the Chevrolet in Philadelphia and bought a Ford in Detroit.

We couldn't find a rental house there, so for $13,000 we bought a house in suburban Birmingham—the first we'd ever owned. I settled into a routine of driving downtown to the *Life* office in the Fisher Building on mornings when I wasn't out calling on prospects or clients around the state. There were no trains or buses to speak of in Detroit; if you wanted to travel anywhere, you drove.

We had been there a few months when something went wrong with our car. I took it back to the dealer to have it checked, and while it was in there the automobile dealers of Detroit were closed by a labor strike. Thus my car was stuck at the dealer's for eight weeks, with the engine out, up on the block. So there I was—without wheels or money in a city where (a) I knew no one and (b) a car was necessary for survival.

The first day my car was gone, a colleague from the office gave me a ride home. But the next morning I had no way to get downtown. The only apparent option was something I had done often in college: hitchhiking.

So about eight o'clock I walked out on Hunter Boulevard—which ran only about a hundred yards from our house—and went to the corner by a traffic light and stuck out my thumb. Much to my amazement, the first car that passed—a large, beautiful Cadillac—screeched to a stop.

The driver was an older gentleman with white hair. He swung open the front door and said, "Get in, young man."

I got in the car and closed the door. "Where are you going?" he asked.

"I'm going to the Fisher Building."

"Well, I work in the General Motors Building right next door," he said, "so I'll take you right there."

"Wonderful," I said.

We drove on, making small talk.

"Do you live out here?" he asked.

"Yeah," I said. "I live just about where you picked me up."

"Oh," he said. "Where are you from?"

"I'm originally from Philadelphia. I spent four years in the Navy, and I recently got out, and now I'm working for *Life* magazine. They've just sent me out here. I'm going to be in advertising sales."

Since he had shown some interest in me, it seemed only right to return the favor. "Are you a native Detroiter?" I asked.

"Oh, yes," he said. "I was born here and I've lived out here all my life."

"Where do you live?" I asked.

"In Bloomfield Hills, out near the country club."

I was impressed. "There are some beautiful homes out there," I said. "That's a very nice place to live."

We drove on a little longer. "Are you in business out here?" I asked.

"Yes, yes."

"What company are you with?"

"Well, I'm with General Motors."

"Oh," I said, "really! What do you do at General Motors?"

"Well," he said, "I guess I'm sort of in the administrative part of things. I have to coordinate activities and I have to select people."

"Gee, that's a funny job," I said. "I never heard of anything like that. Do you have a title?"

"Yes, I have a title."

"What's your title?"

"I'm the president."

"The president of General Motors is Charles E. Wilson," I said. "Are you Charles E. Wilson?"

"Yes, that's me. I'm Charles E. Wilson."

I was dumbfounded. "Oh my God," I said. "Please don't tell my boss that I asked you who you were."

"I'll do more than that," he said. "I like you, young man. Are you having breakfast this morning?"

"Well, I haven't had any yet."

"I want you to come up and have breakfast with me," he said.

Thus I wound up having breakfast with Charles E. Wilson in his private office, and afterward he phoned my boss, Robin Morton—who'd been trying to see Wilson for six months—and said, "Mr. Morton, I have your Mr. Longstreth up here, and he tells me you're very anxious to see me. Why don't you come over at three o'clock this afternoon?"

Now, in no time that story circulated all over the company: Charles E. Wilson had picked me up hitchhiking, and as a result I'd arranged for my boss to see him. This was at a time when General Motors wouldn't talk to anybody from *Life*, because we had done a cover story on Walter Reuther, the labor leader, during the great General Motors strike of 1946.

It was really quite funny: From my chance meeting with Charles Wilson came a recovery of *Life*'s relationship with General Motors. My boss was a very skillful man, and he and Wilson hit it off, and they set up a meeting at which our chairman, Henry R. Luce, came out and met Wilson. The end result was that we got GM's advertising back, and I got noticed at the company's highest levels.

Eight years later, when I ran for mayor of Philadelphia, Charlie Wilson was Secretary of Defense in the Eisenhower administration. As a major national Republican figure, he came to Philadelphia and made a speech in my behalf at Convention Hall. When my supporters first asked Wilson to speak for me, he recalled our meeting without any prompting.

"I know exactly who he is," Wilson said. "He was hitchhiking one day. I picked him up. Sure I remember. Longstreth. Big tall fellow."

Now, why on earth did Wilson pick me up in the first place? That's a good question, and I raised it over breakfast that first morning in his office.

"Gee, do you pick up people every day?" I asked.

"Hardly ever," he said.

"How come you picked me up?"

"I don't know. I just sort of stopped, and I figured you didn't look like the kind of person who'd be doing this regularly, you must have some problem or something, and I liked your looks, so I picked you up." I had been lucky—and not, by any means, for the last time.

WHEN I FIRST GOT TO DETROIT, I found out that like all young salesmen, I was given the accounts that were too small or too far away for the senior salesmen to be bothered with. The accounts outside of the Detroit metropolitan area had been neglected for several years—at least partly because during the war *Life*'s paper supply had been rationed and thus the magazine hadn't had much space to sell. My predecessor had gone off to war and hadn't been replaced until I came along, so when I arrived it was the first time many potential advertisers had been contacted by *Life* in seven or eight years—almost like starting from scratch. By contrast, our big competitor, *The Saturday Evening Post,* was covering the territory and seemed to be getting everything.

My biggest prospect was Kellogg Cereals in Battle Creek. Kellogg had a huge advertising budget and seemed like a natural for *Life.* But I wondered: Why would *Life* give such an important account to a green kid like me? I soon found out.

On my first visit to Battle Creek I called on Kellogg's advertising manager, a fellow named Ralph Olmstead. He and I hit it off right from the very beginning, even though he was twenty-five years older than I was.

"Thacher," he told me, "*Life* is the best magazine there is. We ought to be advertising in *Life.* I believe it. Our salesmen believe it. Our advertising agency recommends it regularly. But we have a block here, and you might as well find out about it, because until that block is removed, we're not gonna get anywhere."

"What is it?"

"Earl Freeman. He's vice president for marketing. He's been in the job for a long time. He's a tremendous marketing man, one of the best in the world. He's extraordinarily powerful in the company."

Freeman's objection to *Life,* Olmstead explained, had to do with *Life*'s wartime allocation of advertising space between Kellogg and its biggest competitor, the Post Cereals division of General Foods. *Life* had allocated its space on the basis of each advertiser's prewar ad volume. Before the war Kellogg had done more cereal advertising in *Life* than Post Cereals had. But whereas Kellogg produced only breakfast cereals, Post's parent company, General Foods, produced a broad variety of products and used several times as much space in *Life,* all told, as Kellogg did. Thus when General Foods got its space allocation from *Life,* it decided to devote most of its allotment to ads for Post Cereals at a time when Kellogg's was precluded from buying more space. The theory behind space rationing was that everyone had to make sacrifices during a war, but General Foods saw the rationing arrangement as an opportunity for Post to catch up to Kellogg by taking advantage of General Foods' larger allotment.

Earl Freeman was angry with *Life* for acquiescing to this scheme. He contended that the rationing should have been based on how much space an individual product had used, not how much the parent company used. "I'll get even with you bastards," he had been heard to say. "As soon as the war is over, I'm never going to advertise in *Life* again."

Thus when I arrived on the scene, the war had been over for two years and Kellogg had not run a line of advertising in *Life* since V-J Day. "I can buy everything else," Earl Freeman insisted to his colleagues. "I don't need them!" And that's what he was doing—buying ads in every general-interest magazine except *Life,* despite the best efforts of everyone in Time Inc., from Henry Luce on down.

"If you ever want to be a hero," my boss said to me when I got back to the office in Detroit, "get Kellogg's."

I wanted nothing so much as to be a hero, so I went after the Kellogg account just the way any kid would. I knew I had the best product, and I knew a lot about my product, and with the innocence of youth I felt certain that if I persisted I could get in to see Earl Freeman and make my case.

Little did I realize that I wouldn't get in to see him by normal methods. I could see Ralph Olmstead; I could see Ted Swann, Kellogg's director of sales; I could see Kellogg's ad agency; I could even see Watson H. Vanderploeg, the president of Kellogg. But all to no avail. When I went in to see Mr. Vanderploeg, he just threw up his hands. "Mr. Longstreth," he said "don't talk to me about advertising. That's all Earl Freeman's job. Go see him."

"Mr. Vanderploeg, he won't see me!"

"Well, that's your problem," he replied.

How could I sell Freeman when he wouldn't see me? I was stumped. Religiously, every month I went to Kellogg; every month I saw everybody there who would see me and made my presentations; and every month they'd say, "Thacher, this is all wonderful, but Earl Freeman's the guy. You've got to see him." But Freeman would either be in his office with the door closed or he'd be out of town.

I tried everything. I learned that Freeman belonged to the Rotary Club in Battle Creek, so I joined the Rotary Club— only to discover that he rarely went to meetings there because he traveled so frequently.

I found out where his house was and called there twice; he wasn't there. His wife was very cordial to me. But then Freeman's secretary sent me a letter: "Please don't go to Mr. Freeman's house. If he sees you at all, it will be at the office." Every time I visited the Kellogg headquarters I left my card with Freeman's secretary. And at least once a month I wrote him a letter and called him on the telephone. But he never took my calls or answered my letters.

This went on for two solid years: Freeman knew who I was and knew I was knocking myself out to see him, but I had received no communication from him at all.

Then one day, en route to a luncheon engagement in Kalamazoo, I figured I might as well stop in Battle Creek, since it was on the way. I went into Kellogg's headquarters, made my customary rounds, shook hands with my acquaintances there, got my customary rejection from Freeman's secretary ("No, Mr. Freeman will not see you"), and went downstairs and out to the parking lot. It was a very hot day, and as I drove past the front entrance I felt a yen for a Coca-Cola. So I pulled over near the entrance, called to the guard—whom I knew pretty well by this time—and asked if I could leave the car there for just a minute. I left the engine running and dashed into the building.

Well, the sun was very bright that day. And as I ran from the bright sunlight into the building, past the receptionist to the Coke machine behind the stairwell, the relative darkness of the indoors momentarily blinded me. As I raced to the machine, I realized to my horror at the last moment that a man was standing there about to take a drink.

I was moving too fast to avoid him. With my head down, I hit the poor fellow, lifted him up in the air, and smashed him down on the ground, causing him to slide across the floor. He ended up against the side wall there, half stunned, with Coca-Cola all over everything.

The guy looked kind of groggy. "Jesus Christ!" he said. "Help me up! Do you always hit people that way?"

"Oh, I'm sorry," I stammered. "I came in out of the darkness, I didn't see you at all, and I apologize . . ." I was trying to wipe the Coca-Cola off of his clothes, but he was visibly annoyed. He was also, I noticed for the first time, a big man, large enough to take a shot at me if he had wanted to. As my eyes gradually readjusted to the indoor light, I thought to myself: I'm glad I don't have to see this guy very often.

Luckily, my victim got his temper under control. "You know, you really hit me a shot," he said. "I haven't been knocked down like that since the Chicago game in '27."

I laughed. "Oh, were you a football player?"

"Yeah, oh yeah," he said. "I played tackle for Michigan for three years."

"Oh, I played football in college, too," I said. "Matter of fact, I played end for Princeton for three years."

"What games did you play in?" he asked. I explained, and he recalled that he had seen Princeton play Michigan at Ann Arbor in 1932. "You guys put up a hell of a battle," he said. "You nearly beat us."

We talked a little bit longer, and then he asked, "What are you down here for?"

"Well, I'm down here to call on Kellogg's," I said. Then, emboldened by the apparent gridiron camaraderie I shared with this stranger, I added, "Actually, it's really funny, I've been trying to see Earl Freeman for a couple of years and I've never made it."

"Who are you?" he asked.

"My name is Longstreth."

Suddenly his voice turned ice-cold: "Longstreth? Thacher Longstreth?"

"Yes."

"With *Life* magazine?"

"Yes."

"Well, I'm Earl Freeman."

My jaw literally dropped; I wasn't ready for this at all. "You're Earl Freeman?" I gulped.

"Yeah. I guess you figured the only way you were gonna get to see me was to knock me down. Wasn't a bad idea at that, was it?" He paused a moment and then motioned toward the stairs. "All right, come on upstairs with me. Let's get this out of the way. I'm tired of all this bullshit—letters and phone calls, you going to my house. Whatever you have to say, come on up here and say it."

We went and sat down in his office. He closed the door behind us, looked at me, and started to laugh. Laughter! "Christ, kid," he said. "I take my hat off to you. You're some salesman. Well, you've got your chance now. Don't blow it."

"Mr. Freeman," I said, "I think I'm there. I don't think I'm gonna have to say anything about *Life* that you don't already know. All I have to do is get you to want to be in *Life* more than you *don't* want to be in *Life,* and I suspect that maybe you've started to feel that way already."

He looked at me and his eyes filled with tears. "You know, I remember when I was your age," he said. "I knew it was there, and I knew . . ." And he started telling me about his experiences as a young salesman, which were very similar to mine, and the next thing you know, the two of us were laughing away together.

Finally I got up to leave. "Don't go," he said.

"Mr. Freeman," I replied, "I think I'm pretty close to getting an order from you. But I want you to give me that order when you feel in your heart that you want to do it, and not because you might be carried away at the moment because of this wonderful experience, which I will always treasure."

"Call me in two weeks," he said. "You don't have to come out here. Just call me in two weeks."

As I left the building, I suddenly remembered that I had left my car at the front entrance with the engine running. But Charlie, the guard, assured me there was no problem: "I turned your engine off for you, Stretch," he said.

"Charlie," I told him, "you could have taken the car and driven it all over town. That's how good my meeting was."

Two weeks later, when I called Freeman, he asked, "Would twenty-six pages be a good starter?"

Well, twenty-six pages was the biggest order of new business anyone at *Life* had come up with in years. So I became an overnight hero in the company—except that in this case, as with most "overnight" heroes, the overnight success had actually been years in the making.

Earl Freeman and I subsequently became good friends, and after six months he used to offer me a job every time I went to see him. One day, after I'd been going out there for about a year, he asked me, "Do you call on Post?"

"Yes I do," I said. Post Cereals, Kellogg's hated rival, was right around the corner in Battle Creek.

"Well, we're coming up with an ad schedule next year where we're going to be in every issue of *Life*. We're going to come in with Grow-Pup"—Kellogg's dog food—"and we're going to increase some of our ads to spreads. So we're going to be one of the ten biggest advertisers in *Life,* and it's your doing. You're very important to us now, you know. You've worked with us on the merchandising and everything, you know everybody in the place. You won't come to work for me, but I don't want you calling on Post. How would you feel if I called your boss and said that I would like to have you limited to our account—your only cereal account?"

I said that was fine with me, and that's what he did. From then on Kellogg was the only cereal company I called on, which was a high compliment. And my relationship with that company lasted as long as I stayed in Michigan. Unhappily, my friendship with Earl Freeman didn't last as long as I would have liked: He died of cancer half a dozen years later.

But it was a classic example of what can happen when tenacity is combined with good luck—and, of course, with the knowledge to do the right thing when the opportunity arises. I was like a running back in football: When he sees a hole, he cuts for it. His teammates' timing and blocking have to be right, but the ball carrier himself has to go when he gets that opportunity. If he stumbles, or if he cuts too far inside, then he doesn't make a big gain. I know I was lucky when I crashed into Earl Freeman. But I also know that I didn't blow the opportunity once it fell into my lap. From that point on I knew that I was going to be a very good salesman, no matter what product or idea I was hawking.

CARL WILKINS was the sales manager of Gerber Baby Foods, which was based in Fremont, Michigan, about fifty miles north of Grand Rapids, which was itself 150 miles west of Detroit—

that is, really nowhere. I had never met him, and *Life* had never had any business from Gerber. So my first call on Wilkins involved driving far out of my way to see a stranger at an unknown company in a remote and unknown town—the classic "cold call" that's every salesman's nightmare.

The receptionist announced me and I was told to go on upstairs to Wilkins's office. Wilkins was a tall, lanky, friendly fellow. After we shook hands and exchanged pleasantries, he said, "Let me ask you a question. I haven't seen a *Life* salesman in—God, it must be ten years. And I don't know why I'd ever see one, because *Life* is really not a publication we would ever advertise in. We advertise to young mothers. We could buy young mothers in *Parents Magazine* or *Good Housekeeping* far cheaper than we could buy them in *Life.* So you really haven't got much of a reason for being here."

But we sat and talked anyway, and he took me around and introduced me to everyone, including Dan Gerber, the president—all very friendly, lovely people.

By the time we finished making the rounds and began strolling back to his office, it was about a quarter to five. "I guess I'd better say goodbye," I said. I had a two-hundred-mile drive back to Detroit.

Suddenly I remembered that my car was out of gas—had run out of gas, actually, as I came down the hill into the Gerber parking lot. One other problem: I never carried much cash with me in those days, and I had only 80 cents on my person. So I had no money and no gas (and no credit cards, which barely existed in those days). And I was in a town where I'd never been before and where I knew no one aside from Carl Wilkins.

"Awful nice to see you," Wilkins said when we got back to his office. "I'm sure we'll get together again some time."

I took a deep breath. "Mr. Wilkins, I wonder if you could do me a favor."

"What's that?"

"Well, I've got to go back to Detroit tonight."

"I can show you the way."

"No, no—it's not that," I said. "I'm out of gas."

"Well, come on—I'll show you where the gas station is, right next to our parking lot."

"But I haven't got any money either."

"What?"

"No, " I said. "I really need ten dollars to buy gas."

He sat down and started laughing. "My God, kid," he said. "I know we're not much of a prospect, but you must have given up on this one before you even got here." He pulled out his wallet. "Come on, here's ten bucks. Give it back to me the next time you see me."

I got a lot of business from Carl Wilkins before I was through. And later on he said to me, "You know, you showed us that *Life* was a good buy for us. And you were a big tall friendly kid. But what really made an impression on me was when you borrowed ten bucks from me the first time you ever saw me. I figured, 'Wow, that guy's really got guts.' You weren't the least bit embarrassed or upset or anything about it. It was almost as if, wasn't it nice that I was going to loan you ten dollars, because some day you'd do the same for me."

We were close friends thereafter, and my throwing myself on his mercy was what had broken the ice between us. Maybe I wouldn't have been so lucky if I'd tried to borrow $10 from someone else. But in that case maybe I wouldn't have tried. As with Earl Freeman, an adverse situation turned into a big break—partly because I was lucky, and partly because I knew how to take advantage of my luck.

MY BOSS in the Detroit office was Robin Morton, who had been publisher of *Liberty* magazine, a defunct competitor of *Life*. He was an extraordinary man—brilliant, marvelously articulate, entertaining, a tremendously competent and exciting mentor for a young salesman to break in with. He was then in his mid-forties—about twenty years older than I. Once or twice a year I'd take him around the state to meet my major accounts, so we spent a lot of time in the automobile together and got to be good friends. I adored him, as I was wont to do with my bosses throughout my career—Jimmy Thach in the Navy, Robin Morton at *Life,* George Barnard at the Aitkin-Kynett ad agency, Fred Gloeckner at the Winchell Company. All were very dear friends, and Morton was the man I admired most of the people I knew in business.

He was also the man who gave me what may have been the best advice I ever got. In the process of working on my accounts, I developed relationships and started getting job offers from the companies I called on. Some of these offers were merely intended to flatter me, but others were genuine and specific.

One of the latter was Shakespeare Fishing Tackle in Kalamazoo, which I had brought into *Life* and which offered to make me a sales representative for about twice the money I was making at *Life.* I was flattered by the offer and the money, but I had no real interest in selling fishing tackle—I don't fish. On the other hand, if I rejected the offer I might offend the folks at Shakespeare and thus lose their business for *Life.*

What to do? At Nancy's suggestion, I asked Robin for his advice. He told me what he'd probably said to hundreds of others like me.

"When you're good as a salesman," he said, "you're going to get a lot of job offers, because the fact that you are good is demonstrated over and over again. You can be a good manufacturing man or a good legal counsel or a good financial vice president, and only a few people in your company—and none of your customers—will know about it. But when you're a good salesman and you're out calling all over, everywhere, your boss knows about it because it shows up in your sales, and your customers know it because you demonstrate to them on a continuing basis your ability to market your product. So you're going to get a lot of job offers, and that's wonderful—but mostly because, if a man wants to hire you, he is going to give you accessibility to himself that makes it easier for you to sell him your product.

"Now, you're going to have to learn to handle this situation, because it's going to come up over and over again. Sometimes you can laugh off a job offer; sometimes you can pretend you didn't hear it, particularly if it's over lunch and drinks. But when it gets to be the honest, genuine thing, you must always look at it, if for no other reason than to avoid being rude. Besides, you never know when something that's really good will come along, and if you haven't examined it, you may have ignored something that in the long run may actually be a lot better for you and your family. But when you reach the final decision—whether or not you should take the job—that's when the easy solution will always lend itself to you."

"Well, what is that?" I asked.

"Unless you know—the moment the job is described—that you want it," Robin replied, "don't take it. When the right job comes along, you won't have to think about it five minutes. If you have to agonize, if you have to discuss it with people, if you waver back and forth—don't do it. The only time to change jobs is when it's so clear to you that you don't even have to think twice about it."

In effect Robin was suggesting what I had been doing all along but had never before consciously articulated: following my initial instincts. The ideal job offer—the one that I wouldn't have to spend even five minutes thinking about—did indeed ultimately come my way, but not for another fifteen years.

ONE OF MY COLLEAGUES in *Life*'s Detroit office—an older salesman named Bill Curran—was undergoing a period of anger at the company; our bosses were putting more pressure on him than he thought he deserved. At about this time each of us salesmen received a letter from Shep Spink, the vice president for advertising sales, in which he urged each of us to pick out a particular potential account, make a run at it, and write a letter to Spink telling him what we had done to land the account. Once this exercise was completed, each of us received a form letter from Spink saying, "Thank you very much for the documentation you sent me and your interesting efforts to try and do this sale. I appreciate it very much. Sincerely, Shep."

On the day these letters arrived, I got to the office early and saw the letters, which had been opened the night before by the secretary and placed on the appropriate desks. Just out of curiosity I peeked at the other salesmen's letters; the text of each one was identical to mine.

So I went back to Curran's desk, inserted his letter in the typewriter, and typed a postscript across the bottom: "Perhaps if you had put a little more effort into this, it would have been a more successful enterprise." Then I put an "S" underneath— as Spink customarily signed himself—and placed the letter back in its original spot on Curran's desk.

He arrived about an hour later, a happy-go-lucky guy, full of "Hello, Hazel! Hi, Stretch, how are ya? Hi Fred!" Then he picked up the letter and I watched his face turn red. "What the hell's this? Jesus Christ!"

He stormed over to my desk, waving the paper before me. "Look what that son of a bitch did! If I had tried a little harder! Jesus Christ! I spent—I'm gonna call him—I'm gonna tell him—" He was frothing at the mouth, he was so angry.

"Will," I cautioned, "don't call him. You'll be playing right into his hands. All he's trying to do is get you angry."

"What does he think I am?" Curran said. "Some twenty-seven-year-old kid? Excuse me, Stretch, I didn't mean you. But goddammit, I'm forty-nine years old. I don't have to take this shit. I'll get him fired." He went on and on in this vein.

Just out of sheer coincidence, right in the middle of this

tirade a secretary came in and announced to Will that Shep Spink in New York was on the phone for him.

Curran stormed out of my office—about to spill his job, his pride, his career in one phone call—and I panicked.

"Will," I said suddenly, "do me a favor?"

"Sure," he said. "What's the matter? I gotta go talk to Spink."

"Don't talk to Spink until you talk to me."

"What are you talking about?"

"Believe me. Tell her you'll phone him right back."

So he did. Then he turned to me. "What are you talking about?"

"I wrote that," I said.

"You wrote it?"

"Sure, I wrote it."

"You son of a bitch," he said. "You really pulled one over on me." He sat down and started to laugh. And he kept on laughing. When he walked out of my office I heard him telling everyone, "You know what that kid did? That's the best one I've heard in a long time."

Then he went in and called Spink. As it turned out, Spink was phoning to congratulate him personally on his outstanding effort. I had had no idea that was going to happen, of course; it was sheer coincidence.

But that was a practical joke that Curran never forgot. He's past eighty now, and just the other day I phoned to wish him a happy birthday. "Why, you son of a bitch!" he bellowed when he heard who it was. "You know, no day passes by that I don't think of you. I'll never forget what you did to me. I must have told that story a thousand times. I love it. I love you."

Funny, isn't it, the things that survive in your memory when all the accumulated aggravations of a lifetime have been forgotten? Practical jokes to me are the funniest things in the world. I can never get enough of them—either to play them on someone or to have them played on me. I never resent being made a fool of myself; I accept that as part of the game.

In my own business life, each day is like a blackboard filled with annoyance and frustration—a phone call from somebody who's rude to you; a customer's refusal to return your phone calls; your subsequent discovery that the customer isn't going to give you the order he promised you last week; your wife phoning with some domestic problem at home, furious because you forgot to get something that you promised her you would get; or a call from the teacher at school to tell you that your kid is going to flunk if he doesn't shape up, and why don't you spend more time with your children and less time on that ridiculous job?

But then somebody phones and tells you a funny story, or a friend or associate comes in with some ridiculous situation, and you start to laugh, you get laughing hard, and the next thing you know it's as if the whole slate is clean—you took an eraser and wiped off the whole thing. All the discouraging impact of a dozen little annoyances is gone; it's as if you're starting all over again. To me, that touch of humor has always been the leavening force of my life.

During my Detroit days at *Life* I covered the state of Michigan—a big state where the temperatures got bitter cold in the winter. In those days I was friendly with a *Good Housekeeping* salesman named Wayne Wilcox, and he and I had cooked up a scheme to beat the cost of living by traveling together. In this manner we could charge our respective companies for gas for two cars while using only one; we could share a hotel room while charging our companies for two; and what's more, we'd have each other's company on the road. It seemed like a good idea—not only for the money we saved, but for the opportunities it presented for mutual tomfoolery.

One day in midwinter I was making a sales call and he

waited for me outside in his car. He kept the motor and heater running—and, as a joke on me, he locked the doors and went to sleep. Thus when I came out of the building, frozen, I couldn't get into the car.

This struck me as an excellent opportunity to test a scientific theory I had once heard. In the subzero arctic cold, I urinated into the crack in the door—first on the driver's side, then on the passenger's side. I took care to do it quietly enough that I didn't awaken Wayne. Then I went back inside the building and waited. If the scientific theory was correct, the urine would freeze so that the car doors would be impossible to open—locked or unlocked. Which is exactly what happened.

After a while I went out to the parking lot again. This time I made enough noise to rouse Wayne from his slumber. I feigned innocence regarding any problem with the car.

"Come on, Wayne, " I said. "The guys inside want to see you. They're gonna buy us some coffee."

"Oh, wonderful," he said. He unlocked the door and tried to get it open—and of course, he couldn't. Ultimately he had to roll down the window and squeeze his corpulent body through the window—one of the funnier sights etched in my memory. Once outside, he tried to pull the door open—without success, of course.

"I can't understand what happened," he said. And to this day I don't think he does.

ONE OF THE THINGS I always liked about sales was that a productive salesman can come to work every day in a lavender coat and dark glasses and shave his head, and nobody's going to object.

Once at a *Life* sales conference I heard one of my colleagues—probably drunk—speak incredibly rudely and disrespectfully to two high-level executives. When the meeting was finished, I asked my boss, Robin Morton, "How does Dick get away with that?"

"It's simple," Bob replied, "He sold over three million worth of advertising space last year. If he ever gets down to the point where he sells only half a million worth, they'll fire him the next day, because those guys hate his guts. But as long as he produces, there's nothing that anyone's going to do about it."

From then on, most of my work involved selling. I didn't want to be a high-level private-sector executive with such grim bottom-line responsibilities that I could never let my hair down. I haven't found many business people who know how to make use of humor. I don't mean they aren't humorous—plenty of business people have wonderful senses of humor and like nothing more than a good laugh. But I don't see very many executives using humor as a day-to-day management tool. It's almost as if they believe humor is something to be turned off when you walk into the office in the morning and turned on again when you leave the office at night.

Of all the carefree, happy-go-lucky guys I know, very few are businessmen. This comes as no surprise, of course: Business is so demanding and places so much pressure on people who reach a high level within a company that it's almost as if they're not allowed to laugh.

At *Life* we had a sales executive named Ford Perine—a great guy whose only visible flaw was his prodigious snoring. One night at a sales convention at the Southern Pines Hotel in North Carolina, a group of us salesmen were sitting around in the lobby after dinner telling stories when Perine announced that he was going up to bed.

Perine always took a single room at these meetings because of his snoring. The Southern Pines was an old hotel, only three stories high, and Ford had a room on the second floor. After he left our group, we got to talking about Perine's snoring. Finally I said, "You know what we really ought to do? There's a hose, a fire hose, right outside that door. I'll bet you we could get the nozzle on top of the transom and we could blow him right out of that bed."

So we went upstairs, got the hose, and pushed the nozzle up over the transom. I was the only sober one in the group; of the other guys, one was holding the chair, one was unrolling the hose, one was turning on the water. The first blast of water hit Ford right in the chest and rolled him out of the bed on the floor, and then we chased him around on the floor with this big column of water. Once he woke up he was screaming, "Help! Help!" We turned off the hose, rolled it back in, and ran off. Ford never knew who did it. He won't until he reads this.

When I was a little boy my mother admonished me to be sure that people were laughing with me, not *at* me. "The big problem with you," she told me some time later, "is that you don't care whether it's *at* or *with,* as long as they're laughing." And it's true. I've always felt that making people laugh, including myself, was one of the greatest gifts that a person could have. But I guess it's hurt me in terms of career advancement. If I'm one of two people being considered for a job, for example, the other guy would almost always be selected— although I might be the superior person—simply because so many business people feel threatened by humor. The executive who's making the choice thinks: If a guy is that dependent on humor or derives that much pleasure from it, he must be a lightweight. There can be no real depth in that fellow, because if there were depth he wouldn't be laughing all the time. To which I would reply: If important people were really as deep as they claim to be, they wouldn't be so serious so much of the time.

MY THIRD YEAR IN DETROIT —the year of my breakthrough at Kellogg—everything fell into place for me. I had a tremendous year. All kinds of business—not only from Kellogg—fell into my lap. I couldn't have stopped it even if I'd wanted to.

It was just at this time—July 1949—that Morton called me into his office. "New York wants to know what kind of business you've got coming along during the next five or six months," he said.

"Gee, Robin," I told him. "I'm about to take a swing around the territory, and I think I can pick up another fifteen or twenty pages. I'm ready to really bust through."

"Let me give you some advice," he cautioned. "If I were you, I would try and hold that business up until next year."

"What do you mean?"

"Well," he said, "you've brought in an enormous amount of business this year. You've catapulted yourself from sixty-seventh on the sales list to the top, and no man in his twenties has done that in the history of the company. You're already the most talked-about young salesman in Time Inc. You're going to be asked to be the principal speaker at the next sales meeting"—the highest honor that a salesman could have. "And there's nothing you can do this year that's going to make your year any better. But the older salesmen are now saying, 'Well, sure, anybody can have a lucky year. Let's see how he does next year.' So what you've got to start worrying about right now is doing better next year than you've done this year, and the year after and the year after, because that's the price that a salesman has to pay. Nobody cares about what went on this year. They want to know what's going to happen next year, and the year after."

He told me the joke about the guy who bails his best friend out of debt in college, pays the medical bills when the friend is hit by a car, and finances the friend's fledgling business. Years later, when the guy is broke and his friend is successful, he asks his friend for help, only to be rejected because, the friend reasons, "What have you done for me lately?" It was the first time I had heard that joke or the syndrome it represented. And by gosh, I went back to my territory and did everything necessary to shift my potential new business into the following year. As a result, I finished the following year three pages ahead of the previous year—not much of an improvement, but something I never would have achieved if Robin hadn't warned me. And it did answer the big question about me within the company: "Longstreth's all right, but he's a flash in the pan. Other fellows have had one big year before. Let's see what he does those following years." Now I had two big years in a row, and from then on I could do no wrong. They knew I was as good a salesman as they had in the company; it was just a question of where I wanted to go.

Or so it seemed. I still had a lot to learn. In 1949, just as I was coming into my own as a *Life* supersalesman, the doctors advised us that Nancy was suffering from multiple sclerosis. The doctor in Detroit told me she probably would not live more than five years.

CHAPTER 7
BACK TO MY ROOTS
(1950–53)

NANCY. In eight years of marriage my spunky wife had demonstrated that she was more than just another pretty debutante; as a mother, homemaker, and organizer she was a woman of iron will and indomitable determination—characteristics which helped her fight her disease and which blossomed years later in her subsequent careers as a real estate broker, political worker, civic activist, and corporate director.

Perhaps most important, she was the perfect mistress when it came to civilizing her overgrown adolescent of a husband. Once in the fall of 1943, when Nancy and I and our baby daughter Anne were living in a little cottage near Quonset, Rhode Island, during my naval training there, I'd gone down to New York with three friends for a baseball game on a Friday. We stayed overnight and went to a football game the next afternoon. I'd told Nancy I'd be home Saturday night, but after the game my friends wanted to go out on the town. So instead of catching a six-o'clock train and getting to Quonset around ten, we caught a two-o'clock train and didn't arrive in Quonset until six o'clock Sunday morning. Nancy had had no idea where I was, and when I finally phoned her Sunday morning from the naval air station, she was furious.

"You son of a bitch," she shouted over the phone. "I'll fix

your wagon. I'm taking Anne, we're getting in the car now, and we're going down to Philadelphia. And you can come and get me when you decide you want to live like a human being!"

I didn't think she was serious, but I was about to learn that Nancy was not one for idle threats. I had no car and no way to get home. When I phoned home again a few minutes later, there was no answer.

I rousted out one of my colleagues from the New York jaunt. "You bastards have gotten me into real trouble," I said. I told him I had to get over to our house in nearby Wakefield to see if Nancy had left. I persuaded him to take one of Quonset's little two-seater trainer planes for student pilots and fly over our house to see where Nancy was. So he got into the pilot's seat, I sat behind him, and we took off.

About five minutes later we were over our house in Wakefield. We flew down low over our house in order to take a look in the garage. Our Chevrolet convertible was not there.

"Where do you think she's gone?" my buddy asked.

"She's probably on her way to Philadelphia."

"How would you go?"

I pointed out the driving route, and he took off in that direction. Sure enough, about twenty or thirty miles down the road, we spotted Nancy in the convertible, Philadelphia-bound. We flew close to the car and swooped down as low as we could, and I leaned out the window as we went roaring by, shouting, "Don't go! Please don't go! Don't go!"

As angry as Nancy was, after a few minutes of this she started to laugh. Finally, she gave us a wave, made a U-turn, and headed the car back to Wakefield—satisfied that she had made her point in a manner which, as you can see, I've never forgotten.

This is not to say that I didn't require occasional reminders, which Nancy always stood ready to provide. A few years later—shortly after we moved back to Philadelphia from Detroit—

Nancy's brother John Claghorn and I were playing touch football at the local high school, and we got home that evening an hour later than we'd promised Nancy we would. We arrived to find the whole house seemingly shut down: All the lights were off and all the doors and windows were locked, as if the occupant had gone away on a long trip. We were wearing sweatsuits and had no keys. We beat on the front door, but nothing happened.

"Do you think she's asleep?" John asked.

"No," I said. "She's not asleep. She's just mad."

I told John I knew of a window at the back of the house where we could get in. At my insistence, John climbed through the window first. As soon as he stuck his head through, Nancy whacked him with the broom handle.

And now the doctor in Detroit had told me that this vigorous and youthful woman had five years to live, and worse: Before that time, he said, she would lose physical control of herself as well as her ability to function as a housewife or mother. He strongly advised me to go back to Philadelphia, where she could be among her family and familiar surroundings. If we did that, he said, Nancy's chances of living and remaining active longer would be somewhat enhanced, and that seemed to him the kind of life I ought to plan on. But that kind of life would inevitably curtail my ambitions of upward mobility at Time Inc.

Surviving abject poverty in the Depression had convinced me and my brother that we could cope with whatever hardship life might hand us. And when I first learned of Nancy's illness, my initial instinctive reaction was that somehow things would work out. But this was devastating news. Nancy was the strong half of our marriage, the take-charge partner. I was a guy who never did any work around the house; she did it all. To think of such a dynamo withering away was more than I could bear.

My long hours in my car between customers on upstate

Michigan roads left me with plenty of time to mull over my situation. One day, while driving outside Jackson, I found myself talking to God. "I'll make a deal with you," I said. "If you'll let my wife live a reasonably decent life, I'll devote a substantial portion of my life to multiple sclerosis." In that moment it became clear to me that, given the sudden change in my family's circumstances, I couldn't climb the traditional corporate ladder and be a proper husband simultaneously.

When I explained my situation to my superiors at Time Inc., they responded wonderfully; for a big company, Time Inc. had a great heart. They moved me back to Philadelphia in the summer of 1950. We bought a house in Chestnut Hill, where we've lived ever since. And *Life* got me off to a running start in Philadelphia by giving me a number of large local accounts—for example, RCA and N. W. Ayer, the big advertising agency—and a territory that stretched from Washington and Richmond in the south to Scranton and Wilkes-Barre in the north.

It was a somewhat more sophisticated group of accounts than I had handled in Michigan and involved much less traveling: I didn't have to drive as far or spend as much time away from home, and I hardly ever had to be away overnight. I had done well by my company and the company had reciprocated—which, in theory, at least, is the way the system is supposed to work.

As for my deal with God—like so many of my other spontaneous decisions, that worked too. In the fall of 1950 I started a Philadelphia chapter of the Multiple Sclerosis Society as a vehicle to raise money for research. At first I ran it out of my home, but after a few years I found an ideal executive director in a multiple sclerosis victim named Dorothy Randall. She had been deserted by her husband—a common scenario with MS: Often the prospect of functioning as a lifelong care-giver, with no hope of a cure, causes the healthy spouse to bail out. She happily took the job and opened our first office—although I could only afford to pay her $7,000 a year—and she stayed on the job for fifteen years until she died. Today our chapter raises $2.5 million a year for multiple sclerosis research.

In 1951 I became the youngest board member of the national Multiple Sclerosis Society, and as I traveled up and down the East Coast for *Life* the society would give me names of possible contacts, whom I'd phone in my free moments to pitch them on the idea of forming an MS chapter in that particular city. At least three of the chapters I helped start in this fashion are still going strong.

As for the other side of my bargain with God—I'm happy to report that Nancy is still at my side at this writing, more than forty years after the doctors told us that she had, at most, five or ten years to live.

BY THE LATE WINTER OF 1952 I had advanced rapidly as a *Life* salesman. My sales performance had been spectacular. I'd become the best speaker in the Time Inc. sales stable, so I was often asked to give talks before corporate management. I'd been picked twice to address the annual sales meeting, an honor reserved for the person who'd had the greatest sales success during a given year. I'd come to know all the top management people at Time Inc. and had become friendly with them. Thus it seemed clear to me and everyone who knew me that I was on a fast track and headed for great things within the company.

Although it was known in some circles that I was bound to be inhibited by Nancy's condition, miraculously that seemed to have straightened itself out: There'd been a complete recovery from her bad attacks of MS; she was going through an extended remission period; and both of us were looking at each other and thinking, Maybe the doctors were wrong. Maybe this didn't happen. Maybe we don't have to be as careful as we thought.

We loved being back in Philadelphia, loved the feeling of

belonging that we get there—a feeling we've never had anywhere else in the world. By this time our children were at
Chestnut Hill Academy and Springside School—fitting into
things, happy with their friends. Everything seemed to be going
our way. The euphoria was epitomized for me by one glorious
twenty-four-hour period in the spring of 1951 when I was
asked to go up to New York to give a speech to the entire
Time Inc. management group about my latest coup: selling
RCA one of the largest ad schedules in Time Inc. history.

I delivered this talk in the Time Inc. auditorium to about
150 people, including all the corporate big shots and the middle-
management people. It was my chance to be exposed to the
whole Time Inc. group, and it was also really the first time in
my life that I discovered my talent as a public speaker: how
easy it was for me to command an audience under appropriate
circumstances and hold them in thrall for twenty or twenty-
five minutes—to make them laugh, or quiet them down, or
get them talking to each other, or make them cry—whatever
I wanted to do, I really could do it. As I spoke and observed
my listeners' reactions, I realized that I could do more than
simply make a sales presentation and elicit enthusiasm from
potential customers for a specific product: I could actually
influence people's emotions.

That same weekend, Time Inc. was holding a marketing
conference for salesmen and their wives at Shawnee on the Delaware, a resort in northeastern Pennsylvania. The company's
top management men had planned to drive there from the
meeting in New York at which I'd given my talk. The president of the company, Roy Larsen, and Andrew Heiskell, the
publisher of *Life,* and a couple of others got into one limousine
and found they had an extra seat. Howard Black, who was
executive vice president in charge of sales, called to me, "Why
don't you join us?"—as if it were the most natural thing for
me to do. So I, the young space salesman, got into the limousine with five of the top brass of Time Inc.—all of them

congratulating me on my speech. It was more exhilaration than anyone could ask for in one day, but more was still to come.

We got to Shawnee about seven o'clock and ate a magnificent dinner, and then some of the salesmen started to play poker. I'm a reasonably good poker player, and I held unusually good cards that night. I played all night, and I won $1,000. Remember, $1,000 in 1951 was like winning the moon. It was the most cash I've ever held in my hand at one time, before or since. Thus I had experienced the excitement of my speech, the drive with the company brass, the wonderful dinner to fill my stomach, and then this incredible all-night poker game and these enormous winnings. When we finally broke up the game to go in for breakfast, I remember I ducked into the men's room and locked myself in a stall so I could count my money without being seen. Then I returned and sat in on some meetings, receiving yet more congratulations for my talk the previous evening.

That afternoon we played a softball game—a traditional end-of-conference activity at Time Inc., where we had a lot of good young players. In this particular game I played center field and made nine or ten catches which under ordinary circumstances I never could have made, particularly after a night without sleep. But this was one of those days when my adrenaline was working full-blast.

My first time at bat I hit a home run. Then I hit a double and then another double, and in my final at-bat I hit the ball so far you couldn't have believed it. As I rounded the bases, the outfielders relayed the ball back into the infield, and as I charged toward home plate I realized that ball and I were going to arrive at precisely the same time. I weighed 230 pounds then, and the catcher blocking my path was a little guy who seemed to be paralyzed with fear. It would have been an easy matter for me to knock him over (after all, I had once done that unintentionally to a big fellow like Earl Freeman) and score a run. But at the last moment I realized that doing so might hurt a friend. So instead of sliding into the catcher, as he crouched down low to protect the plate, I leaped up and *over* him, completely missing home plate, so that he was able to scramble around and tag me out.

It was the only thing that went wrong for me in that twenty-four-hour time period. But even that mishap redounded to my benefit. Howard Black, the executive vice president for sales, saw the whole thing. "That was a very nice thing to do, not to bang into that guy," he told me. "I know you could have scored that run. That's a class move."

I went back to my position in the outfield for the last half inning. My team was one run ahead. The last batter hit a fly ball to me, which I caught for the final out of the game; I ran in to join my teammates in celebration at the pitcher's mound; and just at that moment my wife and four children, who'd driven from Philadelphia to pick me up, drove onto the grounds and my children came running across the diamond, shouting, "Daddy! Daddy! Daddy!" It was the perfect hero's finale.

I remember getting into the car, driving back home, and trying to convey to Nancy my exhilaration at the weekend's combination of personal triumphs, any one of which by itself would have been small potatoes next to a job promotion or an election victory or a military conquest. But within the context of my life and the way things all fell together, it made for a glorious twenty-four hours—perhaps the most gratifying twenty-four hours of my life before or since. Consciously or subconsciously, my life thereafter was guided by an awareness that the biggest things in life are not only the great achievements but also frequently the small pleasures.

ONE THING that didn't change over the years was my love of tomfoolery and my penchant for snaring myself in embarrassing situations. When I worked at *Life* I had a lot of appliance and home furnishings accounts, so each January and June for nine years I'd head for Chicago to attend the furniture show at the Merchandise Mart or the appliance show at the American Furniture Mart. It was a great opportunity to make contact with corporate presidents and sales vice presidents whom I couldn't see under ordinary circumstances. I'd stay at the Conrad Hilton Hotel—an enormous building, then the largest hotel in the world. For some reason, going back and forth from my room to the lobby and then walking to the Merchandise Mart and back always put me in a lighthearted mood.

One evening about 1951 I was set to have dinner at the Hilton with the people from Masland Carpet—a family-owned company in Carlisle, Pennsylvania, whose president had been a friend of mine at Princeton. I'd come back from the Merchandise Mart to my room, cleaned myself up, and made some telephone calls before proceeding to the dining room to meet the Maslands. It was a June night before the age of air conditioning, and the transoms over the doors to the rooms were open for ventilation. As I walked down the hall from my room to the elevators, I heard a female voice say through one of the transoms, "If that motherfucker lays a hand on me, I'll chew his balls off." I was astonished and amazed: I had never heard a woman speak that way before in my life.

Then the other female voice said something along the same lines. Curious, I stopped and walked over to the door to listen to their conversation. "That goddam phone hasn't rung for fifteen minutes," I heard one of the women grumble. "I don't know what we have to do to get any business in this goddam town."

Even with my sheltered background, I was able to deduce that these women were prostitutes. I'd never had any personal experience with a prostitute, so I was fascinated. The language, the rough attitude of these women, the fact that they were talking in loud voices and making no effort to be discreet—it all seemed so exotic and enticing that I couldn't tear myself away.

The doors of the Conrad Hilton rooms were old-fashioned not only in respect to their transoms, but also in their large keyholes—large enough that you could peek through and see something. So I leaned down and looked through. Within the perimeter of my vision I could see part of a woman who was standing there naked. She was speaking to somebody across the room, out of my line of vision. I figured if I got down on my knees and changed my viewpoint a little, I could get a better view. But my glasses prevented me from putting my face too close to the keyhole and the doorknob. And of course I couldn't take my glasses off because I couldn't see without them.

As I kneeled down and tried to position myself, the woman started walking toward the door—more into my field of view. I took off my glasses to try to get my eye a little closer to the keyhole. In the process, I must have brushed the doorknob, because all of a sudden the woman pulled the door open. And there I was, on my knees, with my face up against the doorknob—a peeping Tom, caught in the act. And there *she* was, bare-ass.

With the benefit of thirty-seven years' hindsight, I imagine their loud conversation was probably a stunt deliberately intended to drum up business by luring impressionable fellows like me. In any case, the woman stood there with her hands on her hips, looking down at me. (I never did get a look at the other woman; she was at the other end of the room.)

"What the hell are you doing?" she said to me.

Well, the question and my position and the whole episode were so ridiculous that I started to laugh. I said the first thing that came into my head: "I'm looking for my contact lenses. They've dropped on the floor"—which was ridiculous on its face, because I was holding my glasses in my hand.

"Jesus Christ," the woman said to her partner. "I've heard 'em all. This turkey's looking for his contact lenses. Did you ever hear anything like that in your life?" Then she turned to me. "Now, when you *find* them," she said, "knock on the door and I'll give you some good action." Then she slammed the door in my face.

MY BUSINESS CAREER was progressing so well that, like my father during the 1920s boom, I barely considered the possibility of pitfalls ahead. Yet in the back of my mind I knew that sooner or later I'd have to face the fact that I was only a salesman in *Life*'s Philadelphia office; I wasn't in management. My boss in Philadelphia, Malcolm Scott, was a man I liked very much. But he wasn't good enough to be promoted and he wasn't bad enough to be fired, nor was he old enough to retire very soon. So my prospects for advancing to even a minor management job as head of the Philadelphia office were blocked by the likelihood that Malcolm would be in that job for some time to come.

I had no specific goals in the company at that time, and that bothered me a bit, but I did nothing about it. Instead, I simply applied my energies to increasing my sales volume.

Then one Monday morning in early March 1953, I got a telephone call from Clay Buckhout, *Life*'s director of advertising sales—my big boss. "Thacher," he said, "I'd like you to come up and have lunch with me today, if you will."

So I took the train up to New York and had lunch with Buckhout, an unusual occurrence—it had happened only once before, when the company was talking about moving me from Detroit to Philadelphia. He'd been very kind and decent to me then. He was not a very demonstrative man, but a solid citizen and an excellent, highly respected advertising man.

"Thacher," he explained, "I just want to tell you that we are expanding our operation in Chicago. We're going to move Bud Redpath, who's head of the St. Louis office, to take charge of the Chicago office. We're going to take Jack Morrissey, who's currently head of the Chicago office, and put him in charge of a big mid-America regional operation. And we're going to need a new man to head up the St. Louis office. We'd like you to take that job."

St. Louis was a small office—smaller than Philadelphia. On the other hand, I would have been the youngest office manager in the company. It was obviously a step up. They would put me out there to run that St. Louis office for a couple of years, by which time one of the big office jobs would be available and I'd go directly to that office. So Buckhout's job offer was the logical next step on the ladder of advancement within the sales department.

Still, I wasn't about to leave Philadelphia to move to St. Louis, especially when I'd just returned from Detroit because of Nancy's illness. And I recognized that my superiors in the company didn't really expect me to take the job. In effect they were sending a message: "It's yours if you want it. But if you don't want it, you're still perfectly all right in Philadelphia. We admire what you're doing, we like your work, and thanks a lot." It was above all a gesture of recognition; it was not the kind of situation in which a company tells someone, "If you don't move, your career's dead."

I turned it down on the spot and went back to Philadelphia without much regret—just appreciation that they had been kind enough to offer me the job before I turned it down, as they must have known I would.

That was Monday. The next day I got a call from Andrew Heiskell, the publisher of *Life* and the person in top management I probably knew best and liked most—a young, very attractive fellow who was later married to Madeleine Carroll, the movie actress. "I'd like you to come up and have lunch with me," Andrew said. "There's something I'd like to talk to you about."

So I returned to New York on Wednesday and talked to Heiskell. He had no idea that I'd been offered the St. Louis job (there was no reason why he should have). "We've watched you," he said, "and we're impressed with where you're going. But you're moving ahead too far too fast to come up the classic route in sales. You really are beyond that right now. We have more important plans afoot for you, and we don't want to waste another four or five years of putting you through the sales route. What I'd like you to do is to come up here and work for me, as assistant to the publisher. I'd like you to put in about a year or a year and a half doing that. Then in the meantime we're going to start a new publication, right now called Project X. A sports magazine." This, of course, was subsequently born as *Sports Illustrated*. "In the initial stages we're asking Harry Phillips"—he was the publisher of *Time*— "to come in as the publisher of Project X. It'll probably be another two years before we have anything other than a small task force working on that. So while you're working for me during that year and a half as assistant to the publisher, you'll also be part of this Project X sports magazine task force. Then when we start the magazine, you will leave me and go over and become assistant publisher of Project X, working under Harry Phillips. Harry's going to keep that job for two years before we start the magazine and for another two years after we start it. Then, assuming all goes right, you'll be the publisher of Project X."

For someone who was just thirty-two years old, this was a fantastic opportunity. I couldn't have asked for a more exciting job, especially with my sports background. And to be ticketed, at that stage of the game, for a year and a half of experience working for Heiskell, so I could begin to understand matters of finance and production to go with my sales experience, and to have that much confidence expressed in me—it was a very wonderful thing.

Heiskell said the company was perfectly willing to put me up in an apartment in Manhattan where I could stay during the week, thus enabling my family to remain in Philadelphia. "You don't have to make any definite move here until you've had an opportunity to evaluate the situation," he said.

Eventually, however, I knew that the job he offered would involve a move to New York. If you're the publisher of a major national sports magazine, you have to live where the publication is based. But Heiskell's offer also meant that it would be at least four or five years before I'd have to move to New York.

I asked him to let me think about that. I went back home that night, talked to Nancy, talked to the children, thought about it, and made a decision. The next day I called Heiskell and turned him down.

"Bob," I said—Heiskell's nickname at that time was Bob— "I'm so flattered. On the other hand, I've talked to my wife and my kids, and they really don't want to go to New York. They don't feel it's a place where they want to live. They don't want to move to Princeton or New Haven or somewhere and have the long commute. We're just provincial people; we like it here."

When I said no to that job, I knew that I was pretty well cutting myself off from *Life* magazine and Time Inc., because if you turn down a wonderful opportunity like that, obviously management concludes, "Well, he wants to be where he is more than he wants to be where he might be with us, so we really can't count on him anymore." They don't fire you, but from then on you're never going to get any more good opportunities. You have to adjust to that.

Friday of the same week I got a telephone call from Wes Pullen, who had been two years ahead of me at Princeton and had played football with me. He had gone directly from

Princeton to Time Inc., had compiled a distinguished war record aboard PT boats, and then had rejoined Time Inc. as assistant to Roy Larsen, the president. During his experience with Larsen he had been steered into a special assignment to look after Time Inc.'s broadcast properties, which were just starting to develop. Time Inc. had bought several radio stations, which were owned and operated by the company, and now Time Inc. was beginning to look at television. The company had reached an agreement with Wayne Coy, then chairman of the Federal Communications Commission, whereby Coy would resign from the FCC to run a TV station in Albuquerque as a 50 percent partner with Time Inc. Pullen wanted me to move to Albuquerque to be Time Inc.'s representative on the station staff.

"You'd become the number-two guy at the station," he explained, "and at the end of two years, after you've had a chance to learn the television business from the ground up"—at this stage of the game nobody knew much about it; there wasn't any place to learn it except to be in it—"we have an option to buy the television station in Denver, and we would like you to go up and run the station in Denver for two years. Then, with that background and experience in television"—which at that time would have been as complete as anybody's in the country—"you would come back to Time Inc. and we'd make you vice president in charge of the broadcasting division—assuming you cut the mustard, of course."

That wasn't quite as attractive to me as *Sports Illustrated,* but it offered the excitement of living out West, together with the assurance that I would return to civilization and a high corporate position later on. Nancy and I and the children actually gave that idea a lot more attention and discussion than we had given either of the other two proposals. But over the weekend we finally reached a decision: Come hell or high water, we were going to stay in Philadelphia.

Time Inc. did indeed subsequently enter a joint partnership

in Albuquerque with Wayne Coy and did acquire a TV station in Denver. But I wasn't part of that picture.

I called Pullen on Monday and told him my decision. That night, after dinner, I said to Nancy, "Tomorrow I'm going to go out and look for a job."

"What do you mean?" she said. "You've got a job. They must love you."

"Yeah," I said. "But the love ended today. From here on in, I may become a legend in the company as the guy who turned down three big jobs in one week. The fact of the matter is I'm also through. So I'm going to leave."

And I did, within six weeks.

It turned out that emotionally, finding a job was easier than leaving Time Inc. Once I started looking around, I discovered all kinds of opportunities. I took the one that seemed most attractive—a job with a personal friend as a partner in an advertising agency—and went up to New York a couple of weeks later to resign from Time Inc. It was a traumatic occasion. I cried—real tears. I was terribly upset about leaving this company I loved so much. But I loved Philadelphia too, and there was no way I could have both.

MY NEW JOB didn't last long because I left it to run for mayor of Philadelphia in 1955. After I had been defeated in the 1955 election, I had to look for a job again. (I wasn't going to go back to the advertising agency, where my former partners were still bitter that I had left them to run for public office.) At that time I got a call from Howard Black, who had been my very close friend and benefactor at Time Inc.: It was he who had made it possible for us to move from Detroit to Philadelphia after Nancy's illness had been diagnosed. He had that feeling toward me that you have for somebody you've helped, and I had the feeling of appreciation that you have for somebody who's helped you.

"I'm just calling because I understand you're out of a job," he said, "and I know you're broke. I know you've got a lot of debts that you incurred while you were running for office. I just want to tell you: If you want it, your old job—with a five-thousand-dollar raise—is waiting for you there in Philadelphia. We'd love to have you back, we'll make the opening for you, and you can stay a day or you can stay the rest of your life—it's immaterial to me. I don't think you'll want to do this, but I just wanted you to know, if you had worries or if you're concerned about how you're going to feed your children, you can start that job tomorrow and you can stay as long as you want. Time Inc. is always here for you to come to if you wish."

That's not the way very large companies ordinarily behave. And I was enormously touched. But I said, "No, Howard, I don't want to do that. I'll be all right. I have no fears that I won't find something. I've never been out of a job before, I've never been broke, and I'm a little scared, and your calling like this is wonderful, because now I'm not scared anymore."

Even after I left, Time Inc. was still looking over my shoulder. Other people may tell horror stories about big business. Not me. When I joined Time Inc. I joined a family—which is why my leaving was so painful.

CHAPTER 8

POLITICS I:
GETTING HOOKED
(1936–54)

MY MOTHER AND FATHER had always been Republicans—even in 1912, when they helped the Democrat Woodrow Wilson win the election by splitting their votes between two Republicans (Father voted for the conservative William Howard Taft and Mother voted for the Bull Moose challenger, Teddy Roosevelt). So I developed a sense of loyalty to the Republican Party that's pretty old-fashioned and not terribly intelligent. But there wasn't anything I could do about it; it was in my genes.

My Republicanism went hand in glove with the other critical institutions that made me what I am: Haverford School, Camp La Jeunesse, Princeton University, the United States Navy, and Time Inc. It was an emotional attachment that would not let me free.

Few people maintain that kind of political attachment today. And the process works both ways: Companies, schools, political parties, and the military no longer display the same degree of loyalty to their members as *they* once did. Part of the change probably has to do with size: The world when I was a kid numbered a billion people; now it's five billion people. The world's population has grown so enormously in sixty-five years that the numbers—and the consequent crowdedness, combativeness, and protectiveness—have changed people's attitudes and comprehensions of loyalty.

But to me, loyalty was always the most important quality a person could possess. I admired it most in other people, and I desired it most in myself. If I were loyal, I felt, that would compensate for my other shortcomings.

While most of the country shifted to the Democrats after the Great Crash of 1929, my parents remained Republican all through the Depression and even through 1936, when President Roosevelt won all but eight votes in the electoral college.

That was the year my prototypical political hero, Alfred M. Landon, arrived on the national scene. If you're a Republican candidate in Philadelphia—where you're usually up against a three- or four-to-one ratio of registered Democrats to Republicans—you can be forgiven for choosing strange heroes. I figured that anybody who carries only two states in a presidential election (as Landon did in 1936) and still survives it (as Landon did almost to this writing, more than half a century later), outliving his victorious opponent by forty years, he's my kind of guy. He understands what politics is all about. What the hell—all Roosevelt did was become famous, gain entry to the history books, and die at a relatively early age. Conversely, imagine all the fun Alf Landon had since 1936 telling jokes and stories about his defeat.

It was at Haverford School that I launched my political speaking career. The 1936 presidential elections took place during my senior year there. Just about everyone at Haverford supported Landon against Roosevelt—which may give you some idea of how out of step Haverford was with the rest of the country. In any case, shortly before election day the school held a mock vote and chose four of us to speak in behalf of the four leading candidates—FDR, Landon, the Socialist Norman Thomas, and a fourth candidate named William Lempke, a political madman whose solution to the Depression was to print $100 billion in new money and spread it among the populace.

I was assigned to speak for Lempke. I concluded my talk by declaring, "Here is a fresh political concept—so rational, so reasonable, so practical, so certain of success that anyone who does not vote for William Lempke simply doesn't care about America." It was absurd, but Lempke got more votes in our Haverford straw poll than Roosevelt did.

And so I recognized at that time that I possessed some magic power to influence people to do imbecilic things on occasion.

I was probably the best public speaker at Haverford School. I was the best at Princeton, and I was the best at *Life* magazine when I worked there. They used me all the time to make presentations all over the country. In one such *Life* presentation, I used to take off my shoes and throw them at the audience, and I'd toss out dollar bills stuffed in my pockets—all to promote the concept that (a) creative advertising ideas must be combined with (b) shoe leather in order to produce (c) money. Even today, I'm still approached in airport terminals or on New York streets by people who say, "I remember you—I heard you give a talk back in 1951. I've never forgotten it—particularly the part where you threw the money."

My success as a salesman and speaker had led me to believe that this sales ability, combined with a little luck, would get me into elective office, just as it got me into Earl Freeman's office. But I failed to understand that there were factors over which a political candidate has no control. In fact, some of the qualities that I naively presumed were my greatest advantages—like enthusiasm, youth, a good education, and a WASP heritage—turned out to be political liabilities in Philadelphia.

With equal naiveté I overlooked the difference between seeking office in prep school or college and seeking office in the real world. To run for the class presidency at Haverford School or Princeton meant that you allowed your name to be introduced as a candidate. But you never made a speech; you never issued a paper; you never held a rally. You merely stood for office and were elected by acclaim, on the assumption that everyone knew who you were—not because you campaigned, but because you were popular. And one office invariably led to another.

Thus I developed the notion that running for office was simply a matter of being a good guy and waiting for the right people to acknowledge your goodness and offer you an office. This notion was reinforced in 1952 when Dwight D. Eisenhower was elected president without really trying: The politicians and the people came to him—on the basis of his war record—not vice versa.

The same notion was further reinforced in 1955 when, out of the blue, two leaders of Philadelphia's reform Republican faction walked into my house and asked me to be their candidate for mayor. In my innocence, I believed that all I had to do to be elected was to demonstrate my worthiness to hold the job—just be a good fellow and treat everybody nicely and they would make me mayor or senator or president or whatever.

I subsequently learned, of course, that in real politics you are never evaluated for yourself alone, but for such characteristics as your religion, your race, your age, your sex, your economic status, your geography, and your issues, all of which collectively are far more important than you are yourself—unless, of course, you are an Eisenhower. And I was no Eisenhower. Most important, I found, if you are a Republican in a Democratic city, people may like you and respect you, but they will not vote for you.

THE COMPENSATION of my political naiveté was that I was in good company—at least in Philadelphia. It was through my "aunt" Mable Pew Myrin—my mother's prep-school classmate—that I got to know Mabel's brothers, J. Howard Pew and Joseph N. Pew, Jr., who was always referred to as J.N. Through their ownership of the Sun Oil Company the Pews were (and probably still are) the richest family in Philadelphia. J. Howard and J.N. were always very aloof, very reserved, and I never really broke through their outer facade. As a boy I had gone to Mrs. Duer's Dancing Classes with J. Howard's daughter Frances Pew, and I knew her brother George, who was slightly older than I was and whom I had held in awe by virtue of his large touring car and the speeds with which he drove it around the back roads of the Main Line.

I never knew J. Howard very well because I was just so scared of him. I'd occasionally go over to his estate for a party or a get-together, but when you heard J. Howard coming, you somehow always got out of the way. He had a puritanical objection to smoking or drinking (I didn't smoke or drink either, but at least I seldom objected to anyone else's indulging) and a frightening facade—which was a shame, because behind that facade, which few people ever penetrated, was a basically shy man with a delightful sense of humor and a high degree of generosity.

The Pews had plenty of money to invest and give away, but unlike other wealthy families they never delegated the responsibility to foundations or committees; they personally decided where it was going to be spent. In effect they divided areas of authority among themselves: J. Howard made the business decisions, J.N. the political decisions, and their sisters Mabel and Ethel the charity decisions (a fifth Pew sibling, their brother Arthur, died before I was born).

J.N., because of his long interest in politics, was probably the most worldly of the four. But by any other standard J.N. was dogmatically conservative—and almost as innocent as I was. He was a rich man who fancied himself a connoisseur of gutter politics; a dedicated conservative Republican who put his money where his principles were; but also a man who, for all his money and interest, never became an effective player of the political game.

I first realized this one day in the mid-1950s. I was walking down a Philadelphia street with J.N. when a seedy-looking fellow sidled up to us and said, "Hi, Joe!" Not "Mr. Pew" but "Joe." J.N. greeted this man by name and we continued on. After we were out of the fellow's earshot, J.N. told me his story.

Gabe, as the fellow was called, was a lowly gofer who'd made a precarious living on the fringes of politics. During the 1936 campaign the Republican Party in Philadelphia faced the prospect of virtual extinction amid Democrat Franklin D. Roosevelt's expected landslide victory over Alf Landon. "I was afraid that the whole Republican organization was going to turn in for Roosevelt," J.N. explained, "and that we would lose not only the national election, but the local and state elections in the following years."

To hold the party together sufficiently to produce a respectable showing at the polls—FDR's victory was already a foregone conclusion—J.N. hit upon a bizarre strategy: One week before the election he would bet $50,000 on Landon to carry Philadelphia. "If we made such a bet," he explained, "the word would get out among the committeemen that there's a lot of Landon money around. And politicians being the way they are, they'd start wondering, 'What do they know that we don't know?' And guys who might sell out Landon would decide to work for him after all, in the belief that he had a chance of winning."

Rather than place a single $50,000 bet himself—lest he make his strategy too obvious—J.N. gave the $50,000 to Gabe and instructed him to spread the money around in numerous small bets on Landon. Gabe argued against the scheme—"Save your money," he told J.N.—but J.N. insisted.

Thus Gabe disappeared with the $50,000, which J.N. had written off as, in effect, a campaign contribution. He didn't see Gabe again until three weeks after the election—in which, of course, Landon was soundly trounced, locally as well as nationally. Gabe walked into J.N.'s office totally disheveled and hungover; he looked like he'd been in a fight. When J.N. asked what had happened, Gabe replied, "J.N., to be honest with you, I was a little upset about your throwing this money away. I know you've got a lot of it, but it just doesn't seem right to bet on a sure loser. So I took the money and got drunk. And I've been drunk for the past four weeks. I stayed drunk for a week before the election, I was drunk all through the election, and I've been drunk ever since. So I never got a chance to bet any of your money. Now, I've spent seven hundred and thirty-five dollars, but there's forty-nine thousand, two hundred and sixty-five left. So here it is." And Gabe handed the money back to J.N.

"I think," J.N. told me in recalling this story nearly twenty years later, "I have a right to call him the only totally honest politician I ever met."

Both J.N. and his brother J. Howard loved to lecture people. They supported me generously in my campaigns for various offices. But particularly in my first run for mayor in 1955, when I was only thirty-four, J.N. felt I needed not only money but also a certain amount of guidance in running my campaign. Periodically I'd get a call from him and go to his office at the Sun Building on Walnut Street, where he'd give me another $10,000 campaign contribution and lecture me on how it ought to be spent. Some of his advice was useful, but much of it was not. The Pews weren't noted for backing winners; most often they backed losers, which was consistent with their staunch conservatism and their willingness to support candidates they liked, regardless of the candidates' prospects for victory.

"Thacher," J.N. told me at one point, "of course you haven't got a chance of winning this election. But my family and I are going to put a good deal of money into this, because we've known your family, you're Republican, and we know you're good stuff. You're too liberal, but you'll learn as you get older. We just think people like you have got to be supported."

After I lost the '55 election, J.N. called me in again. "You turned out to be a lot better than I thought you were," he said. "You've got a lot on the ball politically. You can go far if you wish. But not around here. You're going to have to move."

"What do you mean?" I asked.

"You move out to the Midwest—or Colorado, Utah, Wyoming, or one of those places—and I'll help you get established out there. Then we'll run you for the Senate and you'll get elected. And in Washington, who knows what'll happen?"

That was his advice. When I said I didn't want to move, J.N. lost all interest in me. When I ran for the Senate in '62, he supported me, but without the same zeal: I wasn't prepared to make the sacrifice of moving, and thus I had flunked J.N.'s test.

Had I been more ambitious politically, I would have changed my party and become a Democrat in Philadelphia—either that, or I would have moved somewhere else where the Republican label was an asset rather than a drawback, as Joe Pew wanted me to. And had I been a Republican politician twenty years earlier, I'd have been a shoo-in in Philadelphia. So in politics, at least, the luck of circumstances didn't work for me as it had in the private sector—and also, of course, I wasn't willing to pay the price of political success.

But no one could have taught me these lessons. I had to learn them from experience.

MY FIRST REAL FORAY into politics came in 1940—my senior year at Princeton—when a twenty-nine-year-old New York lawyer named Oren Root appeared on campus. He had come to recruit campaign workers for Wendell Willkie, the obscure Wall Street lawyer who was challenging the favored Senator Robert Taft of Ohio for the Republican presidential nomination. Oren's surface credentials were impressive to any undergrad: He was a Princeton man himself, and his great-uncle, the statesman Elihu Root, had served in the cabinets of Presidents McKinley and Teddy Roosevelt and had won the Nobel Peace Prize in 1912. Oren himself was chairman of an organization called the Associated Willkie Clubs of America.

I never made a rational decision that Willkie was the better candidate. Root simply got to me and my colleagues before the Taft people did, and his presentation to the campus Young Republicans convinced most of us that working for Willkie would be pretty good fun. When he called for volunteers, about forty of us raised our hands, and away we went. If Root had asked us to work for Taft, we'd probably have acquiesced with the same alacrity. What mattered wasn't so much the candidate as the excitement of getting involved in a political campaign for the first time.

The forty Princeton students recruited by Root—plus God knows how many from other nearby schools—were dispatched to Philadelphia that June to pack the Republican convention for Willkie. As they say, the rest is history.

From his headquarters room at the Bellevue-Stratford Hotel on the eve of the convention, Root instructed us to report for the next four nights to seats in the gallery at Convention Hall. Upon a secret signal relayed to us by various Willkie operatives spread around the auditorium, we were to begin stamping our feet and chanting, "We want Willkie!" There were a few hundred of us, and the impact was amazing: The first thing anybody knew, it sounded like the whole place was screaming for Willkie. To be sure, organized "spontaneous" demonstrations are nothing new in political conventions, but

I've never seen one that was organized so well and so effectively.

At the end of each session, we volunteers would return to the hotel, where Willkie's aides had set up banks of telephones—a relatively new technique at that time. Root and his people stationed each of us at a phone with a page torn out of the phone book, instructing us to go down the page and call every number. The moment somebody answered the phone, we were to say, "We want Willkie!" and then hang up.

By using every available spare minute to make thousands of these phone calls, Root hoped to get everyone in Philadelphia talking about Willkie—especially cab drivers, waiters, bellhops, and other people who might come in contact with convention delegates. The cumulative effect, it was hoped, would persuade the delegates that Willkie's forces were everywhere and could not be denied. Which is pretty much the way things went: Willkie won the nomination. And had it not been for the war and Willkie's loss of his voice during the general election campaign, he might very well have upset Roosevelt that year.

RETURNING TO THE PRINCETON CAMPUS for my senior year that fall, I was approached by someone from the New Jersey Republican organization. They had a list of those of us who had worked with Root at the Philadelphia convention; now they asked if we'd be willing to work on election day as poll watchers in Trenton, which was one of those ten-to-one Democratic bastions.

They were particularly interested in recruiting physically large people, the sort who wouldn't be easily intimidated in the tough part of town, where votes were most likely to be stolen or rigged. I was six foot six. So I signed up.

We were given a two-hour training session on how to prevent votes from being stolen—what to look for, not to let two people go in the voting booth at the same time, and so on. But of course college boys out to prevent fraud were no match for people who'd been *committing* vote fraud all their lives.

A bus from Princeton dropped fifty or sixty of us off at polling places in a predominantly black section of Trenton. Black people then were very strongly for Roosevelt, but all the officials in the precinct where I was assigned were whites of Irish descent.

We reported in to the judge of elections, received our poll watcher certificates, and then set about the grim work of preventing votes from being stolen by the nefarious Roosevelt forces. But to our surprise, we encountered no resistance whatever. The precinct elections judge was a charming old leprechaun who greeted us with apparent friendship and enthusiasm.

"Ah," he exclaimed in a thick Irish accent, "sure and isn't it nice that the bhoys have come down from Princeton to hulp us out here."

And: "Bhoys, it's woonderful for you ta do this. I'm an older mon now, I don't hahve the energy I used to, so to hahve you people here is most enjoyable for me, and I welcome your presence."

Then: "I hope they hahven't told you any bahd stories about me. As you can see, I'm a harmless old fellow. I like the world. I love the world. And I particularly love young people, and I'm goin' ta tell you all about how these things work."

He proceeded to explain to us the polling system and the books (this was before the days of voting machines; you voted on paper ballots with pencil), and the nasty tricks to look out for.

"There are some people that'll try ta cheat in there," he solemnly advised us, "and you've got to watch very carefully what they'll write. That's the only time, you see; ya doon't have to worry about any other time, 'cept when they put in the X. You watch them when they put in the X and make sure they're puttin' the X on the right kind of ballot and only doing it on one ballot and signing in the proper place and seein' that the signature matches with the signature in the book. There's nothing else to worry about."

When we went in and sat down, this charming gent fetched each of us a Coke. We waited awhile, but no voters came in. Finally we asked him where they were.

"Oh," he replied, "this is a strange district here. They all come in very late, later on in the day. Don't usually come in until nightfall or something near there. You won't have anything to do during the day. You getting bored?"

"Well, gee, there's nothing going on," I said. "I'd felt there'd be people coming in and lots of excitement and stuff."

"I'll tell you what," he said. "They're playin' a movie down the way a little bit called *The Great McGinty*. Why don't we all go down there? I'll come along with you. There's nothing going on here."

We figured, if *he's* coming along, it must be all right for us to go, too. So the judge and the two of us from Princeton and three or four other precinct officials went off to the movies. Admission was a quarter, but the good judge generously treated us all. *The Great McGinty,* starring Brian Donlevy, turned out to be a film about cheating at the polls. Most ironic.

It was perhaps eleven in the morning when we went into the theater and one o'clock when the film ended. But when the lights went up, the judge and his cohorts weren't there. We walked back to the polling place—about five minutes away—and sure enough, there was our grandfatherly election judge sitting there with a beatific smile on his face.

"Did you bhoys like the movies?" he asked. "I stayed for a little bit, but I saw it lahst night and didn't have to see it again."

We said we'd enjoyed the film and sat down again to wait

for voters. But there were none to be seen. Finally I went over to the chief judge.

"Sir," I said, "it's after three o'clock now, and nobody's come in since we got back."

"Ah, no," he replied. "We're all through. We're all finished!"

"What do you mean, finished?" I asked.

"We voted everyone!"

"What was the count?"

He ruffled through his papers. "Oh," he said, "let me see here. We voted four hundred and thirty-six people . . . and let me see . . . Mr. Roosevelt, that great man, that great president, he got four hundred and twenty-three votes. And the other fellow, your fellow, he got thirteen."

"But where . . . when did the people come in here?" I asked. "I didn't see them."

"It musta happened when you were at the movies."

"You told me that they didn't come in 'til late afternoon," I said.

"Well, that's the way they usually do it. But today they seemed to have come in a little bit earlier. Don't know why it happened, but that's the way it was."

"Can I see the register?" I asked.

"Why, certainly you can. Let me show it to you. See, here are all the registers . . . and here are all the signatures, and here are the votes, and here are all the signatures on the votes, and here are all the people they voted for. And you can count those and you can count these . . ."

I counted them. Everything was in order.

"No need for you to sit around here, " he suggested. "You might as well go back to Princeton." We took his advice and hitchhiked back to school.

Obviously, we had done no good and the entire precinct vote had been rigged. But how? Nearly half a century later,

I'm still not sure. Most likely the judge had canvassed the neighborhood the night before and got everybody to sign the dossier so that he had all the signatures. Thus none of the voters had to come in; all he had to do was sign the votes—and he had six or eight of his friends on hand, so they'd have different-looking signatures. We didn't know enough to check the signature on each vote against the signature on the dossier—but if we had, I'm sure the judge would have found some other cock-and-bull story to lay us off. Thus my first experience in the world of politics did no good whatever to the people I was supporting.

FOR YEARS AFTERWARD I had no real involvement with politics. I went off to war, returned, tried to make a living, went out to Detroit, where I didn't know anybody, and came back to Philadelphia, preoccupied with my wife's multiple sclerosis. So I had no involvement or interest in politics at all until 1952, when I got a call one day from Tom Wood, an investment manager friend of mine—and a friend at Haverford School—who was the Philadelphia chairman of Citizens for Eisenhower. At his suggestion, one day in the early summer of 1952 I walked into the Citizens for Eisenhower headquarters on Walnut Street and volunteered to work.

I was greeted with great enthusiasm by a receptionist who wrote my name on a file card and said I would be hearing from them shortly. Nothing happened, so I returned about a month later. This time a different receptionist greeted me. I said I had offered to volunteer, and again she asked me to fill out a card. I said I already had, and she said I would be hearing from them shortly.

Another month went by and I went back yet again. A third lady was at the front desk. I told her I didn't want to go on filling out cards until the election was over.

"Well, if you're *that* anxious to work," she said, "the warehouse out in back, where we keep all our materials, is in terrible shape. How about going out there and cleaning it up?"

She must have thought she was calling my bluff. But I walked back into the warehouse, which looked like the Augean stables. I took one look at things and knew that the task was far beyond my powers. I phoned Nancy—it was not beyond *her* powers—and told her to catch the next train into town. She did so and came over to headquarters, where I pointed to the mess out there in the back. "They want me to clean this up," I said, "and I really don't know how to start."

"Just get out of my way," Nancy said. Then she took over and cleaned everything up, and by the end of the day the place was spick-and-span. As her reward, next day she was made office manager for the local Citizens for Eisenhower headquarters on Walnut Street.

In the meantime, I was immediately demoted to her assistant—that is, I did what she told me to. And since she wanted to work harder than I did, I absented myself from the campaign headquarters and went back to my business. But one night in September 1952, headquarters got a call asking for someone with experience in public speaking. I'd done a certain amount of that, so I got on the phone.

The caller identified himself as a Republican ward leader from Kensington, a blue-collar section of Philadelphia. "We're having a big meeting of our committeemen tonight," he said. "We're going to have about a hundred people here, and my speaker has just pooped out on me. Can you give me a speech?"

"Sure," I said.

So I gathered a lot of the Eisenhower leaflets at headquarters and boned up on them, and that night I gave my first political speech ever before this ward group in Kensington. To my amazement, they liked it—and next thing I knew, I was inundated with requests from ward committees to come and give speeches on the Eisenhower campaign.

In fact, the very next night I was enlisted to speak in the Far Northeast section of the city for a committeeman who proposed to drive me around with a truck and a loudspeaker. Of course, that's quite different from speaking before an audience in an auditorium under relatively controlled circumstances, and I had no idea what I was in for. I simply rode the elevated to Bridge Street—the end of the line—where he met me, and together we headed for the Northeast, which in those days was relatively wild country. Although it was within the city limits, there were still farms up there, complete with cows, pigs, chickens, and a few people.

For my first speech, we drove to what appeared to be an almost totally isolated spot. I assumed my companion was kidding me, or else he wanted to try me out on two or three of the farm animals before exposing me to people.

But sure enough, after a while a small crowd assembled around the truck—maybe twenty-five or thirty people in all. I couldn't understand it—we were out in the middle of nowhere. The ward leader looked at his watch. "Okay, kid," he told me. "Give 'em hell."

I spoke for about three minutes. Then a trolley came along, and my entire audience boarded the trolley and disappeared. I suddenly realized why I'd been taken to this desolate spot: This was a trolley stop, and small crowds gathered whenever a trolley was due.

We did a couple of these three-minute numbers. Then my partner had another idea. "Now the movies will be letting out," he said. We went to a nearby movie house and waited. Sure enough, pretty soon a few hundred people came pouring out of the theater. So I gave a three-or-four-minute talk there. Then it turned out that most of the moviegoers had parked their cars in a lot across the street, so we immediately scampered over there and did yet another little talk.

Thus I learned that the trick of speaking on street corners was not to announce the speech and hope people came; you went where the people were and gave the speeches. Before long I got quite good at street-corner speeches. I was completely relaxed at it and went all over the city of Philadelphia. In some areas I was very well received (which I loved), in some areas I was very poorly received (which I didn't mind), and in others I was totally ignored (which I hated).

As soon as we pinpointed the areas where nobody cared—particularly about sidewalk speakers talking from truck platforms—we stopped going there. An upper-class community like Chestnut Hill, for example—nobody was out at night. Or West Philadelphia and along City Line—middle-class areas where people stayed home at night and there was no reason to be out on the street. But if you went to a big shopping intersection like 5th and Olney, for example, or 52nd and Market, or Germantown and Chelten avenues, you got big crowds. They were hurrying from one place to another, but if you were reasonably forceful, you could usually stop them. Sometimes I had five hundred or six hundred people listening to me extol the virtues of Dwight D. Eisenhower for two to three minutes.

I remember speaking in some of the black areas, which were then nowhere near as large or as numerous as they are now, but were still substantial. They were all for Stevenson—all Democrats—and I would get heckled. There the listeners didn't just toss words at me; they threw objects, too—usually fruit. On one occasion, when a man threw an orange at me, I not only caught the orange, but in one sweeping movement I spun it back at him and hit him on the chest. The crowd gave me a big hand. They had no use for me or my candidate, but they seemed to appreciate the fluidity and skill with which I fielded that orange and sent it back to him so fast that he had had no chance to get out of its way.

They also threw coal, which was unpleasant; you could get hurt. I never got hit by any, but it did take your mind off your talk. On the other hand, ducking coal on a speaker's platform in front of a hostile crowd in an outdoor setting with terrible acoustics and two minutes to get my point across was priceless training. By contrast, all the public speaking I've done ever since has been relatively easy. That experience taught me to spotlight my points and to avoid wasting words.

AFTER THAT '52 CAMPAIGN, I laid off politics again. As I have recounted, I left *Life* magazine in June of 1953 and joined an advertising agency. I didn't jump back into the local political scene until 1954, when Philip Sharpless, then chairman of the Pennsylvania Republican Finance Committee, asked me to help him raise money for Lloyd Wood, the undistinguished Republican candidate who ran unsuccessfully against George Leader in the '54 gubernatorial election.

So I raised money—more money, in fact, than was expected from me. And once again I got a chance to be involved in a political campaign. Whereas in '52 my role was active— speechmaking—in '54 I got to work behind the scenes and get a feel of the role of finances in political campaigns. Thus my combination of speaking experience and fund-raising experience, however slight both may have been, brought me to the attention of some of the crowned heads of the Philadelphia Republican Party—crowns which, I now discovered upon my entry into the party's inner circles, were nowhere near as secure as the public believed.

FOR MORE THAN A GENERATION, Sheriff Austin Meehan was the most powerful and influential Republican in Philadelphia. His interest in politics stemmed from two motives: his love of power and his love of people. He exerted a hold on people that had to be seen to be believed, largely because he performed so many favors for so many people.

Virtually every night of his life, Meehan held court in his home after dinner until midnight. A steady stream of supplicants would come to him with problems—usually people looking for jobs or trying to get a street fixed or a son into college. If Meehan felt there was any chance he could help them, he would try. Even after he was voted out of the sheriff's office, he remained on such good terms with the Democrats that he could get things done strictly on a personal basis. The size and devotion of his following was such that when he died in 1961 and I went to his wake, I had to walk nine blocks to reach the end of the line.

To the outside world Meehan seemed the worst possible caricature of the old Republican boss: In an age when lean, youthful reformers were the order of the day, Meehan was fat, smoked a big cigar, and *looked* corrupt, even if he wasn't.

Next to Meehan, the most important Republican force in the city was his temperamental opposite, the late Bill Meade, who derived his power not from his love of people but from his manipulative skill. Meade was smart but disliked (he was subsequently shot but not killed by a jealous husband). He controlled the smaller wards, which—because they were so many in number (although small in size)—controlled the Republican City Committee. Each ward received one vote on the city committee, and thus a ward with five hundred Republicans counted for as much as one with five thousand.

"I'll tell you a funny thing about politics," Meehan once remarked to me. "Anybody will tell you that Austin Meehan never breaks his word, is never vindictive, is never cruel, is always constructive, is generous, is kind. And what do they say about him? They say he is stupid. He's a dumb politician because he is all those things.

"On the other hand, Bill Meade breaks his word, he lies, he cheats, he steals. That makes him a smart politician."

It was true: People always said Meade was smart and Meehan was dumb. But the fact was that one was honorable and the other was not. At the street level of politics, honesty is often stupidity and deceit is wisdom.

Mort Witkin, a trial lawyer, was perhaps the most interesting Republican leader at that time because he had a way with words and was full of clever schemes. Among other things, he was credited with the Republicans' upset victory in the 1953 election for city controller, when he persuaded dissident Democrats that the way to exercise a check on the new Democratic mayor, Joseph Clark, was to elect a Republican controller.

The fourth of the local Republican rulers at that time was Bill Hamilton, a dogmatic, unpleasant man whose family had controlled politics in the Roxborough section for a generation and who ran the 21st Ward—the last ward in the city to go Democratic—as a feudal lord.

By the spring of 1955 these four men had committed themselves to the mayoral candidacy of Hamilton's handsome but undistinguished brother, Wilbur. But other forces were threatening their control. Upper-income WASPs—mostly Republican—were moving in droves to the suburbs, while lower-income blacks—mostly Democrat—were moving into the city from the Deep South. In 1951 the Democrats won control of City Hall for the first time in a century. When the Democrats elected a governor in 1954, the Philadelphia Republican machine's patronage base—the source of the machine's power—all but evaporated.

A youthful insurgent group called the Republican Assembly arose to challenge the machine. These insurgents believed that the party could no longer win elections by relying on armies of patronage workers to get out the vote; instead, the party's future depended on appealing to a new generation of educated, independent-minded voters. It was a time of new ideas bubbling to the surface of the crusty Philadelphia Republican Party—and, as luck would have it, they were bubbling just at the time I was beginning to be noticed in political circles.

Above. The 1955 Philadelphia mayoral campaign. That's me on the left prior to a TV debate with the Democratic candidate, Richardson Dilworth (right). Moderator Mort Farr is between us.

Below. June 1955: President Eisenhower (flanked by Nancy and me) was utterly charming and unpretentious; to hear him talk, *he* felt privileged to be visited by *us*.

Right. 1960: I served as chairman of Philadelphia Citizens for Nixon. Philadelphia might have cost Nixon the presidency that year, but he never said an unkind word to me about it.

Below. 1964: The author, just after assuming my "dream job" as head of the Greater Philadelphia Chamber of Commerce.

Above. I first met Harold Stassen (right) during my moment of glory in the Pacific in World War II; in 1959 I ran his unsuccessful campaign for mayor of Philadelphia. Here we are in 1965. He was one of my unsung heroes.

Below. Nancy was nobody's pushover. Here she's serving as a Republican committeewoman in Chestnut Hill on Election Day 1968—informing the Democrat U.S. senator (and our neighbor), Joseph Clark, that he couldn't vote because he wasn't registered.

Opposite. 1971: Campaigning for mayor a second time. My greatest interest in politics stems from the fun of running for elective office, even when I'm a loser.

Above. I ran against Frank Rizzo (right) for mayor in 1971 and successfully opposed his attempt to seek a third term in 1978. We remained friends nevertheless.

Below. 1984: Philadelphia City Councilman Longstreth on the scene at a major downtown fire. I sent this photo to several close personal friends, with the message, "While you slept."

Opposite above. 1965: With Princess Grace of Monaco, formerly Grace Kelly of Philadelphia. She lost a close friend to multiple sclerosis and helped the MS Society on many occasions.

Opposite below. 1964: With George Worthington (right), whose life I saved during World War II. My beard was a brief affectation that ended when a waitress, seeing it, exclaimed, "Oh, Mr. Longstreth—you're not one of *them!*"

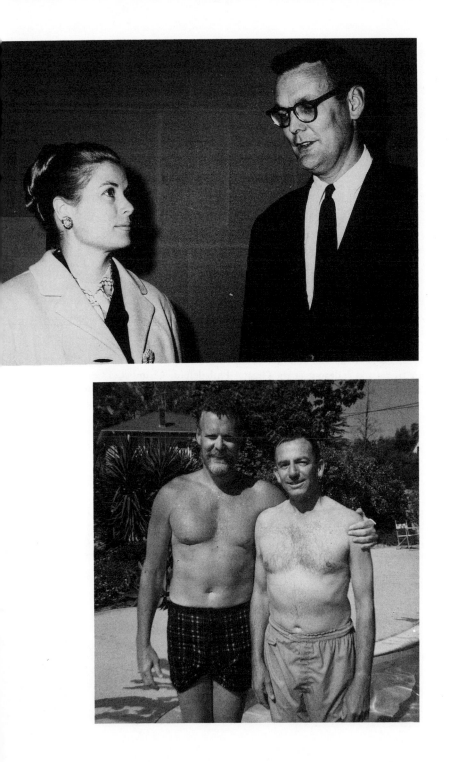

Above. My favorite fall activity: Princeton football games at Palmer Stadium. From left: Chizzy Anderson, me, Miney Anderson, and Nancy.

Below. 1984: An award from Rear Admiral James Flatley (right), son of my World War II superior and hero of the same name. Between us is Dan Noonan, my friend and colleague at the Greater Philadelphia Chamber of Commerce.

Opposite above. 1971: Brother Frank, a prep school teacher in Ohio, and my father provided moral support when I addressed Haverford School's commencement. My father was 90 at the time; he died three years later.

Opposite below. 1971: Nancy and I with our offspring and in-laws. Seated, from left: daughter Ellen Goodwin, Nancy, daughter Anne Anderson. Standing: Howard Goodwin, son William T. Longstreth, Jr., his wife Breck Longstreth, myself, Elizabeth Longstreth, her husband (and my son) Peter Longstreth, and Jay Anderson.

Left. With Nancy, 1974.
Below. With Nancy, 1989. Despite her illness, she's almost as active as ever, thanks to her Amigo electric scooter.
Opposite above. 1986: One of the pleasures of celebrity—throwing out the first ball at a Chicago Cubs-Philadelphia Phillies baseball game.
Opposite below. 1989: A little nonsense now and then: Singing "Makin' Whoopee," with backup provided by other prominent Philadelphians, at the annual "Unstrung Heroes" benefit gala for Philadelphia's Concerto Soloists Chamber Orchestra.

The eternal undergrad: Marching in Princeton's annual
alumni "P-rade"—an event I've missed only three times in
fifty years.

CHAPTER 9
POLITICS II:
RUNNING FOR MAYOR
(1955)

OVER LUNCH ONE DAY at the Racquet Club, two of the insurgent Philadelphia Republicans, John Pomeroy and Frank McGlinn, were discussing the need to find new, independent faces—candidates who could win elections. A friend of mine named Bill Churchman—a Democrat who was also a great friend of the Democratic candidate, Richardson Dilworth—stopped by their table and joined the conversation.

"If you want someone who'll give Dilworth a hard time," Churchman told them, "try the guy sitting right over there in the corner—Thacher Longstreth. He's a big tall guy, a good speaker, has a good war record, athlete in college, he can raise money. There's the fellow you want."

They apparently agreed, because that night they called on me. "We're looking for a candidate to run in the primary on a 'good government' ticket," they told me. "Would you be interested?"

"Well, yes, I guess I would," I said. I wasn't all that sure, actually; most of the political enthusiasm in my home at that point emanated from my wife, who urged me to make the try. Only after I had become a candidate was I bitten by the political bug as thoroughly as she already was.

Next thing I knew, I was meeting with U.S. Senator Jim

Duff and Congressman (later U.S. Senator) Hugh Scott, who assured me of their support. Before agreeing to run for mayor, I asked them to give me a few days to think it over and speak to my business associates. In the best tradition of politics, they agreed—and then they leaked my candidacy to the press the next day, thus leaving me no opportunity to back out. It was a headline story in the newspapers, my partners in the ad agency were furious, and I lost my job there as a result. It was the first political disillusionment among many that were to cross my path over the years. But suddenly I was the independent Republicans' candidate for mayor, challenging the regular party organization.

The independents weren't really anxious for a primary fight. They hoped that if their Republican Assembly selected me as its mayoral candidate, the regular Republican organization would go along with the choice. But the organization refused to support me. My candidacy influenced the organization bosses only to the extent that they realized they would have to match my clean-cut, young-American-boy image with a similarly clean-cut candidate of their own. Thus they were forced to scrap their own preferred candidate—Bill Hamilton's brother Wilbur—and instead run George Williams, a young, attractive lawyer who had been an active assistant district attorney.

Williams was endorsed by the regular Republican organization, which quickly set about dismantling my support. The organization called on Senator Duff, who had persuaded me to run, and told him that if he wanted the organization's support when he ran for reelection in 1956, he'd better get out of town for the rest of the primary campaign. So this man who had led me up the mountain—who was primarily responsible for my candidacy—suddenly disappeared and was seen no more.

Meehan and Hamilton sent the same message to Congressman Hugh Scott, with the same result: Scott returned to Washington and stayed out of sight until the primary was over. So almost from the very beginning of my campaign—

from the moment I had barely decided to run—I found that the commitments politicians make to you count for nothing the minute pressure is applied (not unlike similar commitments made in love and war).

The same held true for most of the "insurgents"—the members of the Republican Assembly. The moment the organization put pressure on my supporters there, most of them—including such outstanding men as Ray Speiser and Judge Nochem Winnet—ran away from me for the duration of the primary.

In the midst of these defections, my strongest supporters—or what was left of them—gathered at Hugh Scott's home in Chestnut Hill to plot our course of action. (That was a classic Scott stratagem: He wasn't present at the meeting, but by allowing us to use his home, he caused me to feel obligated to him even as he was rejecting me.) Of the fifteen men present, almost all of them recommended that I withdraw from the race—and, having thus expressed themselves, they departed, leaving me alone with Steve McLoughlin, Walter Miller, John Pomeroy, and Herb Fogel, who continued to insist that I stay in the race and fight. I myself was shocked at this sudden erosion of my support and began to think about how I could withdraw gracefully without looking foolish.

It was just at this low ebb in my political fortunes, when I was casting about for some face-saving way of retiring to the sidelines, that the organization stalwarts—Sheriff Meehan and Bill Hamilton—invited me to lunch. There Hamilton told me: "If you don't get out of the race, I'm going to ruin you. I'll get you fired from your job. You won't be able to show your face in Philadelphia again, and I will personally see to it that you'll have to move to some other city." Meehan's tone was gentler and more conciliatory, but his message was the same.

Needless to add, their strategy backfired. They made me so angry that by the end of the lunch I told them that I had been looking for some way to get out of the race. "But now," I concluded defiantly, "I feel like a Christian who's been told he must change his religion or go into the lions' den. I don't care if I get beaten by a hundred and fifty thousand votes. I'm going to stay in this thing all the way, and I'll do my best to beat your fellow."

I didn't say it in a vainglorious way, because I really didn't think I had a chance. I just said it because I had been goaded to the point where I felt my back was against the wall and I must retaliate in kind. If instead of pressuring me Meehan and Hamilton had helped me find a way out, I never would have proceeded with my candidacy.

John Pomeroy, my campaign manager, turned out to be a clever and capable political opportunist. He took me to see Jay Cooke, the financier, who was (a) a Princeton man and (b) angry with Sheriff Meehan and Senator Duff because they had worked against Cooke in a gubernatorial primary some years earlier. Cooke and I hit it off personally from our first meeting, and he threw himself into my campaign, bringing a lot of heavy artillery with him.

Through Cooke I gained the support of lawyer Jim McIntosh. He in turn attracted Thomas McCabe, the president of the Scott Paper Company. And McCabe in turn brought in a few financial people. The first thing I knew, we began to get some money, and we spent our first contributions on a special television program aimed at Republican committeemen—almost like a closed-circuit TV program. In newspaper ads prior to the program we urged all Republican committeemen to hear what the new candidate—that is, me—was going to do and why he was running. On the show itself, I delivered a savage attack on Meehan, Witkin, Hamilton, and Meade for "leading the Republicans down the road of defeat."

That might seem like tame material today, but TV was a new medium then, and the program's impact was tremendous. Almost immediately, as a result, we found committeemen coming in to support us. And we raised $100,000 within the next few weeks, while the Williams people—depending entirely on the Republican organization—had raised nothing in the way of either money or supporters.

I began to use television frequently. After several weeks of this high-profile approach, Witkin—the organization's behind-the-scenes manipulator—called Jay Cooke. "Your candidate is really getting to a lot of our committee people," Witkin said. "I've got five ward leaders who say they want to be for Long-streth, and they're holding a meeting with Bill Meade tonight. If you call Meade around ten o'clock, you might find that he's willing to do something with you."

So Cooke got together with Meade—and as a result, Meade and all of his ward leaders and committeepeople defected to my camp. That gave us some of the controlled wards in addition to the independent wards, which had been leaning in my direction all along.

The cumulative effect of all this momentum was something to see. Magistrate James Clothier, who had wanted the organization's endorsement for mayor but had been ignored in favor of Williams, made it a three-way race by declaring his candidacy. That improved my chances, because Clothier was more likely to take votes away from Williams than from me (indeed, I'm told that my supporter Jay Cooke raised some money for Clothier).

Clothier's candidacy made it an open primary. During the last few weeks of the campaign, everything broke my way. When it was all over I had nearly half of the Republican vote and an upset victory—the first time in this century that the Philadelphia Republican organization had been beaten in a mayoralty primary.

RICHARDSON DILWORTH, in the meantime, had faced no opposition in the Democratic primary. I had benefitted from all the public exposure of the Republican primary fight and deluded myself into believing that I might capture the general election as well.

About a week after the primary I got together with Herb Fogel and John Pomeroy over lunch at the Racquet Club. "I think we've got a wonderful chance of winning," Pomeroy told me. "But you must take over the Republican City Committee and run the committee as well as your campaign. Let it be known that if you are mayor you are not just going to run the city, but you are going to run the political organization as well."

I didn't know whether this was a good strategy or not, but I accepted the recommendation because I didn't know what else to do. Bob Duffy had been chairman of the city committee but had resigned during the primary, at Meade's behest, in order to work for me. Now that I had won the primary, Duffy and Meade expected to be rewarded for their support through Duffy's reappointment at the head of city committee. But Pomeroy persuaded me to support someone else for chairman: Pomeroy himself. "This will be acceptable to the Meehan forces," he reasoned, "and we'll be able to present these new young faces to the public as people who have taken control of the Republican Party."

That strategy backfired. The Meade forces thought I had double-crossed them. I hadn't yet wised up to the notion that if someone supports you in the primary, he expects to be rewarded thereafter, and if you don't reward him you are a traitor and an ingrate. On the other hand, the Meehan forces— who had fought me tooth-and-nail two weeks earlier—now declared themselves for me and agreed to support Pomeroy for city chairman.

I became so distraught with all this infighting that at the city committee's annual meeting I made an emotional appeal on behalf of Pomeroy, with a surprise kicker: If Pomeroy was not made chairman, I said, I would withdraw from the race and they would have to find another candidate.

This created a tremendous stir, and for three or four days thereafter reporters followed me wherever I went—the most concentrated dose of public exposure I've ever received before or since. Thus an unexpected side effect of the turmoil in my party was that my name quickly became very well known throughout Philadelphia.

I had not been bluffing when I threatened to resign my candidacy. I was adamant that I would not run unless my man was put in charge of the city committee. On the final day of the deadline I had set, I fully intended to go to the party's headquarters at four-thirty and resign.

That afternoon, Cooke, Fogel, Pomeroy, and Jim McIntosh met with me in Cooke's office. For about three hours they tried to change my mind, without success. But once again, my wife had the final word. At about four fifteen, Nancy phoned to say that hundreds of telephone calls were coming in at home from people urging me to stay in the race and fight. She was almost hysterically insistent on the matter. "It would be a terrible mistake to resign," she cried. "Please don't do it. Please don't do it."

Whether she was right or wrong, I'm not prepared to say. I *am* prepared to say that her comments changed my mind. As far as Pomeroy and the others were concerned, I was a vehicle for promoting their best interests or the city's. But Nancy, I knew, was expressing what she felt would be in *my* best interest. So because of her pleas—and *only* because of her pleas—I agreed not to withdraw.

I did, however, decide to run an independent campaign, outside the structure of the regular Republican organization. Jay Cooke was in charge of it, and John Pomeroy was the campaign manager. The campaign was reasonably successful, except that the Mead people never forgave me. If you examine the election returns in the twenty-five to thirty wards controlled by Meade, you'll find that between the primary election and the general election there was an enormous shift away from me in favor of Dilworth.

Quite a number of the Republican committeemen in these wards were so-called Hessians—that is, Republicans who had become Democrats in 1954, upon the election of Democrat George Leader as governor of Pennsylvania, and who had been told they could keep their state patronage jobs as long as they switched their party registration and worked to get out the Democratic vote.

Meanwhile, I faced another pressing campaign problem: developing issues. After all, I had entered the mayoralty primary with no idea that I would be involved in the general election campaign. My persistence in the Republican primary race was a result of sheer stubbornness on my part and my belief that I was at least providing reform Republicans with some alternative that would keep them from straying to the Democratic camp. But I was an advertising man; I knew absolutely nothing about Philadelphia government. To become the candidate of a major party in the fourth-largest city in the country and to be as ignorant as I was on the subject of city government was really ludicrous.

It wasn't until about mid-July that I began to look at the city and ask, "What are the issues?" and "Why should people vote for me instead of Dilworth?" In other words, the questions which, theoretically at least, were of paramount importance were the last questions I focused on.

That may have been just as well, because the answers weren't very encouraging. Joe Clark, the Democratic incumbent in City Hall, had done a superlative job as mayor. Dilworth, as district attorney, was closely associated with Clark. He had incumbency, patronage, and money on his side, not to mention charm, intelligence, experience, and an aggressive campaign temperament. I was only thirty-four years old and a total novice in political campaigning and city government alike. What could I do?

The first thing I did that summer was to hire Professor Edward Shils of the University of Pennsylvania as my tutor. Shils was an expert on city government, and for the rest of that summer and well into the fall he spent three, four, and five hours a day with me—more than a hundred hours altogether. In effect I got a cram course in city government—and a good thing, too, because during the four-month campaign Dilworth and I had eighteen debates and I gave more than three hundred talks. They were difficult at first, because my knowledge was still superficial at best. But I learned fast.

Early in the campaign, when Dilworth had creamed me in the first four or five debates, he was constantly calling on me to debate him on television; he and his daughter even picketed my headquarters to dramatize the point. But by mid-October I had become adept at handling him in debates and so I accepted his offer—at which time, of course, he retreated from the idea as quickly as he could.

In politics as in the courtroom, Dilworth later advised me, you use whatever advantage you can seize upon. But I was no lawyer, and I was totally unprepared for the aggressive adversary stance that's second nature to any courtroom lawyer.

When Dilworth and I held our first debate before the Philadelphia Real Estate Board, I had never before been so aggressively attacked or insulted at a public meeting. At first I responded timidly; then I blew up; and the ultimate result was that I made an ass of myself. I remember coming home afterward so upset that I cried: My pride had been ripped apart and I felt totally inadequate. I felt like a boxer in the ring against a heavyweight who was so good that he could leave me bloody and battered and I couldn't lay a finger on him.

EVEN WHEN HE RAN against me for mayor in 1955, Dilworth was already a figure of mythical proportions. He was actually a rather shy man except when he drank, at which times he became wild. But he also had a great sense of humor that enabled him to take potentially explosive situations and dissolve them in laughter. Let me provide one small example that took place a few years after he defeated me for the mayor's chair.

Throughout most of the 1950s the executive director of the Committee of 70, Philadelphia's nonpartisan "good government" organization, was a man named Harry Butcher. As a political watchdog task force, the Committee of 70 was by definition critical of whichever party happened to be in power at a given time. Thus prior to 1951, Butcher had provided Democrats like Dilworth with all sorts of ammunition for use against the Republican city administration. But after 1955, when Dilworth himself was mayor, the shoe was on the other foot and Butcher became Dilworth's relentless critic.

This situation invariably strained relations between the two men. Like many another public official, Dilworth's view of civic watchdogs changed once he gained office: As mayor, he argued that the Committee of 70's appropriate function was to support good government (like his), not just to oppose bad government (like the Republicans'). So a certain amount of public friction and rancor developed between Dilworth and Butcher.

Now, Harry Butcher was inclined to take an occasional drink or two or three or more at the Hunt Room, a favorite political watering hole in the Bellevue-Stratford Hotel. In fact, it was not unusual to find Harry closing the place up. One such night, he staggered out of the hotel's Broad Street entrance and down the steps onto the sidewalk, where he began loudly denouncing all the sins and shortcomings of the city, the mayor, the City Council, and anyone else he could think of.

A lone policeman was sitting nearby in a squad car. The cop listened to Butcher's drunken diatribe of him for a while and finally got out of the car.

"You're making a disturbance," he told Harry, "and I wish you'd be quiet and go on home."

Butcher took umbrage and told the cop to go to hell.

"You'd better move on," the cop repeated, "or I'm going to give you a ticket for loitering." (Poor Harry Butcher! By today's standards his diatribe was downright polite. But in those days—unlike today—loitering was a punishable offense.)

Butcher asked the cop why he didn't go catch criminals and leave honest citizens alone. So the cop, having duly issued his warning to Harry, pulled out his ticket book, put one foot up against a fire hydrant, and began to write Harry a citation.

Now, in the course of the conversation Butcher had begun to suffer from the physical (as opposed to the mental) consequences of drinking—that is, a sudden need to go to the bathroom. No bathroom being available, it seemed to Harry a good idea to relieve himself on the nearby fire hydrant—unfortunately, the same hydrant on which the cop was writing the ticket.

The cop, oblivious to Harry's activity, was scribbling away on his ticket pad when he gradually felt something warm on his leg and realized what had happened. Not surprisingly, he was furious. Instead of merely issuing Harry a ticket, he pulled out his handcuffs, slapped them on Harry, bundled him into the back of the squad car, and took him to the police station at 11th and Winter streets.

"I want to charge this man for committing a public nuisance," the policeman announced to the desk sergeant.

"Where?" asked the desk sergeant.

"On *me.*"

This reply caused the desk sergeant a certain amount of amusement. He wrote out the appropriate charges and Harry was taken back to the drunk tank. But Harry was still sufficiently sober to remember his legal rights. "I want to make a phone call," he announced.

"What do you want to do—call your lawyer?" the cops asked.

"No, I want to call the mayor."

"You're not going to call the mayor."

"Certainly I'm going to call the mayor," Harry insisted. "Take me to the telephone."

They took him to the phone. "How are you going to call the mayor?" one of the cops asked.

"I have his private number."

Harry proceeded to dial Dilworth's private number from memory; he had called Dilworth at home many times, back in the days when they had worked together. But those days were long past; what's more, this particular call was made at two in the morning. The specifics of the conversation that followed were subsequently related to me by Harry Butcher and still later were corroborated for me by Dick Dilworth. So I feel reasonably confident of its accuracy.

The phone rang a few times. Then a sleepy voice—the mayor himself—came on: "Yes, who the hell is this?"

"Dick, this is Harry Butcher."

Dilworth was silent for a few moments. "Well, Harry," he said finally, "it's very late at night, you know. Do you have something important?"

"Yes, it's very important. That's why I'm calling."

"Can you tell me in a hurry what's your problem?"

"Well, I'm standing outside of the Bellevue-Stratford minding my own business a half an hour ago. Your Cossacks come along and instead of being out there trying to catch criminals, they're hounding and harassing honest folks like myself. The guy objects to what I'm saying and orders me to cease and desist. I tell him I have the rights of a citizen, I'll say whatever I want to. Next thing you know I'm handcuffed and brought down here and I'm in the hoosegow. I want you to get me out."

"Oh my God," Dilworth said. "Harry, who's there with you?"

"The desk sergeant, Officer Murphy."

"Well, put him on."

So Officer Murphy got on the phone. "Officer Murphy," Dilworth said, "this is the mayor. Mr. Butcher's a friend of mine. Put him in the car and take him to his home. He lives there in Center City. Just let the thing drop—that's the way to take care of it."

So Murphy turned to the arresting officer and explained, "You're supposed to put him in the car and take him home."

But the arresting officer was furious. "Goddam if I'm going to take him home! Tell the mayor he pissed all over me."

"Tell him yourself," Murphy said.

So the arresting officer took the phone. "This is Officer O'Houlihan."

"Officer O'Houlihan, this is the mayor."

"Yes sir, I know. Mr. Mayor, I don't think you ought to let this guy off so easy."

"Why? What's he done? All he was doing was engaging in a little loud talk. I suppose he was drunk."

"Well, no, sir. I was going to give him a ticket for loitering. I had my leg propped up on the fireplug, you know, writing the ticket, and he pissed all over me."

At this, Dilworth exploded with laughter. It was maybe a minute before he suppressed his last giggles. Finally he said, "O'Houlihan, let me ask you a question. What would you rather be more than anything else in the world?"

"Your driver, sir."

"All right, " Dilworth said. "You take Harry Butcher home and get him into bed, and you report to my office tomorrow morning, and you're my driver."

"Your Honor," O'Houlihan told him, "I knew you'd know how to handle this."

I can't think of a more appropriate epitaph for Dick Dilworth: He knew how to handle things. And this was the man I was up against in the 1955 election.

ONE DAY in the midst of the campaign I got a call from Bob Johnson, then president of Temple University and a staunch Republican. He told me that he and General Milton Baker, the commandant of Valley Forge Military Academy and a powerful behind-the-scenes wheeler-dealer in Pennsylvania politics, would be meeting Vice President Richard Nixon the next day at Philadelphia International Airport. He invited me to come along—the beginning of my long and bittersweet relationship with Nixon.

Their limousine picked me up at Haverford School, where I had just given a talk for Alumni Day. As we were driving to the airport, Bob Johnson turned to me.

"You know, Thacher," he said, "you're in the presence today of one of America's great patriots. One of the great men of the country."

I wasn't sure whom he meant, since we hadn't collected Nixon yet. "Oh, yes," I said. "I'm looking forward to seeing him."

"You're right in the car with him now!" Johnson boomed.

I didn't know what he was talking about. "What do you mean?" I said.

"I'm talking about General Baker," Johnson said.

"Oh!" I blurted, realizing my goof. "Oh, yes—oh, excuse me, yes . . . oh indeed, yes, he's a great man!"

"You may not realize it," Johnson instructed me, "but you're sitting in the presence of a man who, as recently as the day before yesterday, turned down the opportunity to be Secretary of the Army."

"Boy!" I said. "Really?"

Then General Baker spoke up. "Yes, indeed I did. Let me show you this letter." He reached into his pocket and pulled out a letter from Charles E. Wilson, who at that time was Secretary of Defense. The letter read:

Dear Milton,

I'm so sorry that your business affairs and other matters will not permit you to accept my appointment as Secretary of the Army. You would have made a great secretary. You are a great human being and an American patriot.

Sincerely, always your friend,

Charles E. Wilson

When I'd finished reading it, Baker turned to me. "What do you think of that?" he asked rhetorically.

"Oh, gee," I said. "I think that's terrific."

"Well," he said, "I'd like to have done it, but I've got too many other things here that I've got to do. . . ."

A few minutes went by, and then General Baker broke the silence: "You realize, Thacher, of course, that you're in the presence of one of America's great patriots and great humanitarians."

This time I was a few minutes older and wiser. I knew the general wasn't speaking about himself or the chauffeur; we hadn't yet picked up Nixon; and he couldn't have been talking about me. So he must have meant Bob Johnson.

"Yes, oh, I know," I gushed, hoping not to commit the same mistake twice. "Bob Johnson is a wonderful patriot. I've always admired him tremendously. Matter of fact, he worked for Time Inc. before I did."

"Well, you know," General Baker said, "Bob Johnson has just been offered the job of Secretary of Health, Education and Welfare in President Eisenhower's cabinet."

I thought: My God, will we have to go through this letter routine again?

But Johnson demurred. "Oh no, Milton," he insisted. "You go too far. I was talked about—it was talked about—I suspect if I had wanted it, it could have been arranged. But no—I'm not worthy. I'm not worthy to the degree that you are!"

"Oh, no, Bob!" General Baker rejoined. "On the contrary, *you* are such a marvelous person. I've always felt that the opportunity to spend time with you is really the most important time I've spent in my lifetime. . . ."

I listened to this Tweedledum-and-Tweedledee routine and thought to myself, My God is this what politics is all about? And of course it *was*. I began to understand that as ridiculous as this conversation seemed, still there was a point to it: Each man was massaging the other's ego; each was reaffirming his loyalty to the other regardless of whatever pressures each might encounter in the future.

Much later in my political career I understood that in politics, where so much is flux and duplicity, you needed to be reassured almost every day that somebody loved you. Contrary to popular belief, politicians rarely lie to each other; they just avoid each other when they have to double-cross each other. In 1967, for example, Philadelphia's Republican chief, Billy Meehan, encouraged me to believe that I would be his party's candidate for mayor. For months thereafter I didn't hear from him—and when I finally sat down with him and asked if I was still his man, he told me he had changed his mind because the polls were in the other guy's favor. He never lied to me; he simply didn't go out of his way to keep me posted. Thus when two politicians haven't seen each other for a while, they feel compelled to repledge their mutual allegiance. And that was what was taking place in the limo between Johnson and Baker.

Finally we arrived at the airport and got Nixon into our car. I had read so many bad things about him in the press—about his slush fund, his Red-baiting, his dirty campaign tactics, his "Checkers" speech in 1952, his uneasy manner with people—that I was amazed by the initial impression he made on me. I've rarely met anyone with whom I felt more comfortable more rapidly. From the moment he got in the car, I was captivated.

We went back to Bob Johnson' s house, where Nancy joined us for dinner, and Nixon started talking about his campaigns. He told a story about thimbles—how he'd always given away thimbles as campaign souvenirs and how effective they were. "As a matter of fact," he said, "I'll bet if you asked Bob Johnson right now to give you a thousand dollars so that you could buy five thousand thimbles, he'd say yes—particularly if I also asked him."

Johnson grew red in the face. "Of course, Mr. Vice President," he stammered. "Of course!" I've since been told that this was the first thousand dollars that anybody had squeezed from Bob Johnson in his life. But it worked; Nixon was that way.

A few days later, Nixon phoned me. "I kind of got the feeling the other day that you'd like to meet Ike," he said.

"Oh, my God, " I replied. "There's nothing I'd like more."

"Well, we'll set it all up," Nixon said. "You come on down here. You're gonna see him."

So I went to Washington and spent an hour alone in the Oval Office with President Eisenhower. I found him utterly charming and unpretentious; to hear him talk, *he* felt privileged to have *me* come down to visit him. Ike made much to me of his eagerness to bring young people into the Republican Party; he said he liked my providing a new Republican presence in a Democratic stronghold like Philadelphia. He related the plight of Philadelphia Republicans to his military experiences—how the stubborn refusal to give up had produced victories in situations where defeat had been expected. And of course we talked about football—Ike recalling how his West Point career was curtailed by a knee injury.

Nixon subsequently joined us, along with two senators and my Philadelphia friend Congressman Hugh Scott—and once again I got a lesson in the art of politics.

After we'd milled around shaking hands and exchanging small talk, someone said it was time to take the photographs.

"All right," the photographer said, "Mr. Longstreth, you get in here with the president so I can take my picture." At that moment Hugh Scott was standing at the other end of the room, and I thought that perhaps he'd like to be in the picture with me and the president. I was about to call over to him but saw he was engrossed in conversation with two other men, so I said nothing. The photographer raised his camera . . . and in that instant just before he snapped the picture, Scott somehow managed to leave his conversation at the other end of the room and slip in between me and Eisenhower. I still have a copy of that picture: Scott is grinning between us; you can see all of Eisenhower and all of Scott and hardly anything of me— and that was the picture which appeared in the newspapers. The remarkable thing wasn't merely Scott's sixth sense about when the picture-taking would begin; he also understood intuitively how the photo would be cropped by the press, and he positioned himself accordingly.

Afterward, Nixon invited me to have lunch with him, and again I found him delightful and candid as he regaled me with stories about his campaigns. The lunch group that day included Senator Jim Duff of Pennsylvania, Senator Edward Martin of Pennsylvania and a friend of mine named Russell Train, who was there at my request because he hadn't met Nixon and he needed Nixon's approval to become a Federal District Court judge—approval which was shortly forthcoming.

Somehow we got to talking about television and its impact on elections. Even then I think Nixon might have felt forebodings about what TV imagery would do to him five years later when he ran against Jack Kennedy for the presidency. But at the time the focus of our conversation was Estes Kefauver, the Democratic senator from Tennessee, who had risen from relative obscurity to national prominence—and a shot at a presidential nomination—all as the result of the televising of crime hearings held by his Senate crime investigation committee.

Duff asked Nixon what he thought of Kefauver.

"I think he's a phony," Nixon said, and then passed on a story he said was told to him by Richard Russell, the senator from Georgia. "Richard Russell said to me, 'Testes Kefauver, that sanctimonious son of a bitch—he walks through the South with his prick in one hand and his Bible in the other. And if he can't convert 'em, he fucks 'em!' "

I was surprised—and amused—to hear such talk from the vice president of the United States about a distinguished senator. But I was flattered that Nixon felt sufficiently at ease to tell that sort of story in front of me.

Nixon subsequently came to Philadelphia twice to campaign for me and accompanied Eisenhower on another occasion. He really gave me all the support I could have asked for. Then, when the election was over, Nixon phoned me again. "Now you need a job," he said. And he knocked himself out to come up with a couple of job offers for me.

A few years later, a friend of mine, a black man, inadvertently got into trouble with the Internal Revenue Service. I tried to get help for him from my friends who were judges and senators and congressmen, but no one would touch it. Then I called Nixon and asked him to intercede for my friend.

"Is the man a good man?" was Nixon's first question.

"Yes, he is," I said.

"I'm particularly anxious to help black people," Nixon told me. "You think he really didn't understand what he was doing?"

"My God, Mr. Vice President," I said, "this guy never got beyond the sixth grade. And if you looked at the kind of paperwork and everything they're expecting him to do, it's just ridiculous!"

And by golly, Nixon had the matter taken care of. But he didn't do it casually. He did it after he had examined it. My friend had to pay a penalty, but the fraud charge, and the accompanying disgrace, was removed.

Another time, Nixon and his wife, Pat, came up to Philadelphia, and I was invited to join them for dinner at General Baker's. Soon our relationship reached the point at which whenever he came up to Philadelphia, he or his secretary, Rose Mary Woods, would phone me ahead of time to tell me he was coming, and on occasion I'd meet him at the train with my friend Frank McGlinn.

In 1960, when Nixon ran for president, he asked me to serve as Philadelphia chairman of Citizens for Nixon. (General Baker was the state chairman.) I accepted that job and worked very hard on it, but we got creamed in Philadelphia—which creaming cost Nixon the state and may have cost him the election. He never said an unkind word to me about it. I have a note which he wrote to me from the airplane on his way back to California the day after the election—a handwritten note from a man who had barely missed the presidency, thanking a lowly campaign volunteer for his unsuccessful efforts.

Nixon wrote me several times from California when he ran for governor there in 1962. When I sent him a donation, again I got a personal handwritten note, attached to the more formal letter.

Then in '68 he phoned me. "I'm going to run again," he said. "I wondered if you were going to be in my corner."

I told him I'd be in his corner all the way. I arranged for him to spend some time with the Pews, whom he really didn't know at that time. When he won the election, he offered me a couple of government jobs—head of the Peace Corps (which Nixon wanted to disband) or head of the poverty program (ditto) or head of the Small Business Administration. But none of those three posts excited me. In the course of a several-hours-long conversation with one of Nixon's transition people, I turned them down. Then Nixon's man asked: "What do you want? What would you like best?"

I said I'd like to be Secretary of the Navy.

"That's spoken for," was the reply. "John Chafee from Rhode Island is gonna take that job."

So I thought to myself: Chafee will only be in that job a short time, because he's going to run for the Senate as soon as Ted Green retires. So I said, "How about under secretary?"

"That might be open," Nixon's man told me. But next day he phoned to report that the next under secretary of the Navy would be John Warner, whose then wife was a Mellon (he was known in Washington then as "Warner Mellon") and who had given $100,000 to Nixon's campaign.

"Okay, " I said. "That's all I have interest in." And from that day until 1988 I never exchanged another word with Richard Nixon; I was never dropped so hard and so fast in my life.

To be sure, I've received several notes from him, and his lovely daughter Julie is a good friend today, as is her husband, David Eisenhower. But from the moment I told his transition man that I was going to stay in Philadelphia and run for mayor, my relationship with Nixon evaporated. He didn't publicly support Frank Rizzo against me in the 1971 mayoral race, but he certainly didn't support me against Rizzo. You might think it was in Nixon's interest to back a Republican against a Democrat, but Rizzo was a Democrat for Nixon, who would support Nixon against McGovern in the 1972 presidential election. So I got no words of encouragement from Nixon when I ran for mayor in 1971—and after I lost I received only a relatively cold letter from him saying, in effect, "Too bad, nice try, and good luck in the future." That's often the way of the great in politics.

BUT I'M GETTING AHEAD of my story. Dilworth and I held our fifth debate of the 1955 campaign at a synagogue in Germantown. Then as now, Philadelphia's Jews were overwhelmingly Democratic. Dilworth had mastered the tactic of seating his loudest supporters—Democratic committeepeople, assistant district attorneys—in the first ten or fifteen rows. They would applaud wildly at everything he said; conversely, when I spoke they would laugh or boo or feign sleep. Dilworth knew that when you're onstage you tend to see only the people in the first ten or fifteen rows, and consequently I came to believe that the whole hall was against me.

Dilworth was also a master at taking everything I had just said and ripping it apart. As a result, it became very important to me to be able to speak last at a debate, so he couldn't rebut me. Somehow or other, he had spoken last at each of our first four debates, and at this fifth debate I was determined not to let that happen again.

Before Dilworth and I went onstage, the moderator called us together. "We're going to flip a coin to see who goes last," he said. He flipped the coin and I won.

"Okay," I said, "I guess I get to go last."

"No," the moderator said. "You go first."

"But I won the toss," I said. "So I get to go last."

"Oh, no," he said. "Here, whenever you win the toss, you go first."

"Every other debate we've had, the guy that wins the toss gets his choice," I said.

"Well,"he replied, "I'm the moderator, and this is how we do it."

I turned to Dilworth. "That's not fair," I said. "You know the way we've been handling it."

"When we're at his place, he has the right to call it," Dilworth said.

I demanded another flip—the winner to get his choice—and the moderator finally agreed. He flipped the coin a second time, I called heads, and instead of catching the coin, the moderator let it land on the floor. "It's heads," he said when he picked it up.

"Okay,"I said. "I win."

"Oh, no," he said. "It doesn't count when it falls on the floor." So he picked it up and flipped it a third time. This time Dilworth won. "Okay," the moderator said to him, "you have your choice."

It was so obviously a crooked call that I was livid with rage. In the debate itself I had to speak first, and I was so furious that I could hardly make my voice heard for the first three or four minutes, because I was struggling not to cry out of rage and frustration.

Dilworth later told me that the moderator was a Democratic committeeman who had approached Dilworth prior to the debate and asked, "Where do you want to go?" Dilworth had said he wanted to go last, and the moderator had replied, "Okay, I'll take care of it." And he did.

BOTH MY YOUTH and the hopelessness of my cause attracted the sort of quixotic young people who frequently attach themselves to lost causes. And Nancy's presence in the campaign attracted many younger women to active roles in the local Republican Party. Over the next ten or fifteen years, a sizable number of Republican committeepeople were men or women who first became involved in Republican politics through me or Nancy. But this new blood really had very little impact on the regular Republican organization, which regained control of the party in 1956 and has run it ever since, first through Aus Meehan and then through his son Bill. For a long while, it was an increasingly shrinking domain. When I ran for mayor in 1955, Republicans accounted for over 50 percent of the city's registered voters. That proportion subsequently slipped to as low as 22 percent (although Frank Rizzo's presence as the Republican mayoralty candidate in 1987 pushed the figure up to 27 percent that year).

After the 1955 election someone asked Dilworth about my future political prospects.

"He has no future," Dilworth replied. "One, he's a Republican in Philadelphia, and there's no future for a Republican in Philadelphia. And number two, he doesn't know how to play dirty. He still thinks the world of politics is governed by the Marquess of Queensberry rules."

With his customary succinctness, Dilworth had sized me up pretty accurately. But he was wrong about my future. I would live to run again for public office in Philadelphia and even win a few citywide elections. And the next time I ran for mayor—as a Republican, of course—one of my most ardent supporters was a Democrat named Richardson Dilworth.

I learned a great deal about politics from Dilworth. But in retrospect it's comforting to think that maybe, just maybe, he learned something from me, too.

CHAPTER 10

THE PRIVATE SECTOR: THE AGENCY GAME (1955–64)

LOOKING BACK, I was blessed in my life to stumble across a succession of people, institutions, and activities to which I was ideally suited, and vice versa. Nancy was just right for me. Princeton was just right for me. So were the Navy, *Life* magazine, elective politics, and the presidency of the Greater Philadelphia Chamber of Commerce. The advertising business, on the other hand, was never quite right for me.

After the emotional roller coaster of the 1955 election year, returning to the ad agency business was something of a letdown. I never really understood the ad agency business very well. I had no background or experience in television production or the creative aspects of radio. I didn't even know much about how to develop a print ad. I learned, of course. But the fact is that I simply wasn't very creative.

Compounding my lack of talent was the fact that my new employer—the Aitkin-Kynett agency—was run by a stern, tough taskmaster, and I had always been accustomed to working for people I loved. Doc Kynett may have been respected, but nobody loved him. When I first went to work for him, he told me, "I do not believe in passing out compliments. That's not my style. I pay you to do your job, and if you do an exceptionally good job, I'll pay you more. The only time you'll hear from me is if you're *not* doing your job."

I'll say this for Doc—he was true to his word. Two years later I landed the Tastykake account—the biggest piece of business in the agency's history. When I came into the office the next day I got a hero's welcome from everyone except Doc. As I floated down the hall on a cloud of euphoria, I saw Doc heading toward me in his customary manner—head tucked in, scowl on his face. He walked right past me without saying a word.

Just as I was thinking, My God, I can't believe this, I heard him say, "Oh, Thacher."

I turned around with a big smile on my face, anticipating his congratulations. "Yes, Doc?"

"Where the hell is the Capital Products check?" he snarled. "It's two weeks late already. Get on that, will you?" And he turned and scurried off down the hall.

Needless to add, Doc's company lacked the warmth I had known at *Life*. When Doc fired someone—as he did frequently—the employee was handed his severance check right then and there and was given thirty minutes to get out of the office. In one case when I was there, a fellow named Miles was fired in this manner. He went back to his office, packed up his belongings, and was heading for the door for the last time when he passed Kynett's office, where a partners' meeting was in session. He opened the door, leaned into the room, and said, "I just wanted to say goodbye to everyone. And as for you, Kynett, everything that Mr. Goldman says about you is true." Goldman was the agency's number-two man; he was sitting in the room with Kynett at that moment, and he was terrified of Kynett. Not all of Doc's firings were so amusing: Before my time at the agency, one fired employee is said to have walked upstairs and jumped out the window; as his body passed Kynett's open window below, legend had it the guy could be heard yelling, "Kynett, you bastard!" all the way down.

Kynett used to distribute the annual Christmas bonuses personally, and thus at the end of my first year he called me into his office for my ritual one-minute audience with him. When I entered the room he got up, came over, and shook hands with me.

"I want to thank you for doing a fine job for us," he said. "I hope you understand that you've only been with us a year, and although we like your work, you haven't really produced anything yet—and we understand that, so there'll be no Christmas bonus for you this year."

"I understand that, Doc," I said, "and it's fine with me."

"You know, you don't really know anything about the advertising business," he continued.

"I know that, Doc," I said. "I told you that when I first came to work for you."

"I know you told me," he replied, "but I didn't believe you. And you were telling the truth." All of this was said in dead seriousness, without any trace of humor or irony.

I subsequently brought in enough business to be elevated to a partnership in the agency. But the longer I stayed in the ad business—and I was there nine years—the less I liked it. The constant turnover of accounts, the lack of loyalty, the endemic phoniness in the industry just weren't my style. I was happy enough there, but in retrospect that happiness pales beside my experience at *Life*—which was pure gold—and the Chamber of Commerce, which was heaven on earth.

ONE DAY toward the end of 1963 I got a call from Dick Bond, who was then chairman of Wanamaker's and president of the Greater Philadelphia Chamber of Commerce. I had a casual acquaintance with him through politics, and he was a man I greatly admired. He asked me to have breakfast with him and with Fred Potts, then the chairman of Philadelphia

National Bank and next in line after Dick Bond as head of the Chamber.

"What do you want to talk about?" I asked.

"I'd rather let you know when we see you," he said.

Thus I went to this breakfast meeting knowing nothing of what it was about—only that two important men wanted to have breakfast with me. I assumed they'd ask me to do volunteer work for United Way or some such thing.

When we had our breakfast—at the now-departed Stouffer's in Penn Center—they didn't beat around the bush. They asked me to become the chief executive staff officer—the official title then was executive vice president—of the Greater Philadelphia Chamber of Commerce. The job wouldn't become available until July of 1964, when the incumbent, Keaton Arnett, was due to retire.

As they explained the duties involved in the job, I found myself thinking: This is almost like being mayor of Philadelphia. It's political involvement. It's working with people. It's dealing with a lot of very important business leaders around town. I'll probably never be mayor—but I *can* be head of the Chamber, with many of the same functions.

I really knew nothing about the Chamber of Commerce; the notion of my heading it had never remotely occurred to me. Yet of all the jobs that had ever been mentioned to me—aside from the mayor's office—this was the one I wanted instantly. I thought of Robin Morton's advice at *Life* magazine: "When the right job comes along, you won't have to think about it five minutes." This was that job, and I knew right away that if the money was right, I'd take it. Even if it meant a small pay cut, I'd take it—that's how right it seemed for me (besides, by this time Nancy had established a prospering career in the real estate business). But I also knew that I had to play a little hard-to-get.

"I'll be dealing with a whole lot of different people at the

Chamber," I told Bond and Potts. "If I take this job, many people will be disappointed that you didn't hire their favorite son, or they'll think I lack the necessary experience. So I've got to have a five-year contract. They've got to know I'm going to be here five years."

"Oh, absolutely," they replied.

Again I put off a definite answer until I had a chance to talk to the Chamber's executive committee—all seventeen members, one at a time. I sounded out each man on his ideas, on how he felt about me, on whether he thought I'd fit in. It was a significant move on my part—not just because it acquainted me with each member, but also because it flattered each of them, so that when the decision to hire me was finally made, everyone was delighted and no one felt he'd been left out of the selection process.

The only problem had to do with breaking the news at Aitkin-Kynett—where I hoped to work until the following July and where, remember, employees were customarily sacked with thirty minutes' notice.

I accepted the Chamber job just before New Year's Day of 1964. But because the job wouldn't take effect for another six months, the Chamber people agreed to keep it quiet so that I could make my own departure arrangements with my agency colleagues and with my clients. That scheme held up no longer than a week. As I was working in my office on a Saturday, I got a phone call from a *Daily News* reporter.

"Mr. Longstreth," he said, "we're checking on a story which we've picked up over the weekend that you're going to be the next president of the Greater Philadelphia Chamber of Commerce, that you will replace Keaton Arnett, and that you're going to take office the first of July."

"I'm sorry," I said, "I'm in no position to comment on that at all."

"Well, have you had any interviews?"

I couldn't lie. "I can't say anything to you at all," I stammered. "This is not anything that has anything to do with anything I'm willing to talk about." So there you are: That told him his tip was correct.

Now, the *Daily News* doesn't publish on Sunday, so I knew I had until Monday before the story broke. Immediately I got into the car and drove out to see my three partners at Aitkin-Kynett. Fortunately, all three of them were home. I spent a half hour in each place, so they knew about it before it appeared in the paper. Then I wrote a telegram to each of my nine clients: "Will be on the phone to you with news about a pending change in my position. Please wait to hear from me before you reach any conclusions." Next I spent all day Sunday phoning them and explaining what was happening. In that way I was able to ease out of the agency without ruffling feathers or costing the company any business.

OUR DAUGHTER ANNE was getting married the first week of April 1964. Late in January I said to Nancy, "As soon as the wedding's over, let's go around the world."

"Are you serious?" she asked.

"When are we going to get a better chance?" I said. "I've got six months now before I have to go to work somewhere else. It's going to take three or four months to get everything cleaned up, but by the first of April everything should be well in hand. What better way to spend the remaining two months than to sail off into the sunset and end up in Tahiti?"

Which we did. It was an eighty-day trip around the world, one of the most enjoyable experiences we've ever had. We still think about it and talk about it every day. And for me, it was the perfect transition between the end of my business life and the beginning of my public life.

CHAPTER 11

POLITICS III:
RUNNING FOR MAYOR
(1971)

AFTER GETTING WAFFLED by Dick Dilworth in '55 I had to decide: What am I going to do? I'd run for mayor and been licked pretty badly. On the other hand, I'd made a good impression. Did I want to remain in politics? Already people were asking: Would you be interested in running for lieutenant governor in 1958? Or: Why don't you run for Hugh Scott's congressional seat?

Well, I wasn't so dumb that I didn't understand why Scott himself wasn't running for his congressional seat—because of the changing demographics in Philadelphia, it was no longer winnable by a Republican. (Indeed, no Republican has won it since then.)

But there were all these offers: "Why don't you take over the Republican Party and become city chairman?" or "Why don't you become the state chairman?" Most of these careers, of course, would bring me no income.

And that's when I went back into the advertising business with Aitkin-Kynett. When I asked Doc Kynett, my boss, what he thought about my being involved in politics, he replied, "You can do anything you want, as long as you do it on your own time and keep your name out of the papers."

Thus over the next half-dozen years I was the Philadelphia

or Pennsylvania chairman of a succession of Republican campaigns—Eisenhower for president in '56 and Hugh Scott for the U.S. Senate in '58, both successful; Harold Stassen for mayor in '59 and Nixon for president in '60, both unsuccessful. I chaired the statewide campaign for Bill Scranton for governor in '62 (successful) and for James McDermott for mayor of Philadelphia in '63 (unsuccessful). My won-lost record was decidedly mixed, and I wasn't running for office myself. But I was keeping my hand in and accumulating political IOUs.

IN 1962 THE REPUBLICAN NOMINATION for senator from Pennsylvania was wide open, for two reasons. First, few people thought the incumbent Democrat, Joe Clark, could be beaten (and that year they were right). And second, as I discovered, nobody in state politics really cares *who* the U.S. senator is. When the elections for governor and U.S. senator occur in the same year—as happened in Pennsylvania in 1962—all attention is focused on the governor's race, because the governor controls the contracts, the patronage, the power. A U.S. senator, on the other hand, is merely one of a hundred different votes in Washington. His job may be prestigious—membership in "the world's most exclusive club" and all that—but the professional politicians couldn't care less about prestige.

So it dawned on me that if I wanted to run for the Senate, I might not face much serious opposition. In those days there were no ceilings on campaign contributions. So I got a big commitment—$50,000—from Raymond Pitcairn, whose family owned Pittsburgh Plate Glass (now PPG Industries). With that $50,000 in hand, I went to see J. Howard Pew and Joe Pew of Sun Oil and got $25,000 apiece from them. Then I got $10,000 from Bob Carpenter, the du Pont heir and Philadelphia Phillies owner, who was a personal friend. These commitments enabled me to drum up another $25,000 in

$5,000 segments from four or five other people. So in the fall of '61 I had about $150,000 with which to kick off a campaign—a healthy sum in those days.

Then right after Christmas I got a telephone call from Raymond Pitcairn, informing me that his brother-in-law, Philip Pendleton, wanted to run for the U.S. Senate. "My sister would be terribly hurt if I supported you," he explained, "and blood is thicker than water. I'm trying to talk Phil out of it—he hasn't got a chance—but until he's out, I'm sorry, I can't keep that commitment of fifty thousand dollars to you."

I felt I had no choice but to phone my other financial backers—all of whom had made pledges to me on the strength of my $50,000 commitment from Raymond Pitcairn—and release them from those pledges. (I sent Bob Carpenter's $10,000 check back to him; he still has it framed on his wall. "It's the only penny I ever got back from a politician in my life," he told me.)

Suddenly I had a candidacy with no momentum. But I got an unexpected boost when the conservative wing of the state Republican Party decided to support Judge Robert Woodside from central Pennsylvania for governor. The party's liberal wing, which was headed by Philadelphia industrialist Phil Sharpless, scouted around for a qualified liberal to oppose Woodside. He settled on my old Young Turk friend Hugh Scott, who by then had advanced from Congress to the U.S. Senate.

"You are a United States senator," Sharpless told Scott, "and I helped get you there. You've got to come up here and stop Woodside. We can't stop him with nobody, but we can stop him with you. But I guarantee that if we can get the guy we *really* want—Bill Scranton—you'll be off the hook. If we can't get Bill Scranton, you're going to have to do it. That's the price you're going to have to pay if you want our continued support."

So now you had—in the newspapers at least—Scott lining

up to run for governor against Woodside. Where did I fit into this Byzantine picture? I soon found out when I received a call from Mason Owlett, a state senator who was also president of the Pennsylvania Manufacturers Association.

"Thacher," he said, "I know you're running for the Senate"—I'd already been to see him. "We are prepared to back you"—which would have been my first substantial support—"but only if you will agree to run in the primary on Judge Woodside's ticket." My presence would give Woodside's ticket the liberal Philadelphia presence it needed to complement the judge's conservative central-Pennsylvania support.

Now, why would conservatives want a liberal like me on the ticket? Remember—no politician cares about the U.S. Senate seat, except as a means of electing a governor. Woodside's supporters would be happy to use a liberal Republican senatorial candidate like me to defeat a liberal Republican gubernatorial candidate like Scott.

"This is a specific offer," Owlett concluded. "I'd like an answer by tomorrow."

I went in to see him the next morning. "Senator, I'll have to respectfully turn your offer down," I said. "I'm a friend of Scott's. I'm for Scott. I can't run on a ticket against him."

"Well, Scott's not going to be for you," Owlett replied. "I'll guarantee that. I think you're being very foolish."

Then I went over to Scott's Philadelphia office to tell him what I'd done. "Hugh, I hope that as a result of this you will support me for the Senate race." I said.

"No," Scott replied, "I won't support you for the Senate. You're from the same division and the same ward in the same city, and you're a white Anglo-Saxon Protestant, just like me. If you were a black fellow living in Pittsburgh, I'd be all for you. But I'm not going to be for you. I'm delighted to have your support; I'll be hurt if you won't give it to me; but I'm sorry, I can't reciprocate."

The Woodside-Scott collision was subsequently averted

altogether when conservative and liberal Republicans agreed, for the sake of party harmony, to withdraw both candidacies and to unite behind a white knight acceptable to both wings of the party: Congressman William Scranton.

So now I went to Scranton and asked *his* support for my Senate candidacy. "Well, I'm thinking things over," he said.

Now I went back to Mason Owlett of the Pennsylvania Manufacturers Association: "Mason, I'd like to get your support for the Senate. You offered it to me once and I want it again."

"No, not any more," he told me. "You've made your bed with those other guys."

"Yeah, but that's all finished," I reminded him. "There's been a compromise."

"Compromise, hell. Scranton's been the one all the time. This was just a maneuver to get him in there without a primary fight with Woodside. It worked—and now *we're* going to get the Senate. We couldn't care less about the Senate, but we're going to get it, and we're going to put one of our people in there."

The PMA's candidate for the Senate, Owlett told me, was a Congressman named Jimmie Van Zandt.

When I went back to Scranton and told him this tidbit, he said, "Well, I know that. And I think Van Zandt's a lousy candidate. I'd much rather have you. But the fact is, I've got to have the support of the conservative wing. And although Van Zandt is a token to them, nevertheless he's a token that they're insisting upon. They don't want you; they want him. And that's the way it's going to be." And of course that's what happened: The Republicans nominated Scranton for governor (who won) and Van Zandt for the Senate (who lost). But it's a curious thing—if I'd said yes to Owlett the first time instead of no, I suspect I would have been the GOP candidate for the U.S. Senate in 1962.

I became the chairman of Citizens for Scranton–Van Zandt.

After the election, Scranton offered me a cabinet job as secretary of commerce. Four years later, when Ray Schaefer became governor, he offered me my choice of cabinet jobs—Commerce or Health and Welfare. But I never had any interest in holding an appointive office. The major share of my interest in politics was always the fun element of elective politics—the persiflage. What you're really trying to do is deceive people in an honest way. You're trying to convince everybody you're for them. And that's pretty hard, particularly if you're caught in something like the abortion issue.

In 1964 I became president of the Greater Philadelphia Chamber of Commerce and dropped out of political campaigns—at least until 1967, when I sought the Republican nomination for mayor. I was outmaneuvered by the ultimate candidate, Arlen Specter, so I ran for City Council and won one of the two minority at-large seats which the City Charter guarantees to the minority party.

For the next four years, in council, I just knew I was going to run for mayor in '71. I resigned from City Council (as required of political candidates under the City Charter), then resigned as president of the Chamber of Commerce and spent all of 1971 running for mayor against Frank Rizzo.

LIKE SO MANY PHILADELPHIANS, I first got to know Frank Rizzo when he was a police captain in the 1950s, striding around Center City with his pearl-handled revolvers. He struck me as a flamboyant and exciting personality, but it never occurred to me that he might be a successful politician—for the simple reason that I had never met a man so willing to express himself in terms that were not only unequivocal but also often inclined to be actively hostile to the person about whom he was talking. I'd been brought up to believe that in any kind of private relationship, with anybody, you either spoke well of someone

or you didn't speak at all—that silence was really the worst
insult that you could deliver, unless you were specifically looking for a fight.

As I grew older and got into politics, I realized that it was
sometimes necessary for a politician to criticize someone else
openly. But I never imagined you could consistently and
emphatically go out of your way to be abrasive—as Rizzo did
when asked to comment on almost anything—and flourish or
even survive as a politician.

I also had been taught that a successful politician is not
elected by his friends; on the contrary, he defeats an unsuccessful politician who is beaten by his enemies. And therefore
the important thing is not to make friends but to avoid making enemies. Rizzo never followed this dictum. He was always
lashing out verbally at whomever he perceived to be his enemy
at any given moment.

I *still* think Rizzo's style will fail most of the time. The
main reason Rizzo became mayor of Philadelphia was that his
style, his flamboyance, his attitudes were ideally suited to a
specific period. It was Jim McDermott, in his losing mayoralty
campaign in 1963, who discovered for the first time that crime
in the streets was the burning local issue: If you could establish
yourself as the law-and-order candidate, you immediately became
a force to be reckoned with. McDermott, the Republican candidate that year, entered the campaign with no money, no
background, no experience, nothing—yet from August 1963,
when he started talking about crime in the streets, he closed
the huge lead that the incumbent, Jim Tate, had enjoyed and
nearly knocked Tate off. Rizzo saw the potency of the street-
crime issue, and I suspect that's when he first decided to run
for mayor.

But he realized that first he had to become police commissioner; no mere police officer, no matter how popular and
flamboyant, could credibly run for mayor. If crime in the streets

was the most popular public issue—well, who was far and away the most visible, the most popular, the most easily recognized authority on controlling crime in the streets? The police commissioner of Philadelphia.

Between 1963 and 1967, Rizzo positioned himself, and then he got his big break in '67, when Jim Tate ran for reelection as mayor against the Republican challenger, Arlen Specter. As Rizzo had foreseen, street crime once again reared its head, and the major campaign issue was whether Rizzo would be reappointed as police commissioner. Specter, hoping to mobilize liberal support, more or less indicated he would not reappoint Rizzo. Tate was smart enough to realize that the only way he could win was to endorse Rizzo without qualification, regardless of how much power Rizzo developed as a result. Which Tate did. And his blank-check support gave Rizzo enough power and momentum so that he carried right on through to become the nominee in the '71 campaign against me.

IT'S IMPOSSIBLE not to like Rizzo if he wants you to like him. The man projects one of the most enormous multidimensional charm packages I've ever encountered. He's funny, clever, entertaining, informative—certainly one of the most amazing people I've ever met. He struck me as a throwback to the elected Roman emperors. That is, if you and I had been members of the Praetorian guard and we had just murdered Caligula, and we had to find someone who'd represent an improvement over Caligula, and we had to do it in a hurry, Rizzo would be the most natural choice because of his combination of bluff, hearty, straightforward exterior—some of which is sincere and some of which is contrived—and Machiavellian interior.

I never really knew him very well before the campaign, but

I grew very fond of him after he became mayor. As police commissioner he was always very polite to me: He always addressed me as "Councilman," he saluted me, and he treated me as if I were a very important person, which of course I liked. He was extremely adroit at flattering you in a manner appropriate to whatever position you held or fancied you held. He didn't do it obsequiously, but in such a way that you felt pleased to be acknowledged by him. You felt that he was an important man reinforcing your importance by paying homage to you.

Once, when I was a member of the City Council's police committee, we held hearings about the police department's budget. Rizzo had argued publicly that the police needed more money; I had argued publicly against any increase in the police budget. My opposition angered Rizzo, but he was sufficiently astute not to hold it against me personally; he recognized that I was simply playing out my role as the committee's lonely minority-party member.

But one particular day—say about 1969—as we were conducting these hearings, Rizzo entered the council chamber with his coterie of police—which on this day included one huge policeman holding an equally huge police dog named Midnight. The dog sat quietly through most of Rizzo's testimony until it came my turn to question him.

When I questioned the wisdom of appropriating more money for the purpose of air-conditioning the police dog kennels, Rizzo replied, "That question can be answered very easily. Sergeant, will you ask Midnight to answer Councilman Longstreth's question?"

The huge sergeant strode to the table where I was sitting and the dog jumped up on the table—his muzzle scant inches from my face—and started barking. Not a pleasant bark. The cameras flashed. I stared.

I didn't turn pale, nor did I roll over in my chair or start to cry, but I *was* pretty uncomfortable for a few seconds. I knew the dog wasn't going to hurt me because I knew that Rizzo would never let that happen. But I also knew that Rizzo had devised this scenario specifically to embarrass me, albeit in a humorous way. I couldn't help but admire the skill with which he had done it. The newspaper picture of Longstreth vs. Midnight was hilarious.

That was really my first experience with Rizzo. When we got into the 1971 mayoral campaign, I was delighted to see him as my opponent. I knew a Republican candidate like me had no chance at all against the usual Democratic candidate— the Democrats' three-to-one registration ratio would bury me. But with Rizzo running, I figured the party lines were out. It would be me against him, and therefore I would have an opportunity to use my campaign skills—whatever they might be—with a real hope that they could make a difference. And my assessment turned out to be accurate: I came much closer than any Republican mayoral candidate usually comes in Philadelphia—within 47,000 votes. To be sure, I finished this close not because I was popular or skillful, but because in some circles Rizzo had many enemies and, in some campaigning respects, he was not terribly skillful.

But as the 1971 campaign progressed, I gradually developed tremendous respect for Rizzo's knowledge and intelligence, particularly his skill at using the political system in a big city. Despite the bitterness of that campaign, I grew fond of him as a person. I liked his sense of humor, and I recognized that his attacks on me were made without rancor. You might say Rizzo charmed me every bit as much as he charmed the rest of the voters.

BY 1971 I had learned a great deal about the city. I'd run for mayor once, I'd been a city councilman, I was president of the

Chamber of Commerce, and thus I had a pretty good idea of what the city was all about and what needed to be done for it. Rizzo, conversely, was a one-issue guy. Deep down, all of his slogans spoke to crime in the streets: "Rizzo means business," "Firm but fair," even "I'll fire Mark Shedd"—a reference to Philadelphia's innovative liberal superintendent of schools. All of these were aimed at white people—telling them, in effect, "I'll stop the black people, who represent the crime in the streets and the problems in the school system and whatever else is bad about Philadelphia."

Thus without trying I became the most popular white candidate in the Philadelphia black community in years—the only Republican mayoral candidate in anyone's memory to carry a majority of the black vote. (Actually, I carried about 85 percent of it.) But my popularity in the black community had little to do with me and everything to do with black fears of my opponent.

My situation vis-à-vis blacks was epitomized one day as I was campaigning along Columbia Avenue. I passed a bar—of which there are many on Columbia Avenue—and as I walked by, the door opened and an enormously corpulent black woman staggered out with a bottle of beer in her hand. She'd obviously been pushed out the door, and as she careened across the pavement she crashed into me and knocked me flat. One moment I was walking along the sidewalk, shaking hands and smiling and waving; next moment I was flat on my back, looking upward through dazed eyes at this woman standing unsteadily over me.

"Y'all right?" she was saying. "Y'all right?"

"I guess so," I said.

"Here, honey," she said, "let me help you up." She pulled me to my feet and looked at me more closely. "You're Thacher Longstreth, ain't you?"

"Yes, I am."

"Ohhhh," she said, rolling her eyes. "I sure hope I didn't hurt *you*. You ain't much, but you all we got."

RIZZO AND I HELD THREE DEBATES that fall—one before the staff of the *Bulletin,* one before the staff of the *Inquirer,* and one on television. In the first debate at the *Bulletin,* I creamed him, and I was amazed at how much more I knew than he did and how much more skilled I was in the debate, and how angry he became as the disparity between us was revealed. I thought I really had him on the run.

As we came out of the *Bulletin* building afterward, Rizzo was walking ahead of me, unaware that I was behind him. "Why in Christ's name did you let me get in there with him?" he was saying to one of his people. "He made me look like a two-bit nothin'. We can't do this anymore. He's gonna kill me. We've gotta do something about it."

That was a Monday. On Wednesday, two days later, we went through the same routine at the *Inquirer.* This time Rizzo was a new man—sharp, astute, in control. I wouldn't have believed it was the same guy. Later I learned that his people had tape-recorded our debate at the *Bulletin*— which I hadn't done—and over the intervening two days they had played the tapes repeatedly, rehearsing Rizzo for about twelve straight hours.

Then he rehearsed in much the same way again after the *Inquirer* debate. By then he had a pretty good idea of the way the questions were going to go. And by the time we did our televised debate the next night, I felt he came so close to me that for all practical purposes he won the debate—because even though I won it (in my judgment), in my situation merely winning wasn't enough: I had to win *big,* and Rizzo had prevented me from doing so.

About all I managed that night was to solidify my support

from the black community. Rizzo inadvertently gave me the opportunity when, during the debate, he asked me, "Why are you calling me Fatso and Bozo, and why are you saying that I am stupid and that I don't know what I'm doing? Why are you doing this to me?"

My answer was, "Well, Frank, if the shoe fits . . ." Apparently that reply broke up black people all over Philadelphia. Rizzo's purpose in asking the question, of course, was to prove that I wasn't the courteous, upstanding civic leader that I pretended to be—that I was down in the gutter with him. Actually, I *hadn't* called Rizzo any of those names: the name-calling had been done by some of my supporters—notably Cecil Moore, the black civil rights activist, who constantly referred to Rizzo as Fatso or Bozo the Clown. In any case, as I heard it from many blacks, the effect of this question-and-answer exchange was that many blacks who'd previously perceived me as a wimp suddenly saw me as someone capable of standing up to Rizzo and mixing it up with him on his own terms. From then until election day, I couldn't go anywhere without blacks swarming all over me. I was their hero, thanks to Frank Rizzo.

ACTUALLY, RIZZO HAS ALWAYS treated black people pretty well; he probably has more black friends and admirers than most liberals have. But in the course of oversimplifying the issues, he tagged himself with an antiblack label, apparently because he and his advisers saw an advantage in catering to white fears. This posture was neither enlightened nor honest, but it didn't surprise me and thus didn't upset me.

What did anger me was the press's insistence on stereotyping Rizzo as a macho cop and me as an effete Chestnut Hill aristocrat. After all, how does one define a macho man? As a young man I had boxed and wrestled and played football; Rizzo had done none of these things. After Pearl Harbor I had gone to war; Rizzo had stayed home. Even in 1971, when both Rizzo and I were fifty, I could lift my weight, do a hundred pushups a day, and walk ten miles without breathing hard, Rizzo was fat, out of shape, and utterly uncoordinated physically. Not that these are criteria for choosing a mayor—but if one of us deserved a macho label, it wasn't Rizzo.

Yet the image stuck in the public mind, and Rizzo capitalized on it.

"You guys want to have some kind of Princeton guy here running this city?" he'd say at Democratic ward meetings during the campaign. "What the hell do you think this Princeton guy knows about it?" I had labored under the delusion that an education at one of the best colleges in the country might be perceived as an asset rather than a liability—especially in contrast with Rizzo's record as a high school dropout. But no such luck. In vain did I protest that far from being an aristocrat, I had gone to school and college with nothing, worked my way through—and if I'd made a little money since then, that struck me as something to be admired, not held against me.

The only exception to my "effete snob" media image appeared in a *Philadelphia Inquirer* column about a softball game I played in that September. "Longstreth's physique," wrote columnist Al Haas, "suggested a man who takes very good care of himself. His six-foot-six-inch frame was trim, and the muscular development of his back, shoulders, and upper arms reminded you of a heavyweight boxer. He did not look like the intellectual fifty-year-old he is." That column was infused with the customary dosage of newspaper-column hyperbole, to be sure. But it was the only time anybody ever suggested I was a reasonably physically potent fellow in my own right, and not just some patsy waiting to be gobbled up by Rizzo the Neanderthal.

Who was more macho? One night during the campaign I walked from North Philadelphia station to Strawberry Man-

sion along Glenwood Avenue—about an hour's walk through
a pretty rough area. I was about to walk back when a passerby
warned against it.

"I'm black, and I live up here," he said, "and *I* wouldn't do
it. You must be either crazy or the bravest man I ever knew."

I thought a little about that and figured it might have some
publicity value.

So the next day I issued a public challenge to Rizzo. "Last
night," I said, "I walked from North Philadelphia Station to
Strawberry Mansion, eighteen blocks, between nine and nine-
thirty, unarmed and unaccompanied. I challenge you to do the
same thing." That enraged Rizzo more than anything that
happened during the campaign, and understandably so: He
knew he couldn't do it.

I WAS VERY BITTER about the way the media played up to
Rizzo. I don't think there was any big city in the country
where one person controlled the working press to the degree
that Rizzo did here in Philadelphia. To be sure, some journal-
ists despised him. But the proportion of reporters and editors
who loved him—far beyond traditional journalistic objectiv-
ity—was extraordinarily high for a political candidate, for a
reason I think I understand: Many people in newspapers—and,
to a lesser degree, in radio and TV—start off on the police
beat. Thus Rizzo, as a prominent police figure over two decades,
had been able to help many young people in the early stages
of their newspaper careers—handing them scoops, taking them
behind the scenes, or pepping up an otherwise dull story with
colorful quotes from his own prolific lips.

He had a tremendous number of friends in the media, and
they favored him throughout the campaign—to such a degree
that at one point my staff made a line count and found that
Rizzo had received more than 30 percent more space in the

papers than I had. In the first three months of the campaign, Rizzo's picture appeared in the *Daily News* exactly twice as many times as mine did. And his name was constantly in the headlines—unlike mine, which, I was told when I complained, was usually to long to fit the available space.

The fact that the papers and TV stations endorsed me editorially—as they did—meant less than the fact that press and broadcast coverage invariably favored Rizzo. The bosses may have preferred me, but the working press preferred him.

This was no idle paranoia on my part. During the campaign a *Daily News* photographer told me, "I love Rizzo, and most of the guys over there love Rizzo. And we're gonna screw you. We're not gonna do it because we don't like you. It's just something in here," he said, pointing to his gut. "I don't know how to explain it to you. I hope you won't hold it against me." I didn't; I was grateful for his candor.

One example. In June of '71 I announced a major recommendation on the school system, developed by my campaign manager, Cliff Brenner, who knew a great deal about the schools. We presented it to the City Council at a public hearing, but it received no ink at all.

Along about September, Cliff said to me, "You know, that was an awful good idea we had. It got shot down because the timing wasn't right—it was June and nobody gave a damn. Let's introduce it again."

Instead of testifying before the City Council, this time we held a press conference. I gave the reporters all the supporting data and literature. Again, not a word appeared.

A few days later I got a call from my fellow Republican Tom Gola, the former basketball All-American who was then serving as city controller. "I haven't seen anything in the paper about that school idea you had," he said.

"No," I said. "Neither have I."

"Well, it's a hell of a good idea. One of the best I've seen. It has direct relationship to the controller's office. Would you mind if I called a press conference and promoted it from a slightly different direction?"

"No," I said, "go right ahead. Hell, I haven't done anything with it."

Shortly thereafter the *Philadelphia Bulletin* ran a big story under a headline which credited my idea to Gola. The story didn't mention me once.

I phoned Sam Boyle, the *Bulletin's* assistant managing editor. "What the hell happened?" I said.

"Jeez, I don't know."

"Well, look at the dates," I said. I noted the date of my press release and the subsequent presence of a *Bulletin* reporter at my press conference. "You responded with not a word in print," I said. "Three days later I give Gola permission to do it, and you have a front-page story by the same reporter who attended my press conference. What am I supposed to think?"

Boyle assured me that he'd look into it and that the *Bulletin* would print a public apology if the facts so warranted.

The next day, on page 3 of the *Bulletin*, I saw the headline "Longstreth Says Gola Steals His Stuff."

Then there was Rolfe Neill, the editor of the *Daily News*. He came to Philadelphia in 1970 and told his paper's advertising agency to create a new image for the *News*—one that would shake the paper's reputation as a sports-and-crime sheet. The theme of the new campaign was: When important people talk, the *Daily News* is there to report it. The TV ads portrayed Mayor Tate talking and Rizzo maintaining order at a street disturbance and Specter campaigning—all, by implication, important people. But mostly they portrayed Rizzo—the macho man of action plugged into the movers and shakers, stalking the streets with a nightstick tucked into his tuxedo cummerbund. None of the ads about important people mentioned me.

I phoned Walter Spiro, a friend of mine whose ad agency represented the *Daily News*. "Walter, where are *my* commercials?" I asked.

"Well, Rizzo was the police commissioner," he said lamely.

"He hasn't been the police commissioner for five months," I said. "He had to resign just as I did. So how come these commercials weren't discontinued five months ago?"

"I don't know anything about it," he said.

"Don't you understand the election rules and things of that sort?"

"The client did that," he said. "They selected the people whom we were supposed to promote."

I took my complaint to Rolfe Neill. He was unsympathetic.

"Everybody knows Rizzo," he said. "Nobody ever heard of you. We're trying to sell newspapers."

It was one of the few times in my life that I've lost my temper. "Rolfe," I shouted, "let me tell you something. I don't know who your boss is, but I'm going to go to the headquarters of the Knight chain"—which owned the *Daily News*—"if I have to. When I leave here I'm going to call him. If he doesn't take action, I can promise you that I'll have a lawyer in here tomorrow, because I know you're off base on this. The only thing I can figure is that you wrote an editorial some time ago saying Rizzo was going to win the election, and now you're trying to prove yourself right. But you're a carpetbagger up here. I'll just promise you you're not going to get away with this."

The following day I got a call from one of Neill's people: "Mr. Neill asked me to call and tell you that the commercials have been withdrawn." Of course, the commercials had already run for four months. Nor did the *Daily News* produce any commercials involving me to even things up.

I USED TO WORK like a dog on Old Newsboys' Day, when prominent local figures hawked special newspapers on street corners for proceeds that went to charity. I was always proud of the fact that I sold more papers than anyone else. When I was asked to participate in the midst of the 1971 campaign, I stood in front of the Union League on Broad Street for more than four hours, collaring my friends and raising over $1,000. Then Rizzo came to replace me, sold papers for five minutes, and handed in $50 from his own pocket.

The next day the front page of the *Inquirer* carried a picture of Rizzo selling newspapers in front of the Union League—and no mention of me. Since then I don't sell papers on Old Newsboys' Day. Even a Quaker can turn the other cheek just so many times.

In the midst of the campaign, *Philadelphia* magazine published an insulting article on me. The magazine had prepared an even more insulting article on Rizzo—which was killed at the last minute and never published.

A week after the election, I was taken to lunch by George Packard, the executive editor of the *Philadelphia Bulletin.* He actually sat across the table from me and cried in frustration as he described a conspiracy at the *Bulletin* to elect Rizzo. He cited chapter and verse and provided names of the alleged conspirators.

"They all got together and they agreed," Packard said. "They were all going to get jobs with Rizzo once he was elected." And they did. Rizzo hired more than twenty newsmen when he came into office in 1972. Al Gaudiosi, a former *Bulletin* rewrite man, was made second in command at Philadelphia '76, the Bicentennial celebration agency, at a $50,000 salary—$10,000 more than the mayor himself was paid. Harry Belinger, city editor of the *Daily News,* was made city representative and director of commerce at $34,000 a year. Lawrence Campbell, a *Bulletin* reporter and rewrite man, became a deputy managing director at $25,000 a year; TV reporter Donald Angell, Jr., became a deputy city representative, also at $25,000.

One of the names mentioned by Packard was Dan McKenna,

chief of the *Bulletin*'s City Hall bureau. That rang a bell. McKenna had interviewed me several times during the campaign, and the subsequent stories he wrote bore limited resemblance to the comments I had made to him. At one point during the campaign I became enraged by a couple of articles in *Time* magazine—my own former company, for goodness' sake—suggesting that my cause was hopeless. I had called a few of my friends at *Time*.

"This is awful bullshit you guys are printing," I had said. "Who are you getting it from?"

"Oh, our stringer in Philadelphia's been giving it to us."

"Who's your stringer in Philadelphia?"

"A guy who works for the *Bulletin*. Name's Dan McKenna." After the election, Rizzo hired McKenna as a deputy city representative at $25,000 a year.

The apparent leader of the Rizzo cabal at the *Bulletin* was the paper's assistant managing editor, the late Sam Boyle. Some time after the election, in a speech before a Temple University journalism class, I said, "Don't talk to me about the integrity of the press. Let me take a newspaper guy, Sam Boyle, and I will spell out to you in specific instances what a screwing he gave me, and the main reason he did it was that he preferred the other guy. He allowed that preference to overcome his objective reporting, which is supposed to be a sacred trust of the Fourth Estate."

Boyle heard about my speech and phoned me in a rage: "How dare you go around saying things like that about me?"

"Sam, what do you expect me to say? All I did was say the truth."

"That's not the truth."

"Sam," I said, "have lunch with me, and I will spell out for you about a dozen instances that I have documented, and then you tell me if I'm lying. And if I am, I'll make a public retraction in your newspaper, under any circumstances that you wish."

We did have lunch, and I went over my complaints one after another. When I got all through, he said, "Well, I'm sure you're wrong on some of those. I want to go back and look them up." I never heard another word.

AFTER RIZZO BECAME MAYOR and I returned to my post as president of the Chamber of Commerce, he and I spent a lot of time together and became quite friendly. He'd call me up and I'd go over and see him all the time; I'd set up meetings for him with business people.

One day Rizzo phone me and said, "I want you to fire Ed Martin." Martin at that time was executive director of the Philadelphia Industrial Development Corporation, a quasi-public agency sponsored by the Chamber and subsidized by the city. Martin had been chosen for the job by Mayor Jim Tate—Rizzo's predecessor—and me.

"I'm not going to fire him," I insisted. "I see no reason to put him out. You may have disagreements with him from the days when you were both in the mayor's cabinet together, but he's done a perfectly reasonable job as head of PIDC. And I'll fight you on this one."

"Now, Thach," he said. "Don't go picking a fight right away. Just talk to some of your people. The guy's no good. I want to get rid of him. I just want you to go ahead and make the change."

"No, Frank," I said. "I'm not going to do it. You're not going to push me around. We're not going to turn PIDC into a political football."

I called Andy Young, who was chairman of PIDC at the time, and told him what had happened. To my surprise, he replied, "Well, you know, Thacher, he's right. Martin's not doing the job. The sooner we get rid of him, the better off we are."

So then I called three or four other guys who were knowledgeable about PIDC. They all said the same thing. I called Rizzo back the same afternoon.

"Frank," I said, "I hate to tell you this, but you're right and I'm wrong. I've called around, and I've talked to people whom I trust implicitly, and they tell me that Martin's not the right guy and we ought to fire him, so we'll fire him."

"Now let me tell you something else," Rizzo said. "After you've fired him, you hire his replacement. I don't want to say a thing about it. You do anything you want, you pick anybody you want and put him in. It's okay with me." (We picked Walter D'Alessio, a spectacular success.) Rizzo would later be accused of turning City Hall into a personal patronage pool, but I saw a very different side of him.

Similarly, a few years later, he phoned me with another request: "I want you to make Fred DiBona the head of the Port Corporation."

"Well, you know," I reminded him, "we had that disagreement back in the days of Martin, and you came out on top. But I don't know anything about Fred DiBona, except that his father's an important judge. And I'm not going to do it. I just am not."

"Look," he said, "do it the way you did it last time. Ask around. See what you think of him. How well do you know him?"

"I don't know him at all."

"Well, get to know him a little bit."

So I asked around and got pretty good vibrations. Then Jack Bracken and I took DiBona out to lunch, and had a long talk with him. I was impressed.

Soon I was on the phone to Rizzo. "Frank, you're right again," I said. "The guy looks pretty good." I suggested we hire DiBona as assistant to the president as a one-year trial. If he worked out in that position, we'd make him president. Rizzo agreed.

A year later I phoned him. "Frank, the guy's fine," I said. "You couldn't have sent us a better man." Little did I then suspect *how* much better: Four years later, Fred DiBona succeeded me as president of the Chamber of Commerce.

In both of those cases, I liked the way Rizzo handled things and the ultimate results he produced. He was anything but the heavy-handed politician; he was an administrator skillfully moving better people into key positions. Was this the real Frank Rizzo I saw, or did Rizzo adjust his behavior when he dealt with me? I can't say; I can simply report my own first-hand impressions, which diverge sharply from those of other Rizzo observers.

TOWARD THE END of Rizzo's second term as mayor I was made chairman of the Powell Award committee, which was empowered to grant a $45,000 prize to the Philadelphian who had done the most for the business community over the past year. When the committee convened, I said, "Fellows, let me tell you something. I think it ought to go to Frank Rizzo."

"Rizzo! Why?"

And I explained. "He's done a lot for business. He's been in there representing us. After Tate, he's just a breath of spring. And he's far more business-oriented than Clark and Dilworth were. We aren't going to find a mayor that's as pro-business as Frank Rizzo for a long time to come, and I think we ought to recognize it."

When they agreed, I pointed out: "The press is gonna climb all over us on this one. If I were you, I'd just refer them to me, because I'm prepared to take the heat and I'm not sure you guys are." They consented—happily—and consequently I took all the blame when the press jumped on the story. What could be more imbecilic, the media asked, than to give a cash award to a mayor for simply doing his tax-funded job?

In the midst of this storm, Rizzo phoned me one day.

"Thach, how are ya?"

"I'm fine, Frank."

"They giving you a hard time about me, Thach?" he asked. Then he said, "I'm not going to take that award. To hell with 'em, Thach! I don't need the money and I don't need the prestige. But I'll always appreciate the fact you went to bat for me."

IN 1978, *RIZZO DECIDED* to seek a change in the City Charter to allow him to seek a third consecutive term as mayor. When he first made the announcement, I went over to see him.

"Frank, I think it's a bad decision," I said.

"Aaah, Thach," he said. "Christ! Do you know who you're gonna get if I get out of here this time? First of all, you're gonna get somebody like Greenie"—Congressman Bill Green, Rizzo's eventual successor—"or someone who won't have the strength to handle the thing. This city'll go to hell. Look at the cities that are doing well, like that Schaefer down there in Baltimore and Daley in Chicago. The ones that do well are the ones that get somebody that works it out and they keep him in there for fifteen or twenty years. Let me get my programs in there, Thach. That's where we need to be."

I told him I didn't agree. "I think it's the other way around," I said. "I think you go decisively downhill from the eighth year on. I don't think your last year's been anywhere as good as your first few, and I think your next year is gonna be even worse—particularly if you lose this thing. And even if you win it, why, twelve years is too long for anybody to be in here, or sixteen or twenty, whatever you'd make it. I'm against you on this one, and I'm gonna do my best to lick you." But I added: "I hope it's not going to affect our friendship, because I treasure it."

"Aaah, Thach," he said, "you're all right. You're doing what you think is right and you come to tell me about it. You've shot square with me all these years. Don't worry. Do whatever you want. It won't make any difference at all."

He kept his word: Although that fall I headed the committee to preserve the city charter and won a huge victory that effectively ended Rizzo's political career—at least as of this writing—he and I remained on good personal terms.

Afterward Joe LaSala, then Rizzo's director of commerce, told me that Rizzo's aides were astounded by his turn-the-other-cheek posture toward me. "Frank was usually pretty vengeful when people didn't do what he wanted them to do," LaSala said. "The fact that you were able to be chairman of that committee and to be primarily responsible for licking us, and to have Frank remain as friendly and as complimentary to you as he was, is a big compliment to you." A big compliment to the Quaker philosophy, too.

CHAPTER 12

THE COMPENSATIONS
OF AGE
(1983–88)

AT A MEETING of industrial advertisers in 1976 I found myself
sitting next to Fred Gloeckner, the chairman of Winchell &
Co., a Philadelphia-based financial printing company. He was
then about seventy-five, but one of the most vigorous, dynamic
men I've ever met. He and I took to each other right away,
and not just because both of us routinely did push-ups every
morning. Eventually I went on his board as Winchell's first
outside director and subsequently became his vice chairman.
But the most important thing Fred did for me was to give me
a new perspective as I headed toward retirement: To Fred, I
was still a young man.

"God, sonny, I wish I were your age," he'd often say. "What
opportunities I'd have!" I was fifty-eight at the time. But Fred
was right—some of my most interesting opportunities were
still to come.

In 1983 I retired as president of the Chamber of Commerce
(my title had since been upgraded from executive vice president) and won election to one of the two minority-party at-
large seats in Philadelphia's City Council, where I'm still serving at this writing. Once I left the Chamber I found, to my
amazement, that all sorts of people felt I could be useful to
them. Since then some ten companies have hired me as a busi-

ness consultant. I also became vice chairman of Fred Gloeckner's Winchell & Co., and subsequently I moved over to the same position at a rival company, Packard Press. These companies hired me not for my printing expertise—I have none—but for my contacts and my ability to open doors. To be sure, this is a talent I'll be able to market only for a limited time, since my contacts are gradually dying off. But to someone who never cared much about money and who never managed to put much aside, it's remarkable to discover, in my late sixties, that without really trying I have suddenly become a marketable commodity—so that, for the first time in my life, I've become modestly prosperous.

About the time I left the Chamber, adman Alan Kalish persuaded Frank Rizzo and me to appear jointly in a TV commercial for the fledgling American International Airlines. The ad was a great success—notwithstanding the fact that the airline subsequently went out of business—and as a result yet another new career landed in my lap. After a lifetime in Philadelphia public life, it developed that I was not merely a prominent personality; I was also an ideal drawing card with which to reach the lucrative senior citizen market, since I've got both gray hair and physical vigor.

I was invited to do TV commercials for a brewery and a men's coat store—strange invitations, since I don't drink beer and never wear a coat. I turned down those offers because I still harbored hopes of running again for mayor, and I wasn't sure that the fun and/or money I'd derive from doing these commercials would justify the damage they'd do to my public credibility.

But in the fall of 1988 I got a call from Philadelphia's TV Channel 10, asking me if I'd do a commercial for Bill Cosby's syndicated reruns, and I agreed. (I'd met Cosby many times, at the Penn Relays and at Temple University, his alma mater.) It was a thirty-second commercial in which I sort of danced across the screen. This led to an offer from Laz-y Boy Chair: When I used that reclining chair to recuperate from a widely publicized broken leg, my picture in the chair was plastered on newspaper ads, direct-mail flyers, and even billboards. A rug dealer saw these ads, called me up, and said, "You did these ads for them—how about doing some for us?" Soon my name and face were selling rugs in newspaper, TV, and radio ads. And Legg Mason, the investment house, hired me to do ads promoting a series of investment seminars.

In none of these commercial endorsements did I solicit the business, and I turned down several offers that didn't appeal to me. I always insist on doing the commercials my own way, which usually involves a little humor. In the rug commercial I did a little dance across the screen and sang a line of "It's a beautiful day in the neighborhood," in the fashion of a spoof.

Some people have questioned the propriety of an elected public official's appearing as a pitchman for commercial products. But the prevailing belief among ethicists these days is that it's all right for a public official to accept work from private interests as long as he discloses it publicly—and what could be more public than a TV commercial? The money I accept for these commercials strikes me as no more improper than the honorariums I accept for speaking appearances. In any case, no one can accuse me of getting rich from commercials: All my commercial fees—like all my speaking fees—are donated to the Multiple Sclerosis Society. The fees augment my income only in the sense that they relieve me of the need to dip into my regular income to make some of my charitable donations.

The real reason I do these commercials is simply that they're fun. Nothing could be more gratifying than to have people stop me on the street and say, "Gee, that was terrific. I had no idea you were that good."

The only complaint that struck me as somewhat valid was a letter from a lawyer who acknowledged that it's perfectly all right for me to do commercials but expressed the fear that I was damaging my credibility as a public servant. In effect he accused me of hurting myself by dipping into my moral capital, and I suppose there's some truth to that. Were I younger and embarking on a career in politics, I'd probably refuse to do commercials. But that's one of the compensations of age: As long as I'm not hurting anyone but myself, my future credibility concerns me less now than my lifelong bottom line: to do good and have a good time.

With or without the commercials, making a living has suddenly become much easier for me. I don't think most people realize, as I have come to realize, the difference between *making* money and *having* money. That is, the papers these days are full of stories about people who earn hundreds of thousands—or even millions—of dollars a year, yet they're actually broke, because their expenses exceed their income. Conversely, it's equally possible nowadays not to make much money but to get rich anyway. I fall into the second category.

In 1976, for example, I got $20,000 after taxes from the sale of a house. By that time our children were out of college and Nancy and I were earning enough between us to meet all our bills, so the $20,000 was really discretionary income—a sizable bundle of cash which, really for the first time in our lives, we could spend as we chose.

But how to spend it? First I thought of buying a car. But my instincts said no—somehow I'll get access to a car without buying one. And sure enough, the Chamber subsequently gave me the use of one of its cars.

About that time I stumbled across something called the Rule of 72, an investment axiom aimed at people like me—who are conservative, who want to save their money and set up a secure future as opposed to a spectacular present. According to the Rule of 72, if you invest money at compound interest, you can take the interest rate and divide it into 72, and the result will tell you how many years it will take your money to double. Thus in 1976 I invested that $20,000 in a mutual bond fund at a 12 percent interest rate. Twelve into 72 is 6— and, sure enough, six years later my $20,000 nest egg had doubled to $40,000; in another six years it had doubled again, to $80,000.

Now at this writing I'm sixty-eight years old. My father lived to be ninety-three. So if I live as long as he did, my original $20,000 investment will be worth more than $1 million. I know that inflation may undercut the value of that million, and I know the interest rate isn't guaranteed indefinitely. But still, my point is that thanks to the financial world's new array of planning instruments, thanks to tax-deferred savings plans, and thanks to the federal government's recently approved catastrophic health coverage, a fellow like me—who for sixty-five years barely made enough to pay his bills and provide for his family—suddenly finds himself in the position where he may become, in his twilight years, moderately rich. And that's a remarkable thing.

AS THIS BOOK is written, Nancy and I are still living in Chestnut Hill. Nancy is confined to an Amigo—an electric wheelchair—but still going strong as chairman of Friends of Philadelphia Parks, still involved in the real estate business, and still a cheerful, friendly hostess whom people come from far and wide to see. Of our four children, one daughter is filling her mother's shoes as a champion real estate saleslady in Chestnut Hill and the other has just gone into the real estate business with her husband in Omaha; one son is a neurologist in Seattle and the other is a successful real estate developer in Philadelphia. And our four children have given us twelve grandchildren, ranging in age from eleven to twenty-four at this writing.

My brother Frank moved away from Philadelphia right after World War II. Although we're still close friends and take trips together occasionally, our lives have moved in different directions and we don't see each other as often as we used to. Still, we speak on the phone frequently, and I admire the way he has directed his life: Since 1948 he has been teaching Latin and coaching track—with great success—at Western Reserve Academy, a private school in Hudson, Ohio, outside Cleveland. He's the "Mr. Chips" of his institution; a few years ago he was voted the best schoolteacher in Ohio. One of the nicer things that's happened to me occurred in 1985, when the school rebuilt its track and named it in Frank's honor. Frank asked two people to speak at the dedication ceremony: Harrison Dillard, the Olympic hurdles champion (and a personal friend of Frank's), and me.

As for me, I'm serving my third term in City Council. I'm probably not going to be mayor of Philadelphia or governor of Pennsylvania or anything else. On the other hand, I had a good run at high office and I wouldn't change places with anyone. I've taken my rewards not in dollars or power but in the discovery that good faith, friendship, and loyalty do mean something in an often capricious world. It has been my happy faculty to find the hopeful side of most situations I've encountered, and as a result I've discovered that you can have a lot of fun even when you lose. Because I've never been afraid or ashamed of losing or of appearing ridiculous, I've taken risks and enjoyed experiences that "successful" people would never try, for fear of failure. Thus if your definition of success is to accumulate the most votes or the most toys or the most power, I guess my career leaves something to be desired. But if your definition of success is having fun, my life has indeed been a smashing success. To the extent that I'm a happy man today, I think it's because I've measured my success by my own lights rather than the world's.

THE FUN AND THE FRIENDSHIP . . .

The lifelong favorite butt of my practical jokes was Sam Lanahan, my friend, classmate, and roommate from Princeton. Sam had married F. Scott Fitzgerald's daughter Scotty, and I had been best man at their wedding. He is a lawyer in Washington and she, before her recent death, was a newspaper reporter as well as a popular hostess who was involved in all sorts of civic and charitable causes. But to me they always remained a couple I had known when we'd all been young and wild, and I never lost an opportunity to be with them.

Most of our clowning has occurred at Princeton reunions, where this kind of thing is expected. At one reunion, for example, we had snapper soup which was so delicious that I noisily slurped up the unfinished portions of everyone around me. Lanahan left the table, picked up one of the huge soup tureens, and stood behind me, without my realizing that he was there. "Excuse me sir," he asked. "Would you like some more soup?" When I happily replied, "Oh, yes!" he dumped the whole tureen over my head.

At the end of that particular reunion, we had changed back into our regular clothes; Sam was wearing a nice tweed coat and gray flannels. I was drinking a Coke as he came over to say goodbye before catching a taxi to Princeton Junction and the train back to Washington. As we chatted, I surreptitiously filled his jacket pocket with Coca-Cola. He was totally unaware of what I'd done, and the coat was new enough to hold the liquid without dripping through the fabric. Sam never realized what had happened until he put his hand into his pocket as he was getting into the cab. All of a sudden I saw his expression change. "You bastard," he said. "If it takes a hundred years, I'll get you."

He still has some catching up to do. One January day in the seventies, I was in Washington for some early-morning business. Because I wanted to say hello to Sam, I stopped by his law firm first thing in the morning—about seven-thirty. No one was there but the receptionist. I asked for Mr. Lanahan but was told he wasn't in.

"Where is he?" I asked.

"As a matter of fact," she said, "They're holding the year-end partners' meeting over at the Metropolitan Club. He'll probably be there until ten o'clock."

I thanked her and sat down for a moment—long enough to concoct an idea. Then I arose, went down in the elevator, walked over to the Metropolitan Club, and told the guard that I was with Wilmer, Cutler & Pickering—Sam's firm. "Oh, they're on the sixth floor," he promptly informed me.

I thanked him and took the elevator to the sixth floor, where I heard a mumbling of voices in a room behind a door. I opened the door and saw about twenty lawyers, including Lanahan, sitting around the table with pads and pencils. One guy was talking; I heard him say, "How much did you get?" It wasn't hard to figure out what was going on: The partners were dividing their profits for the previous year.

I walked right into the room and sat down in an empty chair at the table. Cutler, the firm's senior partner, looked over at me and said, "Who the hell is this?" I said nothing. Lanahan, sitting a few chairs away, said nothing either. But he looked as if he'd like to disappear under the table.

"Excuse me, sir," Cutler said to me. "Are you in the right room?"

"Oh," I said, "this is Wilmer, Cutler & Pickering, isn't it?"

"Yes, it is."

"Well, I'm in the right room," I said.

"What are you here for?" Cutler said.

"I've come for my share of the swag," I said.

Lanahan, who was only a junior partner at the time, was beside himself. And Cutler was furious—his face was all red. Lanahan looked over at me. "Not funny, Stretch," he said.

"You're probably going to get me fired for this one. You'd better go away now."

"Well!" I said, all huffy. "If I'm not wanted . . ." And I got up and left the room without another word.

Cutler never forgot my stunt. I met him formally many years later. By that time he'd come to think of the incident as pretty funny. Indeed, it became a legend in the firm. And of course Lanahan wasn't fired—only shaken up.

But his day (and mine) had just begun. My cousin and Princeton roommate Stanley Pearson had accompanied me to Washington and rejoined me a little later. Lanahan's next appointment that day was a court appearance, as part of the *pro bono* work his firm did. On this particular day Lanahan had been assigned to defend, without fee, a black fellow who had cut a hole in the roof of a supermarket and entered and attempted to burglarize the place. He had been caught cold by the store's security guards, but he'd asked for a jury trial, in the hope that he might elicit more sympathy from a black jury than from a white judge.

So Pearson and I went down to the court to watch Lanahan try this case. When we arrived at the appropriate room, we saw some fifteen or twenty people standing in line.

"Is this Courtroom 23?" I asked.

"Yes, it is."

"Well, what is this group?"

"We're prospective jurors," I was told. "We're being examined by the attorneys."

So I said to Pearson, "So are we."

The two of us gave our names to the bailiff and got into the line. At first we were standing outside the courtroom, but as the line moved forward we got inside where we could see what was happening. Lanahan was questioning jurors in an attempt to keep the blacks and weed out the whites; the prosecutor was trying to get law-and-order types, regardless of race. Finally the guy in front of me stepped into the witness chair to be examined. Lanahan was standing there, writing notes on a clipboard pad and conferring with another attorney. He approved the juror and so did the prosecutor, and the man took his seat in the jury box.

Then the bailiff called out, "Thacher Longstreth." Lanahan jumped, dropped his clipboard, looked up and said "Oh, my God, no!" Here it was eleven in the morning and we were already getting him a second time in one day. For a moment Lanahan and I stood there looking at each other. Then he ran over to the judge, who'd been half-sleeping through the jury selection process. I heard Lanahan say something to the judge, after which the judge looked up.

"Mr. Longstreth," he said, "what are you here for?"

"Well, I'm not sure, judge," I said. "What is this about?"

"We're selecting the jurors for *The City of Washington* v. *John Brown.*"

"Oh," I said. "Gee, I didn't know that."

"Well, what were you in the line for?" the judge asked.

"I'm sorry, your honor, " I said. "I thought I was going to the men's room."

The judge didn't seem sure whether I was serious or kidding. Then Lanahan said something to him. "Young man," the judge said to me, "this is a court of law, and you're considerably out of order. I will have to ask you to leave immediately."

And Pearson and I did. But we got what we'd come for: the look on Lanahan's face when he saw us in the line of jurors—which neither of us has forgotten some fifteen years later.

THE ACCUMULATED DIVIDENDS OF A LIFETIME . . .

One day in 1973 I was driving to Scranton to make a speech. I was late and was really pouring it on. Just before the Scranton exit of the Pennsylvania Turnpike, I passed a police car with his radar on. I glimpsed at my speedometer, saw I was doing eighty-two, and without waiting for a signal from the cop I simply hit the brakes, pulled off the road, and got out of the car. Sure enough, the police car pulled up behind me.

"You know what you were doing?" the officer said.

"Yes sir. I was doing eighty-two miles an hour."

"I'm going to have to give you a ticket."

"I have no argument at all," I acknowledged. "I deserve it. But I don't want you to think I was speeding frivolously. I'm making a speech at the University of Scranton, and Monsignor Murphy told me to be there by noon, and it's ten of now and I'm going to be late. That's why I was going so fast."

The officer looked at me a little more closely. "Aren't you the fellow that ran against Rizzo?" he asked.

"Yeah."

"You put up a good fight," he said. "You're really going to give this speech?"

"Yes, I am."

"I'll tell you what I'm going to do," he said. "I'm going to finish writing out this ticket; I'm going to give it to you. When you get in there, you go see Monsignor Murphy, and you tell him that Patrolman Kelly stopped you up here on the turnpike for going eighty-two miles an hour. You tell him that if he thinks you made a good enough speech, he should take the ticket and send it back to me and that will be the end of it."

Needless to add, that little interlude provided the opening gambit for the speech I gave in Scranton less than an hour later. It got a big laugh, especially when Monsignor Murphy took the ticket from me right there in front of the audience.

Ten years passed. Late one night—after midnight—I was driving home from Harrisburg on the Pennsylvania Turnpike. I was doing about seventy miles per hour in a fifty-five mile zone, listening to the radio and not paying much attention to the road before me. Suddenly I heard a siren and saw the red flashing light in my rearview mirror.

I pulled off the road and got out of my car, as I always do in such situations—the fact that I'm a recognizable figure helps me sometimes in such situations. In this case, the cop started walking toward me in the darkness, but he couldn't distinguish me until he was very close.

"Thacher Longstreth, my God!" was the first thing I heard him say.

I'm accustomed to being recognized and didn't think much of his greeting. "Well, officer," I said, "what was I doing?"

"Oh, you were exceeding the speed limit," he said, "but I'm not even going to make you go see Monsignor Murphy on this one." It was the same officer who'd stopped me that time in Scranton. "Last time," he said, "you were twenty-five miles over the speed limit. Tonight you're down to ten. I think that's pretty good for ten years. So I'll just shake your hand and send you on your way."

THE REWARDS OF LIFELONG FRIENDSHIP . . .

I first met Charles Brown Anderson—"Chizzy" to his friends—in the summer of 1929, when I was eight and he was ten. It was the first of my ten summers at Camp La Jeunesse, a wonderful camp in the Adirondack Mountains run by Henry Blagden. He was essentially a Father Sill type—a natural leader of boys who molded hundreds of us into men in such a way that even half a century later it's impossible to hear his name without feeling tremendous appreciation and love.

On my first day of that first summer at La Jeunesse, Chizzy and I got into a terrible fight—he claimed I had taken his bunk—which ended when he made me cry. Yet from that fight came a friendship which has existed forever since, to the

point where we went to the camp together for years, we went
to Princeton together, our families shared houses at the shore
together, we traveled through Europe together, we've visited
each other repeatedly, and each Saturday in the fall we still
attend Princeton football games together. It's been more than
sixty years since we first set eyes on each other, and we've
hardly missed a week without speaking to each other since.

Chizzy originally lived in Pittsburgh, then in Framingham,
Massachusetts, and more recently in Princeton. Our children
are friends, our wives are friends, we were ushers at each other's weddings—it's the sort of classic friendship that grows
more precious as the years pass.

During World War II, we didn't see each other for a few
years: While I was with the Navy in the Pacific, Chizzy enlisted
in the Army and compiled a heroic war record in the invasions
of North Africa and Sicily. When we came back, I went to
work for *Life* and he got a job in Massachusetts with the Rox-
bury Carpet Company, where he ultimately became president.

Then, during the Korean crisis early in 1951, one day I got
a call from Chizzy: He'd been ordered back into the Army, he
said, and he'd be stationed in Fort Dix. As we got to talking,
it sounded like good news: Fort Dix was located in central
New Jersey and I was in Philadelphia, so we'd be closer to
each other. We decided that it would be fun to get a cottage
at Bay Head, New Jersey, together, move our families in there,
and just live there together for the next six months. In those
days you could rent a cottage cheap on that lovely Atlantic
Ocean beach, so that's what we did.

Let me interject a word here about Bay Head, where we
spent our summers for many years. It was—and still is—a
popular summer retreat for New York and Philadelphia WASPs
who need a place to let their hair down. In the early fifties, we
had a cottage right on the beach, and often in the evenings a
group of us would just go out on the beach, take off our clothes,

jump in the water, come out, put our clothes back on, and return to the house or the party or whatever we'd been doing.

One Saturday at about two in the morning we were all at a party at the cottage of Ella Widener Wetherill, heir to the Widener traction fortune and perhaps the wealthiest woman in Philadelphia. Somebody said, "Let's all go swimming." Since we were only a hundred yards from the beach, we just took off our clothes in the house and threw them in the corners. Then this parade of about fifteen naked people started walking toward the beach.

As we crossed the street, Ella—who was as naked as the rest of us—came over to me and said, "This stuff is hurting my feet—carry me." She just jumped up and I caught her. Girls love to be carried, and I was big enough to carry them, so I often ended up carrying girls—albeit usually with their clothes on.

At any rate, here I was, stark naked, crossing the main street of Bay Head with a naked woman in my arms. As we passed a parked convertible I suddenly realized that a teenage boy and girl were inside, locked in a passionate embrace.

At this moment, Ella leaned over the car, tapped the girl on the shoulder, and said, "Having fun?"

The girl in the car sprang back from her kiss with a loud *pop,* and turned around to see who was there. "Why, Mr. Longstreth!" I heard her say. "What are *you* doing here?"

It was our baby-sitter, who was supposed to be tending our kids at that moment; she was no more anxious to see me than I was to see her. I thought for a moment, and then I said, "I'll tell you something. If you get back there and take care of those kids as you should, I won't say anything to Mrs. Longstreth, and if you don't say anything to Mrs. Longstreth about what you've seen here, we're even-Stephen." Actually, Nancy was right behind me and observed the whole scene. But it just seemed a funny way to respond.

Soon we got down to the water, and I started to throw Ella in, shouting, "I'm gonna throw her in the water! I'm gonna throw her in the water!"

"For Christ's sake," somebody said, "don't throw her in the water—she's got a fortune in diamonds on." And she did—diamond earrings, a diamond ring, and a diamond necklace.

"Oh my God, your diamonds!" I exclaimed.

"To hell with the diamonds," she said. "But if you get my hair wet, I'll kill you."

That was the flavor of Bay Head in a nutshell. And it was here, that spring, summer, and early fall of 1951, that the Longstreths and Andersons lived as a communal family: Chizzy and I and our wives, his four children and my four children, plus three housekeepers we hired to look after us. And we took Bay Head by storm: We *owned* Bay Head by the end of that summer. Each morning I would drive down to Philadelphia to my work, and Chizzy would go to Fort Dix to *his* work. Then we'd come back at night and we'd all enjoy one another's company.

By late August we'd been together about four and a half months with never a harsh word. But one night, about midnight, I heard screaming in the Andersons' bedroom. I rushed to our bedroom door, and as I opened it Chizzy's wife, Miney, ran in and threw herself on our bed, sobbing hysterically.

"My God, Miney!" I said. "What's the matter?"

"Chizzy's going to Korea," she cried. "He's been ordered to Korea."

That was not a place anybody wanted to be in the summer of 1951. The Inchon invasion had taken place the previous fall, and U.S. forces had driven the North Koreans back toward the Chinese border. But in June of that year the Chinese had invaded from the north, and they were kicking the hell out of us. Chizzy had been a very successful forward observer—he knew a great deal about tanks and aircraft—so the Army had decided that instead of using him for training at Fort Dix, it would send him to the front.

My first reaction was that Chizzy could easily make a case to the Army for his staying home: After all, here was a major who had served five years in World War II and had a wife and four children (he subsequently had a fifth), to boot.

"You don't have to worry about anything," I told Miney. "All Chizzy has to do is go down to Washington and tell them."

"He's not going to do that," she cried. "Chizzy says, 'When there's a war, the men fight.' And if they want him to go fight, that's what he's going to do." Which was exactly like Chizzy.

"Miney," I asked, "does he really want to go?"

"No," she said, "he doesn't want to go. But he isn't going to do anything about it. If he goes to Korea, he's going to die, and I'm going to have to bring up these kids by myself. It's not fair. There's only one person in the world who can save him, and that's you."

"Me?" I gulped. "How can I save him? I don't know anybody. I don't have any pull."

"You can save him," she insisted. "I know it. God told me you can save him."

We finally got her calmed down and into bed. Chizzy had been in their room the whole time, angry at her because of the scene she had thrown. So I asked him: "Are you going to do anything or not?"

"I don't believe in doing that," he said. "I believe that the system is such that you do what you're told to do."

"Do you really want to go?" I asked.

"No, I really don't want to go. I'm back in the States again, I've got all these kids—it's kind of different than it was before. And I'm older than I was. But I'm not going to do anything about it."

"Will you be angry with me if I try?" I asked.

"No, I won't be angry. That's up to you. But I won't lift a finger to help you."

So I got in my car—I was so naive, so young, thirty years old and working for *Life*!—and I drove down to Washington. I figured my old school ties could get me in to see Frank Pace, the secretary of the Army: His brother-in-law, Wistar Janney, had been one of my best friends at Princeton. I went to see Wistar, who was then with the CIA in Washington, and asked him to set up a meeting for me with Pace.

"Why?" he asked.

"Because Chizzy Anderson's being sent to Korea, and I want Frank Pace to change his orders."

"Thacher, I can set up a meeting with Frank Pace," Wistar replied. "He knows you and likes you and he'll see you. But he won't do anything for Chizzy Anderson or anybody else. He can't do a thing—I'll guarantee you. It's a waste of your time and his."

That was a great shock; I'd placed all my faith in my entree to Pace and my ability to overwhelm him with Chizzy's story. "What can I do?" I asked.

"Don't ask me," Wistar shrugged.

So there I was, adrift in Washington. Where could I go? Naively—again—I got back in my car and drove over to the Pentagon building. I told myself: If something's going to be done, it has to be done out of the Pentagon. So I wandered into the Pentagon building, which I knew a little bit about— I'd been there a few times toward the end of World War II. I started walking along the hall, looking at the names outside each office, thinking, Maybe I'll see somebody I know.

As its title implies, the Pentagon is a five-sided building, so it's easy to get lost, which I did. At some point in my wandering I saw a sign that read: "Judge Advocate General's Office. General Maurice Kleister." I reasoned to myself that a judge advocate had something to do with justice, and Chizzy's case had something to do with fairness, ergo this was as good a place to try as any.

So I walked into the room. "Is General Kleister here?" I asked the receptionist.

"Who are you?" she demanded coldly.

"My name's Thacher Longstreth."

"What do you wish to see him about?"

"Well, it's kind of complicated."

"Who are you with?"

"I'm with *Life* magazine."

At this her demeanor changed completely. "Oh! Are you really!" she exclaimed. "Well, yes, Mr. Longstreth, I'm terribly sorry, but General Kleister's not here. Can I do something for you?"

"No, I guess not," I said.

As I turned around and started out of the office I saw a side door with a sign that read: "Deputy Judge Advocate, Colonel Gavalas." The door was ajar, and inside I saw a fellow sitting at his desk who had presumably heard my conversation. As I looked in, he looked up. "Thacher Longstreth!" he said brightly.

I had never seen this fellow before in my life. But I answered, "Yes!" just as brightly. He introduced himself as Gav Gavalas and explained that he remembered me from my Princeton football days; he and his then fiancée had watched me play in the Princeton-Yale game perhaps a dozen years earlier.

I saw my opportunity and seized it. "Colonel, have you got a moment?" I asked. "I'd like to come in and talk to you."

It was a total coincidence. But I proceeded to sit down and tell Colonel Gavalas about Chizzy Anderson, about his war record, his large family, his orders to go back to Korea, and what could I do about it?

"Well, let's get his dossier in here," Colonel Gavalas said. A few minutes later Chizzy's dossier was sitting on the colonel's desk. As he looked through it I noticed him shaking his head angrily.

"Dammit, Thacher!" he finally said. "You know your friend was recommended for the Distinguished Service Cross? He didn't get it, but he was recommended for it. Did you know that this is a man whose record of bravery and performance of patriotism is the equal of any I've ever seen? For this man to be put back into war would be a rotten injustice. When I think of that guy Glenn Davis, who graduated from West Point and then abandoned his military career to play football while his classmates are dying in Korea, and now they're going to send a guy like this with four children back there—by God, it isn't going to happen."

He picked up the phone. "General," I heard him say into the speaker, "I want to come down and see you right away."

Together Gavalas and I went down to the office of the general in charge of personnel. Gavalas went inside and closed the door, but from the anteroom where I was sitting I could hear him shouting; he was really stirred up. Finally he brought me in to meet the general. "Tell me something about your friend," the general said. And I did.

When I was finished, the general looked at Gavalas. "You're right," he said. "This would be a terrible miscarriage of justice." Then he turned to me. "Young man," he said, "you go back and see your friend. You tell him, number one, he's not going to Korea. And number two, it was improper of us to have called him back in the first place. He's been back for a year, he's done his training duties, he has discharged his obligations to his country many times over, and he will be back in civilian life in three weeks."

I couldn't believe my ears. "General, are you serious?" I said.

"I'm absolutely serious," he said.

"Well," I said, "but you're allowing me . . ."

"Ordinarily we would simply send him his orders," the general explained, "and that would be the end of that. But any man who cares this much about his friend deserves the right to tell him himself. I think you'd like to tell him."

Well, I got in the car and drove back to Bay Head, delirious with joy. When I walked into the cottage that evening everyone was sitting in the dining room, having supper.

"You're not going to Korea," I announced, "and you're out of the Army in three weeks."

Chizzy's wife Miney burst into tears and I heard his children shouting, "Daddy's going to stay!" In a manner that I never could have planned in a million years, I had worked a miracle for someone who eminently deserved it. It was one of the most wonderful moments of my life.

Now jump ahead four years to 1955. I had quit my ad agency to run for mayor of Philadelphia, and I was hard put to figure out how I'd pay my sons' tuitions that fall at Chestnut Hill Academy, a private school for boys. When I explained my situation to the headmaster, Robert Kingsley, he told me the school would be honored to give my boys scholarships for the fall term; I agreed to resume regular tuition payments in the spring 1956 term, after the election was over.

But when the year came to an end I was still flat on my back financially: I'd lost the election and run up $11,000 in debts, and there was no way I could come up with the boys' tuitions. But I was too proud to go to the school and ask for help again. Yet strangely, when December rolled around I received no tuition bill from the school, nor did I receive one over the Christmas holidays. By the middle of January, with the new term just about to begin, I phoned the headmaster for an explanation.

"Mr. Kingsley," I said, "I haven't received my bill for school yet."

"That's right," he replied.

"Mr. Kingsley," I reminded him, "the deal was that you were going to take care of it through the fall term, and then I would pick it up again in January. So I'd appreciate your sending me a bill. I'll have to make arrangements—I probably can't pay it right away—but I will make arrangements to pay for it."

"You don't get a bill," he said.

"But our deal was only for the first half of the year," I insisted. "How come I don't get a bill?"

"Your bill's been taken care of," Mr. Kingsley said.

I could feel my blood rising. As an occasional politician, I immediately suspected that someone was trying to place me in a compromising position. "Taken care of?" I repeated. "Who by?"

"I'm not allowed to say."

Now I was angry. "I'm not going to accept charity, for God's sake, from somebody when I don't even know who it is," I said. "I'm sorry, but that's no deal as far as I'm concerned. You send me the bill."

"Thacher," Mr. Kingsley said quietly, "this has been taken care of by somebody who's very fond of you. And if I were you, I'd just let it go."

"No," I stubbornly insisted. "I'll never let it go. I'll pay for my own kids."

"Well," he said, "just sit tight for a moment," and he got off the phone.

About five minutes later my phone rang. It was Chizzy. "For Christ's sake," I heard him say wearily, "stop being such an asshole."

"It was you?" I said.

"Yeah, it's me."

"Oh," I replied sheepishly. "Thank you very much." And that was the end of that. Because it was Chizzy, I didn't object. It was our way for a friend to help a friend in need, just as I had done for him.

"I never sent a contribution to your campaign," Chizzy elaborated later, "because I live in Boston and you live in Philadelphia—and frankly, I didn't want you to be mayor because I thought it was going to be too much of a burden. But I care a lot about your kids, and I care a lot about you and your whole family. So when I heard what Nancy had told Miney and Miney told me about the problem of paying for the spring term, I just could see that there was something I could do, and I was very happy to do it."

In the early 1980s, Miney and Chizzy's kids threw them a big party at Princeton to celebrate their fortieth wedding anniversary. They asked me if I would get up and say a few words to the guests. About half of the two hundred or so people present were Chizzy and Miney's friends; the rest were friends of their children—young men and women in their twenties. It was one of those rare opportunities for one generation to sum itself up and pass on its essence to the next generation.

"I just want to make two points tonight that I think are significant about Chizzy," I told the gathering. "Number one, you don't know many heroes in your life. But Chizzy was a hero. You don't know this, because he's never said anything about it, but he was in North Africa and Anzio, and he was at Salerno. He fought the Krauts hand to hand, he saved his men, he took the toughest assignments, he never took a backward step. Guys like Chizzy are why we won the war. As far as I'm concerned, you can have Sergeant York and Audie Murphy—this guy's my hero. And he ought to be the hero of everybody in this room, particularly those of you who are lucky enough to be his children."

Then I added: "My other point is that it's hard for a man to talk about loving another man. It's not looked upon as something you can do without placing yourself under some sort of suspicion. But I love this man, and I've loved him since he was a little boy, and I always will. And it's nice to be able to say it tonight, because I hope that you younger people will understand what a precious thing friendship is, and how the love of another man can be one of the most noble parts of your life."

It took about that long, and it was hard to say it with the tears running down my cheeks. But what made it particularly worthwhile was that young guys came up to me the rest of the evening saying they'd never heard it put that way, and thanking me for teaching them something important.

But it's true—it's a feeling that men don't often express, at least not when they're sober. This may be a male chauvinist attitude, but I believe friendship among men is probably a little stronger than that between women. Certainly it's different. My younger daughter and my older daughter-in-law are two of the closest women friends I've ever seen, but there's still a little jealousy and resentment and anger that surfaces between them on occasion. But Chizzy and I—since that first scuffle at Camp La Jeunesse there's never been a single feeling of anger, jealousy, malice, irritation, or anything else between us. Everyone should be blessed with such a friendship.

THE PAYOFF FOR INVESTMENTS MADE IN OTHERS. . .

About 1967, after I'd been head of the Chamber of Commerce for three years, the headwaiter at a Philadelphia hotel came to my office with a problem. "Big Joe," as I shall call him, was obviously terribly distraught. His only son, a boy of eighteen, had been indicted for a sex offense. The boy would sit in his car outside a girls' elementary school when classes let out; then he'd call to a girl and offer her candy, and if she approached the car he'd open the door and expose himself. Ultimately someone had recorded his license-plate number and the boy had been arrested. There was no question of his guilt. He had pleaded guilty, and now he faced the prospect of a long prison sentence. Could I help him?

My initial reaction was that I couldn't do anything even if I wanted to—which I didn't. I had daughters of my own, after all. "If someone did this to one of my daughters," I remember saying, "I'd kill him."

At this, Big Joe burst into tears. "I'm not trying to excuse his actions," he said. "But when you put a child molester in prison, the other prisoners just beat up on him. He'll be raped and probably murdered before he's through. He's my son and I'm trying desperately to save him. And I can't get anybody to help me. I don't have any money to speak of—I'm a head-waiter. I can't hire a good lawyer. I'm at my wit's end. I just don't know what to do."

In a moment of weakness, I said I'd see what I could do—not really believing I could do anything.

I looked up the name of the judge in the case—who happened to be a friend of mine—and went to see him. But I found him utterly unsympathetic. "Why the hell is somebody like you coming around and speaking for a creep like that?" he asked. "We ought to hang this guy up."

By this time I had persuaded myself that the young man needed psychiatric help—not prison, where he would most likely end up dead. I made my case emotionally but failed to persuade my friend the judge. But a few days later I came back, went at him again, and finally wore him down.

"I'll tell you what I'll do," the judge said. He proceeded to tick off three conditions for placing the boy on psychiatric probation: First, the family of the victimized girl must agree to it; second, the boy must get a full-time paying job at a specified minimum salary; and third, I must accept personal responsibility for the boy's conduct over the next three years.

Well, that was quite an earful. I had set out to perform a small favor for a waiter I knew only from having seen him at various civic banquets. Now I was being asked, in effect, to become a surrogate parent.

I objected that the conditions were too harsh, but the judge was adamant.

"All you bleeding hearts come in here," he said, "you want us to pardon people, and then you walk out the door and that's the end of it. You feel good and everybody's grateful to you, and three weeks later the guy murders somebody."

What could I say? I agreed to his conditions. But of course that was only part of the battle. When I went to see the girl's family, I ran into much the same argument: "Mr. Longstreth, how could a fine gentleman like you be involved in representing a creep like this?"

I explained as patiently as I could that I sympathized with them and that I did not want the boy to escape punishment— I just wanted his punishment to include some degree of rehabilitation. They finally agreed to accept my plan, as long as I fulfilled my obligations to the judge.

Thus the judge placed the boy on probation, and through my advertising contacts I got him a job in the mailroom at N. W. Ayer, the big ad agency. The whole thing worked out well; there were no more incidents, and a few years later the boy got married and had children of his own. He subsequently went into waitering, his father's profession; now he's a head-waiter himself. Today, I'm sure, that whole child-molesting episode is an almost forgotten leaf from the book of his life.

Big Joe, needless to add, was enormously grateful. He came to my office, thanked me profusely, and said he wished he could do something more concrete to express his gratitude. But I told him there was nothing he could do.

About a week later I was having lunch at the hotel where Big Joe worked. As I was sitting at the table, a waiter set two glasses of iced tea before me.

"What's this about?" I asked.

"You always drink iced tea," the waiter said.

"Yes, that's right. I always do."

"Well," the waiter explained, "Big Joe told us that whenever you come in, we should give you two glasses of iced tea."

I walked to the corner of the dining room where Big Joe was standing. "What's this iced tea all about?"

"There's nothing I can really do to express my appreciation," he said. "But whenever you go into one of our hotels, that iced tea will always be there. I won't necessarily be there, but the iced tea will be. And that will say how much I appreciate what you've done for me and my son, and how much my friends appreciate it."

Thereafter, whenever I ate at a downtown hotel, I always got two iced teas—not just at that company's hotels, but at every downtown hotel as the word spread among the waiters' fraternity. It started with the older waiters who were friends of Big Joe's, but after a while the younger waiters picked up the tradition. It still happens frequently today.

Big Joe died in the early eighties. A week after his death I was giving a speech at a lunch to celebrate the opening of the Franklin Plaza Hotel downtown. Sure enough, two iced teas appeared at my place on the dais. The waiter, an older man, leaned over my shoulder.

"Mr. Longstreth," he whispered, "these are from Big Joe."

Epilogue
The House on
Montgomery Avenue

I WAS SIX OR SEVEN YEARS OLD when I learned that there was no Santa Claus. At first I refused to hear it; I cried for a day. Up to that point Santa Claus had been a significant force in my life; now, in an instant, he was gone, vanished, forever. Once the bitter truth sank in, I immediately shared it with my younger brother, Frank, so that he too would know the same pain I was suffering.

Now, in the autumn of my life, I find myself returning to the big house my grandmother built on Montgomery Avenue in Haverford—the house where I was born. Its pull on me is strange, in a way, because I haven't actually lived there since I was thirteen years old. That winter of 1933, when the stock market crash finally wiped out everything for the Long-streths—including even our ability to heat this house, which we still owned (with mortgage)—we moved out of the big house and into the carriage house behind it.

The big house remained empty until 1943, when a man named Dalglish came to my father with an offer: Dalglish would rent the big house and fix it up so he and his family could live on the third floor. The second floor would be converted to offices, and on the first floor the Dalglishes would operate a nursery school. It was an astute use of idle space in the midst of World War II: The burgeoning ranks of defense workers—mostly women—needed a place to park their children during working hours. Under ordinary circumstances, zoning regulations in Lower Merion Township would have prohibited such an arrangement. But this was wartime, so no one objected.

Thus when I returned from the war in 1945, I found my parents still living in the carriage house while the big house was occupied by strangers living in apartments on the third floor and working in offices on the second floor, not to mention fifty little children at the day nursery on the first floor.

Life continued for my parents in this manner. After my mother died in 1958, my father lived alone in the carriage house. The day nursery had become the Gateway Nursery School for three-and four-year-olds, run by another couple, the Hallowells. Then in 1966, my daughter Anne, who was working for the Peace Corps with her husband in Kampala, Uganda, wrote to tell me she was coming home. Her stint in the Peace Corps was over, her husband was going to get a Ph.D. in folklore at the University of Pennsylvania, and they needed a place to live and she needed a job, because her husband didn't have any income.

Entirely by coincidence, at precisely this moment the Hallowells advised my father that they were going to retire and close the Gateway School. They had been paying my father rent of $3,000 a year for the big house—an important part of his income. He phoned me, terribly upset: In his late eighties he suddenly faced the prospect of a sharp drop in income and a huge empty house on his property.

"You know," I told him, "it's the most amazing thing—the Lord must have something to do with this. Anne just wrote me a letter. She's coming home, she needs a place to live, and she needs something to do. I'm going to buy the school and keep it open, and she'll live in the big house where the Hallowells lived."

And that's exactly what happened. From 1966, when Anne returned to Philadelphia, until 1977, when she moved to Iowa, she ran the Gateway Nursery School and lived in the big house. For three generations of Longstreths, this arrangement proved a perfect fit, financially as well as emotionally.

(When Anne left for Iowa, the two ladies who had worked with her took over the Gateway School. I had paid $10,000 for the school in 1966, but when Anne left in 1977 I sold it to her two colleagues for $1 and they established it as a not-for-profit operation.)

In 1968, when my father was eighty-seven, he gave me the big house in exchange for my promise to bear the costs of supporting him for the rest of his life. (He lived another six years, until 1974, when he died at the age of ninety-three.)

Then one day in 1980 I received a telephone call from a builder in Lower Merion Township who asked if I'd be interested in selling the big house.

"No," I replied instinctively. "Hell, no. It's been in the family five generations—a hundred years. I'd have no interest in selling it at all."

"Well," he said, "You know the Vanguard property has just been sold." This was a reference to a well-known school for learning-disabled children located next door to our big house.

"It has?" I said, surprised.

"Yes."

"Where are they going?"

"They're moving their whole operation out to Valley Forge."

I couldn't restrain my curiosity. "What did they sell for?" I asked.

"They got a million dollars."

I was flabbergasted. "A million dollars? It's four acres—that's two hundred and fifty thousand an acre."

"That's right."

"My God," I said, "I've got two acres. Is my property worth anything like that?"

"Yeah," he said. "It's worth about the same thing."

"You mean you're talking in terms of five hundred thousand dollars for that property of mine?"

"Oh, not that much," he said, "because Vanguard had an entrance on Cheswold Lane and you don't, and there are a couple of other differences. I'd say somewhere in the neighborhood of four hundred and fifty thousand."

"Let's talk about it tonight," I said.

He came over that evening. I didn't dicker. "What are you going to give me for it?" I asked. He told me.

"Wow," I said. "I hadn't the faintest idea it was worth anything like that." And right then and there I agreed to sell the big house, knowing full well that I was signing the death warrant for my symbolic birthright.

You see, someone had made the proverbial offer I couldn't refuse. At that point in my life I owned no other assets of any consequence. For years I had been drained by taxes and upkeep on the house, which I could justify in one way or another as long as my father was alive and a school was operating there and my daughter was living there. But once Father died and Anne moved away, the house became a huge mausoleum, occupied only by a few tenants in the upper-floor apartments. My brother was living in Ohio, my sister in Connecticut. *I* couldn't move into the big house—it couldn't function as a home without six or seven servants. I was sixty years old and facing retirement within a few years; I assumed the future would hold declining income for me and rising medical expenses for Nancy. As I saw it, I had no choice but to sell.

A few weeks later I signed the necessary papers at the developer's office in Bryn Mawr. After the sale was consummated, I drove the mile or two out Montgomery Avenue to take a last look at the old house. For about fifteen minutes I sat alone on the front doorstep and cried. Then I walked through the house and around the grounds where I had spent my boyhood, where my father had been raised, and where his mother before him had lived—crying all the way, overwhelmed by guilt feelings.

After an hour or so I went outside, got in my car, threw the house keys into the street, and drove away. Since then I have never traveled past that spot. Santa Claus may be gone, but as far as I'm concerned, the Longstreth house is still standing.

When I drive through Haverford these days, I avoid Montgomery Avenue. And as long as I do that, I'll never have to acknowledge that anything has changed.

INDEX

"WTL" refers to the author. Numbers in *italics* refer to photographs.